Samuel Kelly :   *y*

Seaman

Samuel Kelly:

an Eighteenth Century Seaman

*whose days have been few and evil, to
which is added remarks etc on
places he visited during his
pilgrimage in this
wilderness*

Crosbie Garstin (Ed)

Introduction by Tony Pawlyn

CORNISH
CLASSICS
3

Cornish Classics No 3

First published by Jonathan Cape Ltd in 1925
This edition published by Cornish Classics 2005

Cornish Classics is an imprint of Truran Books Ltd
Croft Prince, Mount Hawke, Truro, Cornwall TR4 8EE
www.truranbooks.co.uk

© this edition Cornish Classics 2005
ISBN 1 85022 303 3

cover image: Packet Ship *Walsingham*
© the Broad Collection at the National Maritime Museum
Cornwall

© Introduction Tony Pawlyn 2005

Cover design by Peter Bennett, St Ives

Printed and bound by Short Run Press Ltd, Exeter, Devon

INTRODUCTION

The original manuscript of Samuel Kelly's story was discovered by Mr. J. A. D. Bridger, one time bookseller of Penzance, and placed in the hands of Crosbie Garstin in the 1920s. Garstin, the celebrated author of the swashbuckling trilogy about Cornish seafarer Ortho Penhale, masterfully edited the account, reducing it from a massive three hundred thousand words or so (equivalent to four novels in Garstin's estimation), to a manageable book of about 85,000 words.

In considering Garstin's introductory remarks about the Falmouth packets, a few words of explanation seem to be required. The actions that Garstin describes all relate to a later period during the Napoleonic & American Wars of the early nineteenth century. Prior to 1790 the packets carried crews of 60 hands in war time, and the surrender of the **Grenville** without a shot being fired, was indeed a disgrace – though in this and later wars, as civil ships, many packets did surrender after a token exchange of fire with their attackers, after first sinking their mails.

Born at St. Ives, Cornwall, in 1764, Samuel Kelly truly was an eighteenth century 'Cornish' seaman – displaying his Cornish roots by calling the Hoyle Bank off Liverpool, the *Hayle* Bank. Put to sea at the age of 14, and retiring in maturity after many years service as the master of vessels belonging to just one Liverpool merchant, his account of his early years at sea is as fresh today as when it was written two centuries ago. While we do not know just when the account was written, it is clearly the reflective work of an older man looking back with some satisfaction on his formative years at sea. Covering his first seventeen years at sea from 1778–1795, this encompasses his first voyage as a boy (acting and unpaid), on board the Falmouth packet **Thynne**, through service on the **Jason**, transport vessel of Sunderland, and terminating at the end of a transatlantic voyage as master of the Liverpool ship **Thetis** in 1794–5.

Kelly certainly lived in interesting times, and over half of his early sea going experience was gained while England was at war with one power or another. Having first going to sea during the American War of Independence, he enjoyed a modest period of peace, before major international conflict again broke out following the French Revolution, and the execution of Louis XVI, in January 1793.

Having enjoyed a good basic schooling at Helston, Samuel Kelly was no illiterate seaman, but neither was he a cultured scholar of the accepted officer class. In this latter respect he clearly had expectations as a boy, and suffered a grave disappointment in his prospects by the financial setback of his father. The chip on his shoulders is apparent on several occasions, but despite this, and cutting the 'the psalm singing' as the late Mr. Bridger put it, his story is both lively and informative.

His account of his years before the mast are as bracing as a dousing of wind whipped salt spray. When he recounts frequently falling asleep on watch on his first voyage, he is still indignant at the harsh treatment dished out at the hands of the officers and his shipmates. Falling asleep while on watch was one of the mortal sins on board a ship: reliving his life as a boy first at sea, his narrative was in no way tempered by his later understanding as a ship-master.

Although written in later life, Kelly worked mainly from journals kept throughout his time at sea. Thus he retains much of the spontaneity of his original observations, on people and places, customs and geography. Spending some time at Charleston, Philadelphia, and New York, his insight into the fledgling years of the United States is novel. This fascinating book is both a refreshing account of an eighteenth century seaman, and a revealing eighteenth century travelogue.

Tony Pawlyn, Chacewater, Cornwall, February 2004

THE 'MERCURY'—FALMOUTH PACKET.

(From a painting on glass in possession of the Falmouth Municipality.)

Contents

Part one

Part two

Part three

Illustrations

Introduction

SAMUEL KELLY's autobiography was put into my hands by Mr. J. A. D. Bridger – the late W. H. Hudson's 'great Penzance bookseller' – having lain in an old bureau in St. Ives for upwards of a hundred years.

Bridger described it as 'intensely interesting – if you cut the psalm-singing.' I read it and agreed with him.

The memoirs were written in three paper-covered volumes. From observations on the cover of the first, I imagine the author originally intended them for log-books. 'H, 1. K, 2. F – . Course W. by N. Wind – . Saw Old Cape Francois bearing South Distant about 4 Leagues. Broached 2nd Barrell Oatmeal and Third Tierce Beef.' 'H, 6. K, 2. F – . hove too. Spoke the sloop *Bermuda* of 12 Guns on a cruise which informed us of St. Marks being Recaptured by the French, at 7 made Sail again,' and so on – a mouse has gnawed the binding.

The neat writing covers both sides of the pages, and, despite its century, is quite legible. The work ran to approximately three hundred thousand words (for the benefit of the uninitiated the average novel numbers about eighty thousand) and about two hundred thousand commas. They flecked the paper like a plague of midges. In eliminating but a tithe of them I have made the full-sized blue pencil look small.   The spelling remains as in the original.

Asterisks were also a passion with Kelly. Wherever I could see my way I have replaced them with the missing letters, but this has not been possible in the majority of cases. Not that it matters to my mind. The young gentle-

9

man who tried to enter a Roman convent, disguised as a woman, and who was next seen in Philadelphia 'dressed in the habit of a Quaker,' translating the life of Frederick the Great, will go as well by the title of 'Mr. W–rr–l' as Mr. Smith.

Then there was the 'psalm-singing.' It was a common disease among retired mariners of that day. Kelly's contemporary and fellow Cornishman, Harry Carter, 'King of Prussia,' undoubtedly the greatest wholesale smuggler these islands have produced, combined rum-running and 'exhortation' with the utmost success, and died a local preacher. John Newton, the notorious slaver-captain, became vicar of Olney, Bucks, and author of the Olney hymns.

The lamentations of these gentlemen rent the heavens, and not without reason, but Kelly, according to his own account, never failed in respectability (apart from the unfortunate affair in the Liverpool tavern), which I much regret as I should dearly like to hear what Captains Ducket and Shaw, those noted privateersmen, had to say to each other that night they dined at the Lamplighters' Hall. Somebody falls off the yard-arm and is picked up little the worse for his ducking, but Kelly must needs moralize on the insecurity of life over a page and a half, ending with a string of Biblical quotations and a hymn. These I have removed at the cost of a second pencil, and in so doing reduced the book by more than one-half.

What remains seems to me a very full description of the life of a British merchant sailor in the late eighteenth century. Everything is here, the hardships he endured, the ports he visited, the cargoes he carried, the wages he drew and paid, the food he ate, the trouble he had with his crews, his observations on winds, currents, seamanship and peccant humanity, during a period when England was almost continuously at war, not with a single nation, but, at times, with four maritime powers at once.

The great naval commanders of those times have had their measure of praise; their portraits hang in galleries, their swords in museums, their names are glorified on the signs of public-houses, but little has been said of the humble merchant masters who kept trade alive through those critical years, driving their ill-found, undermanned little brigs and snows about the world undaunted by the swarms of privateers that lay in wait for them. It is on record that between 1793 and 1814 seventy-eight letters of marque were commissioned in Boulogne alone. Dunkirk, St. Malo, Nantes, Bordeaux and Bayonne stood no whit behind.

I have by me the story of one Thomas Williams, a townsman of Kelly. In March 1804 he, a mere boy, was captured by a French privateer. In May 1814 he was released, having spent ten years in various jails and marched over three thousand miles in chains – ten years of dungeons, rags and semi-starvation! Captain Hugh Crow, who was there, records that in 1794 nearly two thousand prisoners died in Quimper of want and disease. It was the risk of a like fate that all these merchant seamen faced. They faced it to such purpose that by the end of the Napoleonic wars they had made the English the first sea-carrying nation of the world. All honour to Sam Kelly and his fellows!

So much for war, but peace hath also her victories. What

of his winter passage from Liverpool to New York in the slovenly *John?*

Seventeen weeks; lying-to eight days continuously, forty-eight days in all; melting ice for water, keeping the fire going with bits of splintered timber, sitting in darkness to save his last few candles.

'The 23rd December the wind was like a hurricane from the westward,' he writes; 'whilst lying too, at 1 p.m. a heavy wave fell on board before the larboard gangway, which washed our boats out of the chocks, and stove the long-boat, burst in the steerage hatchway, crushed the hen-coops in pieces, broke the cabin skylight, and finally carried away our lee quarter-boards.'

A month later, lying-to again 'About mid-day a sea struck the vessel fore and aft her whole length, which shattered the channel bends, broke the remaining rough-tree and its stanchions, threw the boats again across the deck and stove the long-boat (the second time), split the covering board of the gunwale, broke the larboard gallows stanchion, and two stanchions on the quarter deck, and opened several seams so that I had to fix canvas spouts to lead the water across my bed.'

So on for forty-eight days, eight of them continuous. Nevertheless he persists in his determination not to run to the southward, and at long last crawls into New York, weed-hung, sheathed in ice, his deck swept clean, one hundred and nineteen days out. Ye yachtsmen, who have lain-to for, perhaps, twelve hours, think of that! Ye globe-trotters, who cross the Atlantic in twenty-knot, steam-heated palm-courts, consider!

But I have one quarrel with Sam Kelly – his account of the Falmouth Packets. It is true that he met rough usage in the service, but the times were rough generally. It is also true that the capture of the *Grenville* by the American privateer *Franklin* was a disgraceful affair, but it was the exception, not the rule. He gives the minimum armament of a packet as fourteen guns and sixty men, whereas many of them carried no more than six guns and thirty men, and the guns were almost exclusively nine-pounders – the old brass 'Post-Office gun.'

It is to be remembered that the packets, carrying mails and specie, were most valuable prizes, and, as such, diligently sought after. This being the case, even with the maximum armament, they were but lightly equipped for the work they had to do. Nevertheless they ran their mails year in year out, peace or not, frigates or no frigates, and have as gallant actions to their credit as may be found in the annals of any service, notably the capture of the *Jeune Richard* by the *Windsor Castle;* the heroic defence of the *Townshend* – lasting three hours – against two American privateers. *Bona* and *Tom* (the *Townshend's* weight of metal being as 78 to the Americans' 360, and men 32 to 220), and Captain Anthony's running fight with six Spanish gunboats, during which he sank one and beat off the rest. The 'dissolute and depraved young men' who formed the packet crews had stout hearts in them for all they robbed the Falmouth hen roosts.

Of what subsequently happened to Samuel Kelly little is known beyond the fact that he retired to his native St. Ives, raised a family of six, and, it is supposed, died and was buried there.

But he saw history making in his day, the British evacuation of New York; the foundation of St. John's, New Brunswick; Benjamin Franklin walking the streets of Philadelphia, a gold chain round his neck; Washington, in black velvet, addressing the Senate, and Lord Howe exchanging salutes with Admiral MacBride as the Grand Fleet stood down Channel to drub the French on 'The Glorious First of June.'

CROSBIE GARSTIN

Part one

Samuel Kelly:
An Eighteenth Century Seaman

I

He Joins the Packet Service

A SHORT account of the life of Samuel Kelly, whose days have been few and evil – to which is added remarks, etc., on places he visited during his pilgrimage in this wilderness.

Perhaps it may not be amiss to give some account of my family first. My grandfather on my father's side was a surgeon in the Army, and settled at Birr, King's County, Ireland. My father (Michael) had first a commission in the Army, but turning out gay, he sold his commission and went into the Navy, and was with Captain (afterwards Lord) Rodney, in either the *Tartar* or *Fame* frigates, when he engaged a French ship. He afterwards left the Navy and went into the Merchant Service, and I have heard that whilst sailing somewhere, that during his watch below asleep, in moderate weather, every one of the men on deck was missing, but what became of them no one could tell, whether taken out by another ship, or fell overboard. He was after this in the smuggling trade from Jamaica to the Spanish Main, and was taken by the Spaniards, and sent to the silver mines in Mexico, from which, by the assistance of an Irish priest, he escaped and fled to the Indians. I think he fastened the sentinel in a hammock where he had fallen asleep, and after suffering much amongst the Indians he escaped in a boat, and after many trials arrived at Jamaica. Here he married (at Kingston) one Mary Thomas, with whom he got considerable property, but his wife did not live many years after. He then was Master of a ship called the *General Wolfe*, which was wrecked in St. Ives Bay, Cornwall. Whilst Master of some ship previous to this, he beat off a French Privateer, for which he had a sword presented to him, by one of the Governors in the West Indies.

My mother was the youngest daughter, and was courted by my father when wrecked near St. Ives. Before they were married my father returned to Jamaica to collect his property, and was on his return, again shipwrecked (and uninsured). My parents were married about five years before they had a child, and then I was the first, born in June 1764 at St. Ives, and before I was seven years of age my mother had seven children, and then with the seventh died at Falmouth, from which place my father traded to South Carolina in the ship *Admiral Spry*. Four of the sisters died in infancy.

On the death of my mother, my brother John (thirteen months younger than me) and myself were sent to board at Helstone, with an aunt, about the year 1771, where we continued at school till 1778 (except one voyage I made to Charlestown with my father in 1774 for benefit of my health, after having scarlet fever. There, I often viewed the colonists trained to arms to resist the encroachments of the parent government, which terminated after a long unhappy war in their Independence. The ship was here laden with rice for Falmouth, and on her arrival I returned again to school.)

OLD ST. IVES, CORNWALL.

(From a print in the possession of Mr. J. A. D. Bridger.)

During my voyage I was treated by my father with so much tenderness and indulged with so much fruit, nuts, etc., and brought home such a number of birds that caused me to wish to be placed at sea, when I left school, though I suffered severely from sea-sickness.

All the time we were at Helstone we associated with the most respectable and orderly boys, and lived in a family of the strictest morality. About the beginning of the year 1778, my father married his third wife, Nancy Mitchell of Penzance, and I believe both parties expected each other to have handsome property, which was not the case, and my step-mother, being rather advanced in years, died with the first child, and the infant followed her in a few days. Previous to her death I was removed from school, and placed in the *Thynne* Packet, Captain Robert Johnstone bound to Madeira, the Leeward Islands and Jamaica, she carried fourteen guns and sixty men and boys, and in order to induce the captain to treat me well, I was to have no wages. I was also placed in the mess of the mate and second mate at my father's expense. Notwithstanding all these precautions, I may date the beginning of the troubles of life from this period. The night before the ship sailed I slept on board, but as there was not sufficient room in the place allotted for the men to sling a hammock for each, I had to spread my mattress on a chest. Soon afterwards a drunken boatswain's mate took possession of my bed and left me to shift for myself.

We then sailed and I became sea-sick, which continued some weeks, and for more than seven years I was less or more troubled with this sickness, on leaving the harbours, and also in contrary fresh gales when the ship plunged in a head sea. After leaving Falmouth my messmates took little care of me. I slept or rather lay about upon the deck, in holes and corners, being unable to eat or scarcely crawl, my chest of clothes was thrown down the main hatchway, having no one to look after it, and for want of exertion, by the sickness I became dirty and literally a neglected cast-away.

At length the sailing-master (Sampson Hall, afterwards some years Commander of an East Indiaman from London) took pity on me, and ordered a hammock to be prepared and slung across, under the clews of the seamen's hammocks, and though this was athirt-ships, and not very comfortable, I had here some peace in the night, but the quartermasters finding it in the way of their mess, it was thrown aside in the daytime, and I was therefore obliged to lay on the chests when it was my watch below. Mr. Hall also ordered me to be washed and cleaned, and though he was a severe man, I was happy to be taken some notice of, and he commonly made me hold his quadrant from past eleven till the sun was near the meridian, by which I learnt to take the sun's altitude, and from this time I acted as a midshipman on the quarter-deck.

A few days after leaving soundings we fell in with a fleet bound to the westward under convoy of the *Hussar* and *Montreal* frigates. I was placed in the second mate's watch, and was stationed in the after guard, and as I often fell asleep at night on deck, my messmate (the second mate) used repeatedly to drench me with water, sometimes thrown only in my face, but at other times my clothes were wet through, which made me cold and uncomfortable during the remainder of the watch.

One cold night I crept into the cabin stairs to shelter myself from the winds, but Mr. Hall coming up to see the weather detected me, and ordered the officer of the watch to place me on the poop, in the most exposed situation by way of punishment. Sometimes my face was tarred and blackened when I fell asleep on deck. On our arrival at Madeira the captain indulged me so far as to permit me to accompany him and the passengers on shore to see the town, which I found very pleasant and gratifying. Here we landed a negro boy (Marcus) whom Mr. Hall had purchased on the last voyage to the West Indies for Mr. Bell the postmaster here (as a livery servant.)

On our quitting this anchorage we saluted with our great guns some gentlemen who had come on board to take their leave of the passengers, and in order to make me a warrior the captain appointed me to fire the guns on one side.

Nothing of moment transpired from our quitting Madeira, till the day of crossing the tropics, when preparations were made as usual, for shaving and ducking those seamen and boys that had never before been this voyage. Accordingly about twenty or thirty men and boys were confined below, and the hatchways closed and guarded. After putting a half-crown in my pocket (which was the fine to escape the ducking), I pushed forward to get it over as soon as possible and afterwards to enjoy the sport with the crew. Accordingly after one or two had been shaved, I presented myself at the hatchways when my eyes were closed with a wet cloth or stocking bound round my head; I was then conducted and placed on the edge of a large tub of water, but escaped with a little wetting on the captain's interference. I had then an opportunity of inspecting the actors, and process. Two seamen, representing Neptune and an attendant, disfigured with blacking, flour, and an odd kind of dress, were the shavers, the lather was composed of tar, grease, etc., and the razor an old iron hoop jagged at the edge, like a saw; and what was scraped off the face with this vile instrument, was drawn between the teeth when the person opened his mouth (being blinded). They then threw him on his back into the tub of water while many other seamen poured buckets of water on his face till he had nearly lost his breath, and thus ended the shaving. I also saw the captain's steward ducked from the main yard-arm, three times, while the ship was running six or seven miles an hour, he being obstinate and refusing to pay the fine, but it was an unwarrantable proceeding, and attended with great danger, as the ship was rolling very much.

On our arrival at Barbados, we found laying in the bay His Majesty's ships *Boyne* and *Prince of Wales*, of seventy-four guns each with many frigates and sloops, Admiral Barrington having his flag hoisted in the *Boyne*. Here we learnt that Dominica had been taken by the French, for which island we had an engineer on board. At this place one of our seamen taking the advantage of my simplicity borrowed a great part of my pocket-money under false pretences, and on his going on shore on liberty never returned to the ship; this was a great disappointment to me as I had little left to purchase fruit.

After waiting here a few days we left Carlisle Bay and

proceeded to Grand Courland Bay in Tobago. In this anchorage we discovered a number of pelicans, some of which we shot; they settle in a shoal of small fish, which they catch under the water in their large bill with a bag or loose skin hanging under, and as they raise their head to swallow the fish a number of small sea-gulls are ready to pluck it out of their mouths, therefore it is only now and then they have an opportunity of securing their prey.

From hence we proceeded to Grenada, St. Vincents, Monserat, Antigua, St. Christophers, and lastly to Kingston, Jamaica. As we passed Port Royal, we found the flag to be Sir Peter Parker's in the *Ruby*. My father having furnished me with a letter of introduction to his friend Mr. Daniel Gully, a shipbuilder here, I was kindly received and entertained at his house whenever I had liberty to go on shore; he also took me in his kitareen to see another of my father's old friends, and when I sailed he sent by me the hire of some negroes (which my father had left under his care) together with a present of coffee, cocoa, nuts, and a case of old rum for my father.

We sailed from Jamaica under convoy, and on our arrival at Falmouth, I hastened on shore to see my father, and on my return to the ship, found to my great mortification, that the officers of the Customs had seized and carried off my case of rum, together with some coco-nuts.

This first voyage being concluded, and my father disapproving the usage I had received, removed me to the *King George* packet, Captain Wachope, of fourteen guns for Lisbon. In this ship I continued two voyages, but the treatment I here received was also rough with this difference, that I was now better able to take care of myself. In my watch I was stationed in the tops and was trained to the exercise of small arms, as a marine, and to frequent boxing bouts with the other boys. I had a letter of introduction from my father to the mercantile house of Caffre & Tibbs of Lisbon, with whom I dined when on shore and saw (on a Sunday) the celebrated bull fight, when about fifteen or twenty bulls were fought with men and dogs. Only one bull at a time was introduced into the amphitheatre where one horseman and two or three footmen stood prepared to attack the bulls. The horsemen used a long spear, and the footmen used short darts with pieces of coloured flags on their arms, to irritate the bull. If the bull refused to attack the men, one or two dogs were let loose on him, and once I saw the bull jump in among the spectators, over the enclosure, about five feet high. I also saw one of the combatants so hard pushed by a bull, that he threw himself between the horns of the animal, and held fast round his neck, till several men disengaged him from his perilous situation.

Soon after my arrival home after the second voyage to Lisbon my stepmother and infant died, and as my father was low-spirited, I stayed at home a few weeks and then shipped myself once more in the *Thynne*, Captain Robert Johnstone[1] bound to the Leeward Islands and Jamaica.

[1] This man I met at Liverpool about the year 1791, and he borrowed of me three and a half guineas, promising to repay me on the arrival of his son, daily expected from Dublin, instead of which, on meeting him again on my return to Liverpool in 1794, he informed me that he was unable to repay the money, but if I would take him as my steward he would pay me out of his wages. He was then about seventy years of age and very unfit to go to sea; I therefore declined his proposal. Such are the vicissitudes of this mortal life.

I continued two or three voyages in this vessel during the year 1780 and 1781. On my revisiting Madeira, I was employed to carry the letter-bag on shore, and on my being discovered at the postmaster's door by Marcus (the Guinea negro boy), mentioned in my first voyage, he was overjoyed to see me, and took me to a confectioner's, and laid out some money in cakes for my use. He then conducted me to several houses where he was acquainted, to introduce me as his old acquaintance and conducted me into a sick English gentleman's bed-chamber, under a supposition (as I imagine) that as we were countrymen the interview would be gratifying to both parties. He also introduced me to a man cook in Mr. Bell's kitchen, where I dined with them, and after showing me every civility, I returned to the ship well pleased with the gratitude of this poor African, who probably recollected that I had often given him a piece of gingerbread cake.

After the hurricane in Barbados, I was much surprised on my arrival to behold such an alteration in the appearance of Bridge Town, almost all the coco-nut trees which formerly were interspersed through the town, and made a lively appearance, were now no more. The church (a brick building) was blown down, and the fort and town much damaged.

On our arrival at St. Kitts, the beach presented a melancholy prospect, there being a number of vessels of various descriptions lying on it, irrecoverably wrecked. We lay two or three days in Grasolet Bay, St. Lucia, with Sir George B. Rodney's fleet repairing their damages after an action with the French.

When we lay at Port Royal, Jamaica, our vessel became

very leaky, and heaving in the hold where the water came in, we heeled the ship and found a rat had eaten through the side, at the water's edge. Was it not for a superintending Providence, how few seamen would be spared to old age, considering the perils they go through.

I well remember at this time, being in our cutler sailing from Kingston to Port Royal, when the step of the foremast gave way, and the mast went through the bottom of the boat. We immediately took in the sail, and put a jacket or trousers in the hole, and began bailing out the water, till a frigate's launch came to our relief, and towed us alongside our ship.

In this ship I was stationed when at sea in the main-top, and I imagine I have slept hundreds of hours in this top, even when the ship has been rolling nearly gunwale in, and often pitching with very sudden jerks against a head sea, but through mercy I was never thrown out of the top, and the pillow I made use of was a small box of gunpowder deposited there for the hankerbusses and blunderbusses in case of engaging the enemy. This dangerous box, generally served as a pillow even in thunder and lightning, which is very frequent in squalls in warm climates. The greatest trouble I had in this top was attending the sails that were hoisted on a long top-gallant mast full thirty feet in the hoist, and on this mast I was obliged to haul myself up by main strength, with my hands. When all the sails were set, to take in and out and send into the top, the upper sail (which was termed in this ship, a sky-scraper,) was not only a very painful and teasing employment, but also very dangerous, as this mast used to bend and spring like a coachman's whip.

There were lying at Port Royal, under the command of Admiral Sir Peter Parker, eight two-deckers and several frigates and sloops of war. I saw two seamen flogged through this fleet for desertion, a most cruel punishment, especially as the desertion is sometimes occasioned by severe and cruel treatment. These men were fixed to a kind of gallows in a boat, and exposed to a tropical sun whilst going through their punishment, and I was informed one of the men expired on the same day.

I think the last voyage I was on this ship, while we were at Montserrat, I perceived the silver coin current there to be very black, and on inquiring was informed it was owing to the steam of sulphur issuing from an old volcano in this island.

From Antigua we carried General Birt to St. Christophers; he was the Governor-General of four islands, and on his leaving the ship we saluted him with fifteen guns, which was returned by the forts on shore with seventeen guns.

On my return to Falmouth, being much attached to the sailing-master, Mr. C. Spurrier (who had taken me under his protection to instruct me in navigation, and who employed me to sell his Adventures on shore in the islands), on his leaving the *Thynne* I also quitted her, and we both shipped ourselves in the *Grenville*, Captain James Nankivel, a contract packet, three of which were provided by a Captain Stewart of Milor, under contract with the Post Office. In this ship we sailed for the Leeward Islands the 20th October 1781. Previous to this date I was a voyage in this ship in company with the *Dashwood* for Charlestown and *Roebuck* for Jamaica, it being usual for several packets to sail at the same time for mutual defence, in case of an attack while crossing the Bay of Biscay. Our vessel (Spanish built) was the fastest sailer off the wind, but a most miserable tool in plying to windward; we could spare the *Dashwood* seven sails more than we had set, and even then was the headmost ship. As she had the mail for the Canary Islands, we parted with the *Dashwood* off Madeira, having escaped from a fleet of seven sail which chased us to the eastward of Porto Santo.

Between Madeira and Barbados (the *Roebuck* always in company) we were often chased by cruisers (without effect) and arrived at Barbados the 21st November 1781. The 26th the Cork fleet arrived consisting of seventy-two vessels, under convoy of the *St. Alban* of sixty-four guns and a frigate, and as these were expected, we could sell little of our Adventures, which most of the crews of the Packets are accustomed to trade in.

The *Grosolet* schooner brought our dispatches from St. Lucia, and we were ordered to sail that evening for England. During this passage we had very turbulent weather, and while scudding under a foresail, our vessel broached too, which caused us to be in eminent danger of being swallowed up in the waves, then running mountains high.

While scudding, our velocity was ten miles an hour. When we lay the ship too, she proved one of the best sea boats I was ever in, for though the sea was grown very high, and the waves very turbulent, our deck was as dry as if the weather had been fine. She was short to her breadth and very high, which occasioned her to carry her guns well out of the water. Our complement was fourteen 14-pounders and two 18-pound cannonades, and sixty men.

On one passage many of the crew were attacked with excruciating pains in their bowels, and I believe nearly half our men were confined to their hammocks. This disease our surgeon supposed to be the effect of poison. Accordingly the copper boilers were examined, and a quantity of verdigris was discovered on the inside of the pease copper, which the cook's mate had neglected to clean, as usual. For my part, I escaped by not liking the pease soup, and as I was always fond of administering to the sick, I was employed by the surgeon to assist in dispensing the medicines, and in a few days (through mercy) they were all restored.

At another time by some carelessness, the lead beneath the fire-place covering the deck, was melted, and the fire burnt through the deck, but providentially the carpenter, going into his storeroom in the cockpit, discovered the fire overhead, and it was soon extinguished. Had it not been discovered so early, as the storeroom contained oakum, pitch, etc., the consequences might have been fatal, and our loss never accounted for.

This ship being a contract one, our provisions were of infamous quality, the beef appeared coarse, and such as is cured for negroes, the barrels of pork consisted of pigs' heads with the iron rings in the nose, pigs' feet and pigs' tails with much hair thereon. Each man had six pounds of bread and five pounds of salted meat per week, but neither beer, spirits nor candle were allowed.

When the top-gallant sails were furled we quitted the tops and took our turn to look out an hour at a time at the fore top-mast head for vessels, and as it was *always* blowing weather when the topmen took their turn at the mast-head, the motion at this extreme from the centre, was so great that unless we grasped very fast, it was sufficient to throw us to a considerable distance into the sea, as if we had been ejected from a sling, and the sensation was so disagreeable as if all our entrails were coming up into our mouths.. This often caused vomiting, and made me dislike it so much that I parted with my clothes to those who would go up in my turn. I believe my great coat and hair mattress also went to hire a substitute.

On our arrival in Carrick Road, Falmouth, the captain went on shore with the mail and his Journal, but returned immediately to the ship in consequence of the post office requiring the Journal to be made out in a different form than heretofore. Accordingly the captain applied to the officers to do this for him, but at last he pitched on me. I . therefore set to, and effected the work, which I believe procured me some dinner in the cabin. Before now to get a fresh bit, I have plundered a poor parrot of a bone of a fowl which the steward had given him, and chewed it up sweetly.

Many a time (when wet and cold, and no dry clothes to shift) have I wished myself in any menial situation on shore, but when on the land, knowing my father could not pay a premium with me, nor afford to maintain me while apprenticed, and being naturally proud, I was ashamed to draw back from the Service I was in. During my stay at home between the voyages, my father was very indulgent, and used to say that as I always returned thin and meagre from sea, that he wished me to have any kind of victuals that I fancied, that I might recruit my strength before I began another voyage. My wages I always gave to him, and he still provided my clothes to this period, but now as he had nearly expended his money, he was at last obliged to sell his furniture, and go to lodgings where he became entirely a bed-layer and very low spirited.

My Uncle Wheelwright took my sister Martha to live with him at St. Ives, and as for my brother John, just as I returned from my first voyage, he sailed in the *Cartaret* packet, Captain Newman, for the West Indies.

I forgot to mention that during our stay in Barbados this last voyage, one of our seamen purchased a large baboon, which was a great terror to the negro women there, and which they called 'The Evil.' He was generally kept tied fast on board the ship, at which time the ship-boys used to tease him. One morning, as I was going over the gangway he got loose and seized my arm, and from the affray I came off wounded, he having bitten my elbow severely. He seldom ever dared to bite a man, but generally attacked the boys when he got loose. At sea, when he was at liberty, he used to visit us in the tops, and on his appearance we used to abandon the top and fly to the extremes of the yards. This was great diversion to the men, but was extremely unpleasant and even dangerous to the lads, and had not Providence interfered, in all human probability some in the fright would have fallen from the rigging into the sea. In bad weather the baboon was tied in the galley by the fire, where, from the effect of smoke he generally kept his eyes closed. One day a boy ventured near to blow the fire, when he seized on him and bit his lip severely.

We had a very eccentric boatswain's mate in this ship, who pretended necromancy and dealing with invisible beings. One night he went below in the dark to get something out of his chest, and after lifting up the cover on feeling for the article he wanted, he happened to place his hand on the baboon, which had got loose, and followed him to the chest. Being frightened he let the cover fall on the creature so as to make him shriek, which hastened the retreat of the conjurer, who fled on deck and placed himself abaft the mizen mast, and the fright occasioned him to have several fits even after we arrived in Falmouth, and 'tis to be hoped cured him of his infamous practices.

On my arrival at Barbados, I was employed by the sailing-master to sell his Adventure on shore. Accordingly, being provided with a bag, it was stocked with plated buckles, ribands, men and women's shoes, etc., and taking this on my shoulder, I landed at Bridgetown, and like another Jew, called at the doors and addressed the ladies that I discovered in the balconies, making a tender of my wares. I at length was accosted by an old seaman, who informed me that if I would follow him, he would show me a house where I could make sales. I immediately embraced the offer, and he conducted me to a house near the church, and on entering the door I perceived several women dressed very gaudily, and not liking their appearance, I began to wish myself safe back into the street, but not wishing to give offence, I put the best face on the business and took out a piece or two of coloured riband, which I was determined to ask an enormous price for, but to my great surprise they gave me my price, and having secured the money, I was encouraged to go forward (though they were common prostitutes), and made a good morning's work. I then left the house and in the street, meeting another of our lads with silk stockings on sale, I supposed they would be acceptable to my late customers, and accordingly took him with me, where, he also made sales, keeping a good look for fear of pilferage. In passing again through the town a girl called me and requested me that I would come to her mother. Accordingly I was conducted into a mean room, where I found a woman in bed; she pleaded illness, and said she wanted to look at my buckles on sale: accordingly I opened a bundle (supposed to be a dozen) and gave them to her to look at, but none pleased her. I therefore began to repack them, and finding only eleven, I accused her with concealing a pair, on which she pretended to cry, and pleaded innocence, but she had secreted the buckles in the bed.

At this place going into the cook room, a clumsy landsman kicked over a kettle of boiling water, a part of which entered my shoe, and disabled me for some time from going ashore, but at St. Kitts, though I could not get on my shoe, I tied up my foot in canvas, and shouldered my bag of merchandise again. Here I sold several articles to a watchmaker, who taking the advantage of my ignorance paid me in light gold coin, but my employer on board came on shore and made him account for his baseness. Here we took on board a quantity of cases of Geneva, which was smuggled from the Dutch Island of St. Eustatia to carry to Jamaica as an Adventure, in which, as many of the crew as pleased took a part. On our arrival at Kingston, Jamaica, I was again saddled with my bag, and the sailing-master being acquainted with a man here of the name of Byrne, who often purchased largely from the packets (he being

c

also an officer in the Customs), it was agreed between them that my employer's Adventure should be deposited in Mr. Byrne's store and that I should have my board in his house in order to make sale of the goods. One day, hearing the Earl of Harrington's Regiment was encamped at some distance from the town, I selected such goods as I thought would answer, and set off for the camp, taking also a dozen or two gilt and ivory-headed walking canes under my arm, arriving while the officers were at dinner. I therefore placed myself in a situation to attract their attention, and soon drew an officer from the table, who took one of my canes, and went back to the mess-room. Immediately a number of his companions sallied out and seized on the canes, with which they began fencing, and soon demolished one of the instruments, which rather alarmed me. I therefore entreated that they would not injure my property, on which an officer gave me his word that he would answer for the deficiency. I therefore waited patiently for the termination of the battle, when I sold a number of these articles, for which I was paid by the above officer. Being rather confused in my calculation of the amount by the affray, I retired under a tree to compose myself, and found I had received a trifle more than was due on the canes, and therefore took up my burden and returned to Kingston about sunset.

I was not many days on shore before Mr. Byrne cast his eye on me as likely to be very serviceable to him. He therefore sounded me on the subject, and having promised me a liberal salary, I at last agreed to quit the ship on her sailing. He accordingly purchased a large desk for me to write at, and from this time employed me in his service, when I was not engaged in selling the Adventure.

One day, he having purchased some chests of Castile soap from a ship from Charleston, he sent me with a gang of negroes to bring it home on a handcart, and on our return, being at a little distance from the soap, I happened to look round and discovered a negress named Lucky, depositing some of the bars of soap in the hands of a woman at the corner of the street. This I recovered, and it taught me to look sharp after the slaves in future.

Mr. Byrne had a negro boy about twelve years of age named Cuffee, who was so fond of sugar, that he frequently absconded and resorted to the wharves, where the article lay, and notwithstanding repeated whippings, he ran away twice while I was there. I was therefore dispatched in quest of him, and the first time, on inquiry for a little negro boy with a brass collar on his neck, I was directed where to find him, and I soon discovered his head above a sugar hogshead, and on seeing me he stooped down, but I soon laid my hands on him. The next time he ran away I had more trouble to find him; at last I found him by the side of a large copper rum still, lying by the water's edge. I think he was employed in shaping a stick to get the sugar out of the holes in the casks, and the instrument he made use of was I think either a jawbone of a sheep or pig, as a knife, and looking into the still I discovered that it was his habitation at night, and here he had some molasses in a part of a glass bottle.

On seeing me he ran into the sea, but I made him come on shore and led him home, where he was tied to a large iron weight, and the cook flogged him with tamarind twigs. I saw several punishments inflicted on the poor slaves at Kingston. It is common when negroes offend to send them to the workhouse to be punished. From this house I have seen a gang of twenty or thirty chained two and two; with each there was the back shell of a large turtle on their heads, in which they collected the filth of the streets and carried it out of town. In this employment it was requisite to be quick, as they had a negro driver with a long whip, who frequently exercised his cruelty on the backs of those who were most indolent. On passing through the street I saw a black woman with her hands tied behind her, and on inquiry found she had not washed the clothes clean. One I saw whipped at the cart's tail. I also saw a woman of colour whipped at the corners of the streets for having hired a black man to kill a seaman. While in the act of flogging she lay on her face in the street held down by four negroes, while another negro lashed her with a long whip, and a white man stood by the executioner with a short whip to punish him if he did not treat her severely.

One evening Mr. Byrne returned home with a black eye, which he had received (I imagine) in an affray at a tavern. This confined him at home by day, but at night he went out with a cutlass under his coat, doubtless to wound his late antagonist if he should meet him in a convenient place, but I never learnt the result.

Mr. Byrne's house was in Church Street, but the premises extended back to Jew Alley, where a Mulatto woman (Mary Morris) who was kept by Mr. Byrne carried on a huxter's shop to supply the negroes with a variety of articles, and she had a good trade. Over this shop was my bedroom, where I dined alone, but as the time of the ship sailing drew near, Mr. Byrne thought I had better go into the country, to the house of an acquaintance. But 'He who hath determined the times before appointed, and the bounds of their (men's) habitation' saw fitting to overrule this apparently eligible proposal, and I continued in town.

The sailing-master, wanting to receive bills on London for the Adventure sold, I was dispatched to the Paymaster of the Forces to get a set of drafts for the money, but at night instead of going on board the ship, I retired to my chamber, as close prisoner, leaving Mr. Byrne to account for my disappearance. The captain and other officers called on Mr. Byrne, but what excuse he made I know not, and as the sailing of the ship was now put off, for (I think) ten days, I continued in my bedroom by day, but sometimes ventured down late in the evening. One day under a supposition that I had been imprest by the man-of-war at Port Royal, the surgeon and sailing-master of the ship went there in quest of me, but making no discovery and having some little suspicion that I was in Mr. Byrne's house, they agreed to reconnoitre in the evening. Accordingly they approached the door in Church Street, and seeing one of the boys promised to give him some money if he would inform them where I was gone to. Accordingly he gave the desired information and they passed through the house and came down the yard where I was standing in the shop. I immediately fled down Jew Alley and was followed by the surgeon, who threatened me if I did not surrender (both officers having their side-arms).

I ran a considerable distance, and believe I should have escaped had I not concluded it was best to deliver myself up, not being now so desirous of staying with Mr. Byrne as I was at first. I therefore waited for my pursuer to come up, and on being joined by the Master, we proceeded to the wharf. The captain having gone to bed before my arrival, I spent a very unpleasant night in fear of what treatment I should receive from him next morning, and was exposed in the meantime to the jeers and scoffs of the ship's company.

At length I was summoned to appear on the quarter-deck and received a kind lecture only, at the end of which the captain informed me that had I stayed behind with Mr. Bryne it was very probable I should be brought to the gallows.

The captain now informed me that the honourable Captain Cadogan of the *Licorne* frigate had applied to him to recommend a lad for a midshipman, but as I was not to be found I had lost the opportunity. I therefore informed the captain that my father was averse to my going into the Navy, having been offered that situation in the *Valiant* of 74 guns, before I left school, and his reason was this, that unless midshipmen had opulent friends to support their appearance on the quarter-deck, they were treated with not only neglect but contempt.

We now prepared to sail for Great Britain, and our decks were well filled with sheep, goats, pigs and poultry, there being about twenty passengers going home in the ship, amongst whom were the Earl and Countess of Harrington, the Honourable Messrs. Paulett and St. John. The captain now requested me to take my station in the cabin and messroom, as an assistant to the steward, where I ate the fat and drank the sweet, being fully employed from morn till late at night, and in order to be ready for all calls, my bed was spread under the mess-room table after the passengers had retired to rest.

We had daily two dinners to prepare as the Earl, with a select party, had a mess in the cabin, and the planters, merchants, etc., were confined wholly to the steerage or mess-room, from which latter class, the Earl occasionally invited *some* to partake at his table. I was now become quite a domestic during the passage home.

We sailed from Port Royal under convoy of the *Licorne* frigate to beat up through the windward passage, and was joined off the island of Navassa by another frigate (I think the *Pomona*), who took our vessel in tow, she being only wood sheathed. We got through the Corcos passage in two weeks or thereabouts and the convoy left us.

We were put to an allowance of three pints of water each man per diem, except the passengers. The ship's candles were expended long before the passage ended, and were under obligation to the Earl for wax candles to burn in the bittacle. Train oil was used in the mess-room in a lamp which was suspended over the arm chest.

One night I spread my bed on this chest, and being called on when the lamp was out, I jumped up suddenly against the lamp, the oil from which I received in my mouth, and on my clothes, and made me woefully sick all the next day. Our steerage mess was in the habit of card playing to a late hour, and for enormous sums of money; the loss and gain I think was sometimes from two to three hundred dollars, 'till the captain forbade it.

One night a lamp plate was provided with a mixture of rum and salt therein (by one of the passengers) which was set on fire, to make the whole company present to appear with dismal ghastly blue countenances which I perceived to be actually the case, as every one's face appeared frightful.

Amongst the passengers was a Jew named Levi, who was going to London to have a cancer cut from his under lip, on which he wore a black plaster, and sat at the table in the steerage with the other passengers, selecting such victuals only as he chose to eat, some of which was provided wholly by himself, viz: Jew beef salted and spiced, each piece having a lead ticket fastened to it; he had also a large quantity of rusk and sweet cakes, and always drank out of his own cup on account of his cancer. He dressed remarkably cleanly and was rather a reserved man. I was afterwards informed that he did not long exist after the operation in London.

As we drew near to Scilly an alarm was given by the mate (Evans) that he had discovered the light on St. Agnes and by its appearance he was afraid we were not far from the rocks. The ship's course was immediately altered, and all was in confusion, the passengers running on deck, partly dressed, when behold the supposed light turned out to be the moon rising!

I will here give some account of this man, and the treatment my brother received from him when Mr. Evans was mate of the *Cartaret* packet and the usage I experienced from him in this ship. Mr. Evans had formerly sailed with my father, who discharged him on some account *unknown* to me. He next sailed with my brother, and under a pretence of making him an able seaman, he used to tie him in the weather mizen shrouds, with his face to the weather. He then on leaving the *Cartaret*, shipped in the *Grenville*, where he exercised his cruelty on me.

When I was in Mr. Evans' watch he has at night visited me in the top, if he thought I was asleep, and if he found this to be the case I got a flogging. If the small sails were furled and the top men were ordered down on the quarter-deck during the night watch, it was almost impossible for the boys to keep their eyes open unless employed about something. The log was thrown every hour and if, on the word being given to heave the log, I was not ready, a bucket of water was thrown on me.

If Mr. Evans was in the other watch at night he was on the look-out for my appearance at the relief, and if he found my great coat on, he made me take it off and secured it from repetition. I was, notwithstanding this, too cunning for him by tieing up the tail and making it look like a short jacket.

In the daytime when I had occasion to go on deck when my watch was below he would give me a job to go aloft, to take in, or let out a royal, or some other nonsense to tease me. This was generally done with an appearance of friendship and under a smooth tongue, and all this ill-treatment did not originate from anything I had done. It proceeded from revenge against my father.

We now drew near to Falmouth, and the passengers made me a present of about £4.

The ship was now ordered to be coppered, and a false keel, sternpost and fore gripe was to be added, to make her *keep a better wind.* She was accordingly lightened, and on turning out the water casks, a discovery was made that we had only *one* cask of water remaining on our arrival for about eighty people. Therefore had not a kind providence watched over us, and brought us into our haven, at this critical period, we might all have perished with thirst.

*   *   *   *   *   *

2

His Third Voyage in the 'Grenville'

MY third voyage in the *Grenville* commenced the 12th February 1782, on which day we sailed for Madeira and Charleston, South Carolina.

The 22nd. Saw the island of Madeira, and the next day, being calm, we could not get into Funchall Bay, but a Portuguese boat having come alongside, the captain hired her to carry the mail on shore. Accordingly the bag was handed in, and the captain, with Mr. Shoalbread (a Charleston passenger) and myself accompanied the mail.

These boats belonging to the island are much better calculated to land in the surf on the beach than ships' boats, being made stronger, and the stem so high, as to support a man standing up ready for a chance to spring on shore on the blue pebbles with which this bay abounds. They have also ring bolts for oxen to draw them up on dry land. On approaching the beach, the health officers, after the usual inquiries, permitted us to leave the boat, when the Captain proceeded to pay his respects to the Governor, and I carried on the mail to the post office, where my old friend Marcus was glad to see me.

I was then ordered to an English tavern to get my breakfast off a cold boiled neck of mutton and cold parsnips, for which, with a glass of wine, the captain was charged half a crown.

I dined in the Agent's kitchen, and afterwards walked about the town. I saw a funeral passing through the street in procession, attended by a vast concourse of ecclesiastics and a numerous body of the lower class, bearing in their hands enormous lighted wax candles (though in broad daylight).

Some of the friars carried crucifixes elevated on poles, and the corpse appeared in an open coffin, on *disorderly* men's shoulders, all with great parade, as usual with the Romish Church.

Being curious, I joined the motley assemblage, and proceeded to the church, the ecclesiastics bawling the litanies in Latin all the way. I entered the church with the rest, and as soon as the corpse was placed on the floor, all the lights were extinguished except one solitary lamp, and the windows were not to be discovered, being covered with thick curtains. Everything appeared so awful and alarming, that I began to wish myself out. At last I espied at a distance the daylight through a door that was opened. I immediately proceeded to the spot where I had discovered the light, and soon got into the street, to my great joy.

This is a noted place for bells tingling at night, not for their melody, but to call the friars and priests to prayers, and I believe there is little cessation during the absence of the sun; but what some church, monastery or nunnery are either chiming, tolling or tingling a small or large bell, which is not unpleasant to the seamen on their watch, in vessels lying in the bay. From the anchorage a large monastery with two towers may be seen very high on the mountain above the town. This edifice is often enveloped in floating vapour, and the summit of the mountain appears clear, towering above the clouds, which has a pretty effect from the bay.

The produce of this island consists of wine, onions, walnuts, grapes, oranges, citron, lemons, pomegranates, etc. Here the Adventures in the packets exchange English manufactures for wines, walnuts and onions, which answer in the

West Indies and Charleston. It is customary to allow the seamen to attach from ten to fifteen per cent to the amount of this invoice, and to take this increased amount in payment for the wines: those are generally inferior that they barter in this manner. The traders in these vessels, not being willing that the Madeira wine merchants should get much profit by them, are in the habit of making out what they term salt-water invoices, which is a false document fabricated on the passage to this island, in which they add a profit to every article therein, and this they exhibit as an original and true bill of parcels.

On a former visit to this place, I was on shore with the ship's boat, waiting on the captain, but was ordered to return to the ship without him. As the boat's crew could not be found till very late, the boat was anchored without the surf. At length they all arrived, and on getting into the cutter, a strange man endeavoured to force himself also into the boat, and on being repulsed, he hung by the gunwale entreating to be taken on board, and we were obliged to unloose his hands and let him get on shore as well as he could in the dark. Doubtless the man was a criminal, and wanted to escape from justice.

At midnight a breeze springing up, we made sail for Charleston.

On the 15th March we had lightning from all quarters, and saw a large waterspout at a distance. On the 18th a ship chased us, and on the 19th about eleven at night she drew very near. Called all hands to quarters, after which the ship hailed us, and informed us she was an English cruiser, ordering at the same time our boats to be sent on board, which was attended to, and the boat returned with strange armed men, instead of our boat's crew. On their coming on deck, they informed our captain that the ship's name was the *Trumball* (I believe), an American frigate, on which the captain gave the signal for our mail to be sunk, and surrendered the ship without any further ceremony. Our crew immediately went below to secure their clothes, and all was in. confusion.

I had heard from several seamen that it was useless when captured to endeavour to save many clothes, as they were generally taken away on going on board the enemy. I therefore only filled a pillow-case and abandoned the rest, with all my bedding. On meeting my friend (Mr. Spurier) the sailing-master, he requested I would retire to his cabin in the cockpit and there wait for him. After a while he came and informed me that he was to remain in the prize, and he would endeavour to retain me also. I therefore continued in this retreat most of the night with the door shut on me, but recollecting that there was a cask of walnuts in the cockpit now abandoned by its owner (the boatswain), and being very unconcerned at our capture, I proceeded to help myself to some of the nuts, which I now conceived to be *pro bono publico*. Having taken a quantity, I retired again to my castle, the surgeon's cabin being directly opposite. He was a German, so on hearing me cracking the nuts he became exceedingly angry and reprimanded me warmly, not for taking the nuts, but for being so inconsiderate as to eat this article at a time when he was overwhelmed in trouble. This reproof had little effect as I continued to devour the nuts.

The people having now been removed to the American, at

daylight I came on deck, and on viewing our enemy, found her to be nearly of equal force with our ship. She having eighteen guns and seventy-five men, and our ship sixteen guns and sixty men. Her name was the *Franklin*, Captain Duval belonging to Salem, and I afterwards found that our crew, though less in number was much superior in strength and ability. Had our commander been a man of spirit, and not suffered himself to be imposed on easily, I have not the least doubt but we should have beat her off, if not taken her.

About breakfast-time the captain of the privateer came on board to see his easy prey and to select what he chose to be removed into his ship. He had on a hair cap and a rusty red coat, apparently French cloth, and had the appearance of a Frenchman. I now began to contrive to ingratiate myself into the favour of the prize-master by offering to superintend the cabin and provide the victuals. This pleased him, and I therefore commenced my services.

In the afternoon of the 20th, the boats were hoisted in, and the prize-master (Mr. Potter, the first lieutenant) was ordered to proceed to Boston, and the *Franklin* departed for the Capes of Virginia, to land her numerous prisoners. Those of our ship's crew that were left consisted of the sailing-master, surgeon, a sick man, a boy and myself.

In the course of the day our two officers, having drunk pretty freely, I imagine to drown their troubles and exhilarate their spirits, the surgeon fell asleep in the sun, on the windlass after dinner, and during his nap I believe some person cut away his pocket in which he had some letters. On awaking, missing his pocket, the master being near him, he accused Mr. Spurier with the theft, on which Mr.

Spurier struck the doctor and strained his wrist. As the fight was soon over, and the parties reconciled, the surgeon applied something to the sprain forthwith.

Towards evening the wind began to freshen, till a violent storm came on from the southward. We therefore scudded away before the gale, but I believe it was past midnight before we had secured the sails, our new crew being few in number and of the most wretched description. I exerted myself to the utmost aloft, and on laying out on the main-top sail-yard to furl the sail, for want of active assistance, I was a considerable time wrapped up on the yard in the sail, and was disengaged only from my perilous situation by the topsail providentially unfolding itself again.

After securing this sail, on my descending the main shrouds, they appeared very slack, and on inspection found most of them were stranded. We therefore fixed tackles from the mast-head to secure it from going by the board. During our bustle the main quarter hatch being off, the sea poured down in such a manner as to oblige us to resort to the pump. The guns also having been neglected to be secured, gave way, and we had some trouble in lashing them fast. The prize-master kept at the helm a great part of the night for want of a proper man to relieve him, and on my going down into the cabin, found the water had got in there, and a quantity of cheese being loose, and the wet getting to them, made them so slippery that they were running from side to side almost every roll, which was extremely dangerous.

The next day the wind moderated, which enabled us to put things in a little order. The American officers appeared sober men, as they generally drank water mixed with the

CHARLESTON, SOUTH CAROLINA.

bottled porter, though some of the crew had broached a pipe of Madeira wine in the between decks, and cut up the cheese which they fried in the pan to eat. I now discovered two of my blankets, but my bed had been emptied of its contents by one of our own seamen (as I found afterwards). I now emptied a cask of walnuts into a chest in the cabin, and having discovered a superior cask of Madeira wine in the storeroom, lately belonging to one of our passengers, I broached it for cabin use. I also discovered two boxes of preserved citron, which I took care of for my own use.

The next day (22nd) we were chased by a ship, which gained on us, as we were not in a condition to make the most of our sails. The next morning before day the ship ranged alongside, which we found to be His Majesty's ship *Garland* of twenty guns, Captain Chamberlain. The Americans were now taken out, and a master's mate and crew sent on board in lieu thereof.

The 23rd after the *Garland* had taken from our vessel what they liked, we made sail in company, for our original place of destination (Charleston). Hitherto I had two or three valuable watches of the master's adventure, tied up in the tail of my shirt, to conceal from the Americans, which much incommoded me, from which I was now relieved. I continued to provide the cabin mess, consisting of two officers from the *Garland*, and our surgeon and master, till we arrived at the bar of Charleston.

The American crew were sent to the *Howe* prison ship, and our vessel was placed under care of the Court of Admiralty, who ordered the goods found on board (as Adventures) to be sold by vendue.

D

On our arrival here the *Halifax*, Falmouth, packet was in the harbour, and a few of her men were sent to look after our ship. Soon after this she was again commissioned, and the sailing-master of the said packet (a brother to the captain), was made our commander, who I shall in future call Captain Lofty. This captain was about two years older than myself, and his father (an old captain) lived next door to my father in Falmouth, and before we went to sea, was my intimate acquaintance and boon companion ; but at home, after I had begun to sail in the packets (his brother having pushed him forward, and I having no friend) he began to show his superiority by slighting and totally withdrawing himself from my society. He finding me in the cabin, requested I would continue to act as steward till he could procure a suitable person, and then I was to be made second mate.

We began to pick up a few seamen also, and news arriving in April that Sir George Rodney had defeated Count de Grasse,[1] we prepared for firing a royal salute of twenty-one guns, one half of which I was appointed to fire. In the evening the town was illuminated.

The American army under General Green was not at a great distance from ours, under the command of General Leslie, the latter being encamped to guard the town, at the distance of about seven miles from it, and the American army had cut off most of the supplies from the country, by which means provisions were scarce and the prices exorbitant in the garrison. On Sunday, having liberty to go on shore, my curiosity led me to visit houses, etc., where I had

---

[1] Action fought in the Saintes Passage, between Dominica and Guadeloupe, on April 12th, 1782. – ED.

spent many happy hours at eleven years of age, when here with my father in 1774 and 1775, but alas what a change! I could only discover one person who had been a planter, and now kept a store. Numbers of houses were in ruins, and their once opulent owners, dead, or unknown to the present inhabitants. The markets were thinly supplied, and an egg fetched threepence in a place where I had formerly purchased a live partridge for either a penny or an halfpenny.

The statue of Lord Chatham, erected in the public square, was much defaced by the shot in the siege. The church tower, a wooden edifice, very lofty, was painted black, to prevent its being seen at a distance at sea, it being a landmark to ascertain the entrance of the bar, and was formerly painted white. The wharf in Coopers River, where my father's vessel loaded, was in ruins, and the proprietor's (Mr. Gibb's) elegant mansion was now an hospital. Such are the ruinous effects of war! On the outside of the town lines, where I had formerly walked under the refreshing shade of lofty spreading trees, to visit a pleasant well-regulated tea garden, no trace could now be discovered of either trees or garden, but all appeared void and waste, like the soul of a natural man unrenewed by grace.

We now procured an English cook, and a French steward, both of whom had been planters in the state of South Carolina, and being reduced and unable to pay their passage to Europe, took this method to get there. The Frenchman (Monsieur le Ney) was a decent, well-behaved man who took my berth in a few days after I had shown him the requisite duty. I was now appointed second mate, and was employed to fill the ship's water for our passage home, which we pumped out of a pond above the town, at some distance up a creek, in which a numerous quantity of turpin or sea tortoises were to be seen, swimming with their small heads above water, appearing like snakes, while others were walking on the mud at the riverside.

One day, having occasion to go to the army smithy, about some iron-work, a soldier belonging to the regiment of Old Buffs was in the shop, and on my mentioning that I knew a Captain Casement of that regiment, when quartered at Helston, where I was at school, the soldier replied that at that very time he was Captain C.'s servant, but now his master was dead. This man appeared so happy to see one from the above place, that he pressed me much to visit the camp, and as a person in the shop offered to accompany me on the following Sunday (which is the general day for seamen obtaining liberty), I agreed to walk there with him. Accordingly I arrived there at the time appointed, through a waste sandy country, and on finding the soldier, he conducted us to an arbour in the rear of the encampment, or more properly speaking, hutment, the troops mostly living in huts of their own erection, with gardens behind the same. Here I dined on salt pork, loaf bread and onions, and he had also obtained from the sutling booth some rum to make us welcome. After dinner I went through the front of the lines, which were nearly extended from Ashley to Coopers Rivers (Charleston being built at the extremity of the land where these rivers mingled their waters. The town garrison being Hessian troops).

In the front of the army there were trenches filled with water, and at intervals a passage remained of the solid ground to act as causeway which were commanded by cannon placed on log forts, opposite each space; on the outside of the ditch was a single house, where the General resided, beyond which was the parade ground, protected by an abbatis line, composed of trees cut down with their branches outward, and on the outside of this were the picquets. On the rivers, galleys, mounting heavy ordnance, flanked the encampment. While here, I heard of a deserter from the American army, who offered his musket for a dollar, which I purchased. It was stamped and branded on several parts with the words, 'United States.' I continued here to see the night guard paraded, and then returned towards town. After dark it came on heavy rain which well wetted us, and my musket shared the same fate. On approaching the town lines, we were challenged by a Hessian sentinel, who was in his box, and let us pass in the rain with little trouble, keeping my gun out of his sight.

At this place I have seen at night the whole sky in every visible direction flashing with fire, and which had a most awful and tremendous appearance. This is also a place much subject to thunder and forked lightning, and to prevent damage, the houses have iron rods, or conductors, from the ground to some distance above the highest point of the dwelling, at which extremity the rod is forked with three points, to attract the electric fluid. Formerly the tropical fruits were here in great plenty, supplied from the Bahamas, also the fruit from the Northern States, this place being nearly central.

I had often heard of men being tarred and feathered in America, and I had now an opportunity of seeing it realized.

A negro having stolen a goat, belonging to the Commodore, was stripped naked, his surface tarred over, and then rolled in fowls' feathers. In this figure he was paraded through the streets.

Near our landing place I discovered one day an alligator dead, about six or seven feet long. One of the galleys, up the river, belonging to the Quartermaster-General's department, was surprised and taken by the Americans in the following manner. A boat came down the river in the night, which was hailed and ordered alongside the galley. They pretended to be going to the town with fodder, under which a number of armed men lay concealed, who boarded the galley, and after wounding many of the crew, secured the vessel. The gunner of this galley took the same station in our ship, to get to England, being much wounded in the head and face. To show the folly and wantonness of seamen, it may not be amiss to relate an anecdote of the crew of a privateer. The *Peacock* had returned here from a cruise, and the seamen, having received some prize-money, purchased several watches, and in a drunken frolic, they determined to fry the works on the fire, and were highly entertained to hear such a number of them ticking in the frying-pan.

This is a very unhealthy place in the summer, the inhabitants being much subject to fevers and agues. Oysters were plenty, and the rivers well stored with fish, such as drum, trout, mullet, sheeps-head, shad, whiting, and many others, unknown by name to me. There is a blue-and-yellow crab here, about the size of a man's hand, and they are plenty; the way to catch them is to get into the boat alongside, with a line to reach the bottom, to which any animal substance may be fastened; after lying at the bottom a few minutes, it is drawn up softly, and you will find the crabs fast to the bait, which they will hold fast to the water's edge, then having a cabbage net extended on a small hoop, you place this gently beneath the crabs, and secure them, for they always quit their hold on being lifted out of the water. The fish mostly in repute is the black fish (about the size of an English bream), these are caught with hook and line, by negroes in canoes, without, and to the southward of Charleston bar. These boats arrive at the fishing ground about daylight, when 'tis generally little wind, and return with the sea breeze about mid-day, to the fish market, where those men that have caught the greatest quantity of black fish in a given time receive a bounty. On my first visit here, in 1774, large quantities of turkeys and Muscovy ducks were shipped for the Caribee Islands, now, scarce one could be seen. The deer formerly ran about the streets, with collars round their necks, like dogs, but at this latter visit, I do not remember to have seen one.

About the middle of May we took our passengers on board, with the mail, and proceeded over Charleston bar, where we found His Majesty's ship *Princess Caroline* (Dutch built), of fifty guns at anchor. She had on board a quantity of French prisoners for England. Mr. Evans, our former mate, and my *petty tyrant*, was a passenger with us, but being out of office, and crestfallen, I was treated with civility, in language as smooth as oil.

Lieutenant D-r entered into conversation with us, and finding I was acquainted with his relations in Falmouth he invited me into his cabin, in the poop, where I partook of some refreshments and received more respect from the second officer in this ship, than I experienced from the lowest officer on board my own.

A breeze springing up, we got under way. Made sail for Great Britain, the man-of-war in company. During our passage, we perceived the *Princess Caroline* sheering about in an unaccountable manner, which led us to imagine the French prisoners had risen on the crew, but on inquiry, found the wheel rope had given way, which occasioned the confusion.

My station at sea was, as usual, in the main-top, where I experienced much hectoring and uncivil language from the captain below, who had evidently forgotten himself, and never once during the passage home, gave me a bit of fresh victuals, or even treated me with more civility than the crew experienced from him, though he was even rioting on poultry, hogs, etc.

About the beginning of July, 1782, we drew near the land, and as the wind was now got to the westward, and blowing a stiff gale, it was judged prudent to bear up for Plymouth Sound, to land the mail and passengers. We anchored in the Sound about mid-day, and the captain, after landing the mail and passengers, proceeded by land to Falmouth, leaving Mr. Briton, the sailing-master, in charge, to proceed home with the ship the first fair wind. Whilst we lay here our officer went on shore to Cawsand, to purchase spirits, and I was surprised to see this contraband article carried through the streets in open day, as if in defiance to the laws of the country, and even the soldiers from the camp on the neighbouring heights were the porters to carry about the kegs of brandy and Geneva here. In this port women frequently ply in boats, as watermen, which I believe is scarcely the case in any other part of Britain.

In a day or two after arrival, the wind coming fair, we sailed in the forenoon, and about three in the afternoon arrived at Falmouth. We found the *Antelope*,[1] Captain H. Wilson, an East India packet, laying in Carrick road, and on going on shore was informed that one of her mates had left her. Both the agents and shipbuilder being my friends, they each thought on me, and being applied to for this purpose, I was under the necessity of declining the situation, as I was not only bare of clothes, by being captured, but my father could not now afford to supply me, £100 at least being requisite to equip a mate for the East Indies. I have since seen the hand of Providence, in mercy, preventing me going this voyage.

Monsieur le Ney having now quitted the *Grenville*, and assumed the gentleman, remembering the civilities I had shown him on coming on board the ship, gave me an invitation to dine with him at the principal inn at Falmouth, which I accepted. Having now no home, my father being at lodg-

[1] This ship, on her return to England, sailed from Macao in China, July 20, 1783, and on August 9 following she was wrecked in the night, on a reef near the Pelew, or Palos Islands, in the west part of the Pacific Ocean. This group extends from 5° to 9° north lat., and from 130° to 136° east long.; but not laid down in the English charts. The crew, assisted by the natives, built a schooner on the Island of Oroolong, and sailed in this vessel on November 12 and arrived at Macao the 29th of the same, 1783, where they sold their vessel for 700 Spanish dollars, and returned to Great Britain in the China fleet. The Pelew Islands are the fifth division of the Archipelago, now known by the name of the New Carolines. Captain Henry Wilson was afterwards the Commander of the Missionary ship *Duffe*.

ings, and a bed-layer, I was now under the necessity of living on board the vessel, and as the second mate was in the same state, we now messed together. My wages per month did not exceed 22s. 6d., that being a seaman's pay in the packets, and navy, and I believe our sailing-master received no more than £4 per month, and this station was the zenith of preferment from merit. The Captain being appointed by the Post Office, through Government interest, and in general were strangers in the Service. It was customary to receive 40s. per man after being captured, to replace our clothes and bedding, but this I could never obtain from the Post Office agent here. I began now to be tired of this Service, but, hearing our ship was ordered to London for inspection, I was determined to continue by her till I had seen the Metropolis.

Whilst I was in the *Thynne*, we had nearly lost a stout boy, who fell from the main-yard into the sea. As we were running down the trades at the rate of six or seven miles per hour, and a number of small sails being set, we were afraid to heave the vessel round too, till the canvas was reduced. A hen-coop was thrown overboard immediately, but we had run a considerable distance before the cutter was hoisted out, which providentially picked him up, just as he was exhausted in swimming. He had not seen the hen-coop, nor the boat, till she was near him, as the billows were high, though seeing the ship at a great distance his spirits began to flag, but the boat's crew kept calling to him to cheer up, amongst whom was his elder brother. The tar brush which he had in his hand when he fell, he kept hold of till he was picked up.

Whilst we lay in Falmouth harbour, Captain B. ordered two boats to attend on him at Falmouth quay one morning.

The cutter with seven oars, and the yaul with four, the latter boat was furnished with a fishing net, under the management of the gunner. The cutter was supplied with a cold collation. I made one of the crew of the latter boat this morning. Captain B. brought with him a Mr. O - k, one of his neighbours, and an old companion, and this gentleman had also paid me great court formerly, when I came to Falmouth, at the vacations from Helstone school, but now he too took no notice of having formerly been my companion. We proceeded with the boats to Milor pool in Truro River, and there began to haul the seine, and catch fish; in the meantime our gentlemen left us to walk up the village, they soon after returned in company with another gentleman and three ladies, which I soon found to be a party well known to me at Helstone, viz., a brother and sister of Sir C. Hawkens, Bart., Miss Robinson and Miss Johns. This discovery was very mortifying to me, for though I was dressed clean and decent, I was now only an associate of vulgar seamen, and kept myself at a respectful distance in hopes of being unnoticed. They continued awhile to see the fish caught, and then retired to a small farmhouse to get their dinner. From thence a message was sent from Captain B. to me, demanding my presence to fry some of the fish. But whether this was by way of insult, or from knowing I understood the business, I am at a loss to determine. For he must have been aware that the ladies had formerly known me. However, I went to the house and informed a person that I saw there that it was my opinion women were better acquainted with cookery than myself, and that I did not like to undertake to cook for ladies.

We now got the ship ready to proceed to London, and sailed about the latter end of July, 1782. A day or two after this we got to the eastward of the Wight, and then bore up for Spithead, one of our cables being found imperfect.

On running down to the Mother bank, we passed a ship sunk, which we found to be the *Royal George* (a first Rate), the crew had heeled her a few days before our arrival here, to stop a leak, and by very bad management, and obstinacy after the danger was intimated to the commanding officer on deck, this valuable hundred-gun ship was lost.[1] The Admiral[2] with several hundred men, and (I believe) with about two hundred and fifty women were drowned,[3] many of which, I fear, were ill prepared for an eternal state. The men-of-war near her sent their boats as quick as possible, and were enabled to save a number of the crew, who jumped overboard ; but doubtless many were drawn down in the vortex of water. I was informed that a child was saved by holding fast by a sheep.

After we anchored at the Mother bank, our captain went on shore to Portsmouth and ordered a new cable. Whilst we were waiting for this, the dead bodies belonging to the *Royal George* floated and passed our ship both with ebb and flood tide; many we perceived on the shore at low water, and some I saw fastened by ropes to the buoy of a ship at Spithead. No reward being offered for burying the dead for several days, few people troubled themselves about them. About this time the diving bells were at work on the ship,

---

[1] The traditional story. Actually she sank because her timbers were rotten. – ED.

[2] Kempenfelt.   [3] Losses estimated at 600 souls, in all.

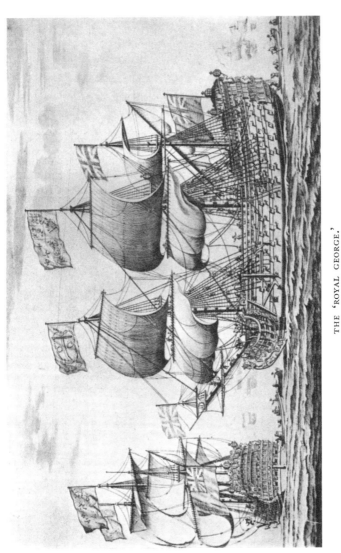

THE 'ROYAL GEORGE.'

and I went several times in the boat with Captain B. to attend the process. There was a large capstan-hoy fast to the masts which we went on board, and here some of the boatswains attending the bells, supposing our boat's crew to be sent there to work, drove me to the capstans. At other times I attended to watch the bells going up and down, keeping a good look out that I did not get the boatswain's supplejack on my back.

The principal bell, in which was a surgeon of an East Indiaman, with a Lascar (native of Bengal) was very large, made like a porter vat, the largest end downward. Round this a quantity of pig lead was fastened on, to sink it, there were small round glass windows to admit light near the top, and a large hole in the bottom for men to enter, under which a board was hung with chains, on which the men stood. On sinking the bell the water rose within, as far as the air pent up would let it, which might be about breast high on the men. In this small space of air they breathed, which was refreshed by the following method.

Two smaller bells were employed to go up and down in succession to supply the large one with fresh air. At the top of each a leather hose was fixed. At the end of the hose was a brass cock, which, when sunk, was pulled into the large bell by a line; they then let in the fresh air, and the foul air returned in its place into the small bell, when it was hauled up again above the surface of the water, to let out the foul air and to fill again with fresh. There were also signal lines held by men who sat on the gunwale of the hoy, and these were led in at the bottom of the bell, near the deck of the ship, and by the surgeon twicking one or other of these lines, the man who held it knew what was wanting. One time the large bell remained under water (I believe) fifty odd minutes, and when hoisted up the air that rushed out was smoking. The Lascar went out of the bell to inspect the situation of the things on deck, and received air from the bell by means of a leather hood covering his head with a hose to the air in the machine. Once the surgeon sent up a message written with a pencil on a clean bit of deal wood, and requested that the boats on the surface might not intercept the light of the sun from the bell.

The hoy was crowded with naval officers from the fleet at Spithead, and the rigging of the *Royal George* was decorated, not with colours, but with dead bodies, who were hung up by arms, legs, etc., which presented a horrid spectacle. These men had floated at high water, and to prevent the tide carrying them away, had been tied fast to the shrouds and mainstay, and at low water (which was the time the diving bell worked), they were suspended several feet above the water. Some people searched the pockets of the dead while floated on the tide. 'Tis more than probable that as this crew had just been paid their wages, that they had been the day before rioting in drunkenness and debauchery, little considering what a change a few hours would make. 'In the midst of Life we are in Death.'

Our ship lay off Ryde, exactly in the stream of ebb that came from the wreck, we had therefore an opportunity of seeing the dead in vast numbers floating by us. Whilst lying here, the sight of so many disagreeables greatly injured my appetite. On receiving on board our new cable, we sailed for the Downs, which I was not sorry for. On our getting as

far as Margate Roads, we had to ride out a tremendous gale
there, and it was very providential that we had now good
ground tackling in having a new cable, or the consequences
might have been fatal.

About the middle of August, 1782, we reached our moorings in Limehouse hole. Near our moorings I had a sight of
a merchant ship built at Archangel, the size of which surprised me. Some of those ships are fifteen or sixteen hundred tons burthen, and at that time were allowed to be
purchased by British merchants. My old ship the *Thynne*
packet being in Taylor's dock, Rotherhithe, many of my
old acquaintances came to visit our crew. The carpenter had
been my messmate, and invited me to his lodgings, he having been always very kind to me, I therefore went to see him.
There he introduced me to a native of Cornwall (in the hat
line) of whom I ordered a guinea hat. This hatter afterwards invited me to dine with him. On the following Sunday
accordingly I waited on him, and after dinner he proposed
to his wife to take tea with a friend in the Fleet Prison, to
which place I accompanied them, and on my being introduced, who should I behold, but the boatswain's mate of the
King George (Lisbon packet), with whom I had sailed, and he
appeared glad to see me. His name was H. Pentire, and
having run into debt to the shopkeeper in Cornwall, for his
adventure, had delivered himself to this prison to clear his
bail. He lived in his own hired room, with his hammock
hung up on one side, and I am well persuaded he had on a
shirt with ruffles. Here I inspected the premises, and found
a very commodious coffee and tap room, with ranges of
galleries to accommodate those debtors who could afford to

hire the rooms. Those who were poor were obliged to pig
in the common room on straw. There was also a yard and
playground for exercise. This prison has been since rebuilt.

Whilst our ship lay in Limehouse hole, our crew used to
cut off junks from the cable, which they sold early in the
morning to the bumboats for purl,[1] and I think the petty
officers had a hand in this nefarious practice. Here our cook,
John Daily, an Irish Papist, having drank to excess on
shore, fell overboard between two vessels and was drowned
late at night. Having hauled our vessel into Limekiln dock
for inspection, our crew was generally on the range, and
many left the ship. A goat that we had on board here went
one day down into the cabin, and ate a number of blank
Press protections, which she found on the locker. On Tower
Hill I saw a vessel on wheels with masts and rigging, called
the *True Blue*, which was used as a rendezvous to enter
seamen for the Navy.[2] I do not think I was overhauled
but twice by the gangs, whilst I was in London, as they
could discover by my conduct that I was not afraid of
them.

Soon after his appointment we heard that our carpenter and
boatswain were in the police cage at Shadwell, being exposed
to the view of the populace. Several of our people set out

---

[1] 'Purl – ale or beer in which wormwood is infused.' – BAILEY's *Dictionary*.
[2] A singular invention for this purpose of pressing, is a ship which is placed
on land not far from the Tower on Tower Hill, furnished with masts and all
the appurtenances of a ship. The persons attending this ship promise simple
country people, who happen to be standing and staring at it, to show it to them
for a trifle; and as soon as they are in, they are secured as in a trap; and according to circumstances made sailors of, or let go again.' – MORITZ, *Travels
Through Several Parts of England*, 1782.

for the spot, to see what they had been doing, and I followed. On our arrival the carpenter appeared much dejected and we found they had been attempting to sell a coil of rope belonging to the ship, and were detected by the police officers in the act. They continued in the cage till the next day, when our captain procured their liberation.

The Underwriters at Lloyds who insured on our ship when captured, hearing she was in the river, requested that our commanding officer would send three of the crew, that were taken by the *Franklyn*, to be examined respecting the captures and the subsequent plunderage. Accordingly the second mate, steward, and myself were ordered to proceed to the house of Leslie Groves (an old captain of the *Thynne*, whom Captain Johnstone succeeded), now an underwriter. On our way through Goodmans fields in the evening, some ladies standing at a door, accosted my companions, like old acquaintance, and they promised to call on them on our return from the examination (both my shipmates were Londoners). Accordingly on our return we visited this house, and on our being seated a bottle of wine was introduced, but I soon found that I was in a Bagnio, and began to be uneasy, though my friends (or rather my foes) appeared quite at home in this community. Seeing one of the females wasting the wine by overflowing the glasses, I reprimanded her, and took the bottle under my protection. Being quite at a loss to find the way to Limehouse, as I was a stranger in London, I continued here a considerable time, in hopes my companions would accompany me to the ship. At length the second mate and a lady quitted the room, and not finding the steward disposed to go with me, I proceeded to the street

E

door, when a female strove to keep me back by force, but I soon threw her aside, and gained the street. (These men had been three voyages in the ship with me, the steward's wife had come to London with him, from Falmouth, and was now at lodgings at Limehouse, and I was informed he had formerly been one of the Press-gang on the Thames, and of course a man of no good principle. And the second mate was little better, having been several years in this low station, without merit to recommend him to obtain a higher, he afterwards became a penny post letter carrier in London, with a bell.) On my getting to the corner of Great Prescot Street, I inquired of a woman my way to the ship; she replied she was going in that direction, and would walk with me; we therefore entered into conversation and proceeded down Ratcliffe highway. On the road she seemed desirous to recommend herself to my notice as a modest young woman, but finding I was not very desirous of becoming further acquainted she bid me farewell, and I found my way alone with little difficulty. Hearing on board that several people were to be hung at Tyburn the next day, I agreed to accompany several of our seamen to see the execution. Therefore the next morning we got to Newgate some time before the prisoners were ready to leave the prison. We kept close to the door round which a large concourse of people had assembled; by and by we heard a loud cry of make room, and on looking round, saw a fat man pressing through the crowd, with a large piece of bread and butter in his hand which he was eating, in the greatest hurry, and on inquiry found he was an assistant to the hangman (Jack Ketch), but seemed little concerned about the office he was soon to undertake. I shall just relate an anecdote of Jack Ketch, and a seaman.

A seaman, being in a public-house, was asked whether he knew such a person, to which he replied in the negative. The man then informed him his name was Mr. Ketch, and that his employment was to hang men at Tyburn, on which the sailor had an inclination to shake him by the hand, and advancing, said, 'How do you do, Mr. Ketch?' to which Jack Ketch replied, 'How do you do, sir? You have the advantage of me.' 'Aye,' quoth the Tar, 'and I intend to keep it, for I am told you use those *very roughly* that you get the advantage of.'

We waited to see the prisoners put into the carts, and then made the best of our way to Tyburn (passing St. Sepulchre's church, where the passing bell was sounding its discordant notes in the ears of the poor criminals). We got near the gallows, in the midst of such an assembly of people, as I had never witnessed before, nor never wish to see again, on such an occasion. The malefactors consisted of a Jew, five or six other men, and one woman (Charlotte Goodall) a servant, who let her sweetheart rob the house of plate. He was also hung by her side, but whatever might have been the guilt of those people, one of my shipmates in company, and who had been our pilot this day, was (I believe) as fit for the gallows as any of them, he being a most depraved wretch, and by his knowledge of the intricate passages of this part of the town, I guess he formerly frequented them for no good.

One night when in my hammock on board, asleep, I felt a cold hand on my thigh, which did not alarm me a little, as there was only one man on board that slept regularly in the betwixt decks. I thought I heard the person retreating from my hammock and called out to ask who it was, but could get no answer. The ship was much infested with rats, which made great noises in the night.

At this time our crew had dwindled by frequent desertions to a small number; four or five Scotchmen who were the most decent and orderly men, still remained, but these, on account of the wages being only 22*s*. 6*d*. per month, were determined to go into the Transport Service, where the wages were £3, and they endeavoured to persuade me to go with them, which I took into consideration. I knew my father had nearly expended the last of his property, and that in all probability he would soon want some assistance from my earnings, which at present were small. I therefore considered an increase of wages desirable. Therefore, having no home now at Falmouth, and no prospect of doing any good for myself in the Packet service, I made up my mind to quit the *Grenville*[1] with the North Britons, and accordingly removed my chest and bedding to Deptford, where the transports fitted out, and this we were enabled to do with safety, by having a protection from the packets.

As I have now left the Post Office department, perhaps it may not be amiss to say something concerning the packets, and their crews, previous to the year 1783. I think there were twenty-four armed packets from Falmouth whilst I sailed in this Service, most of which had from fourteen to

---

[1] This Packet's name was changed to the *Shelborne*, and some little time after the Peace in March, 1783, she was returning to Falmouth with the New York mail and a vast number of passengers, but never arrived, and no one left to tell tidings what became of her.

OLD FALMOUTH, FROM THE NORTH.

(*From a print in the possession of* Mr. J. A. D. Bridger.)

eighteen guns (and two had as many as twenty-six guns),
with crews of sixty men. Some of these ships had clean
coppered bottoms, some had their copper painted over with
white lead, and others had tinned bottoms made of a composition like what is called tooth and egg metal. The first
sort was the best for keeping clean, as seldom any marine
plants or shell fish adhered to the clean copper, but on the
painted copper I have seen many barnacles (a shell fish),
and on the tinned bottoms marine grass and shellfish grew
as readily as on a wood-sheathed ship. I think I have
counted thirteen packets at home at one time. These vessels
seldom rejected any able-bodied landsmen that offered themselves, as they were cheaper than seamen, requiring only
16s. to 18s. per month. These ships were, therefore, recep-
tacles for a number of dissolute and depraved young men,
who were either ashamed, or afraid to continue in their
native place in the county of Cornwall. These new-comers,
having no home at Falmouth, were generally victualled on
board, in the harbour, and slept round the galley fire at
night, without bedding. There might have been from five to
ten of these in each ship, and these attended all calls in the
boats. An officer was appointed to sleep on board at night,
in his turn, but this person frequently neglected his duty and
remained on shore all night, making his appearance on board
early in the morning for a cloak. The non-attendance of this
officer encouraged the new-comers to land about midnight
for plunder, when the gardens, poultry yards, etc., were
robbed. One of the associates remaining on board to make
a good fire, and prepare water to scald off the feathers from
turkeys, ducks and fowls, they then boiled or roasted for

present use, and buried the remainder in the ballast, to prevent discovery. A considerable number of the able seamen and petty officers were produced from time to time, from this nursery. Deserters from the Navy at Plymouth, frequently resorted to Falmouth, where many entered on board privateers and merchant ships. Others shipped themselves in the packets for the West Indies with an intent to desert in the Islands to the merchantmen, from whom they obtained thirty to forty guineas by the run to England. Most of the officers, and those seamen that were married, carried large Adventures out, and brought home in return contraband goods, which were frequently landed in the Cornish coast at night. I have seen our vessel laden deep in the water with this merchandise, and the captain has testified his displeasure at seeing the ship so much like a laden merchantman. A great deal of goods fell into the hands of the Customs, as the officers searched every packet on arrival, and I remember one of the Lisbon packets being seized for having a quantity of tea on board. This dealing in merchandise made the seamen greedy, covetous and scheming, and scarcely any trait of that generosity which is the characteristic of British seamen,[1] could be discovered in this community.

[1] I have been informed that a seaman in London, having received an order on Drummond & Co., Bankers, for his wages, tied the paper in the corner of his neck handkerchief, and by inquiry found the house at Charing Cross, where he requested to see Mr. Drummond, and on being introduced, asked, 'Is your name Drummond?' On receiving a reply in the affirmative, he produced and handed Mr. D. the order, saying, 'There's a tickler for you!! But don't distress yourself if you have not so much money in the house. Give me two or three guineas just for a night's cruise, and I'll call again for the remainder.'

They were likewise addicted to tippling, gambling and pur-
chasing goods abroad from prize-masters and ship keepers.
They were also in the habit of plundering the wharves
in the Islands, and in America, of mahogany, lignum-
vitæ, etc., which they hoisted into the ship and stowed
away in the hold in secrecy, during the night. They pilfered
the taverns in Jamaica of the glasses they drank out of, and
brought them on board, and most things were fish that
came to their hook. When a customer approached the ship
to purchase goods, the sellers crowded to the gangway, each
desirous to secure him to himself. On these occasions the
officers were treated with very little ceremony. In these
vessels the effect of original sin was to be seen in its horrid
perfection, and I saw little or no appearance of religion, or
even morality, while I continued in this service, which was
about four years, and I recollect once being informed at
Jamaica, that two of our pedlars entered the Jews' Syna-
gogue on the Sabbath, with goods to sell, where they
attempted to drive a bargain with some profane Israelites.
If a man-of-war is considered as a floating hell, I am well convinced that a Falmouth Packet (at the time I sailed in one),
was far from being a floating heaven.

* * * * * *

3

He Joins the Transport Service

ON my arrival at Deptford, I went to the carpenter's lodgings to wait till I heard of a berth in a transport. To obtain this my shipmates had employed one Bryan (a crimp and waterman), to be on the look-out for us. Accordingly the next day, three besides myself were shipped in the *Jason* transport, Thomas Appleby, a ship belonging to Sunderland of about 300 tons burthen, and known in the North of England by the name of a barque. Other ships go there under the denomination of Pinks[1] and Cats,[2] which distinguishes their mode of construction or build of the hull. I did not altogether like the countenance of our captain, for notwithstanding he was a handsome man, there was something forbidding in his appearance, and on further acquaintance I found him to be almost everything but what he ought to be.

In the evening I was called into the cabin to sign Articles, where I found the captain's wife and his sister at work, ironing some washed clothes. Here I was taken to task by the female captain respecting my abilities in sea affairs, and at the close of the examination, she pronounced me to be no sailor because I had not served an apprenticeship in the coal trade. I was therefore put under the denomination of an ordinary seaman, and my wages fixed at 40s. per month, whilst my companions (many years older) were to have 60s. This low wage I was not altogether sorry for, as less ability

[1] A Pink is (or was) a vessel with a narrow stern, so built for convenience in working with her quarter guns. — ED.

[2] A Cat was a vessel built from a Norwegian model, with a narrow stern, projecting quarters, and a deep waist. — ED.

would be expected, and my disposition was inclinable to diffidence, having been in the packets almost confined to a particular kind of duty, but now I was to be traversing from mast-head to mast-head, and from one end of the ship to the other, there being no other man before the mast, but myself and three old shipmates, together with master, mate, second mate, carpenter, cook, three young apprentices and a little negro (which our master picked up on a former voyage in Antigua), in all our complement was thirteen. What a contrast was this ship's company to those that I had formerly been accustomed to in the packets! viz., sixty men, or rather more properly speaking, fifty-nine, as I was told the agent at Falmouth received the pay of one man from each ship as a perquisite, which reduced the complement to fifty-nine. The lumpers, who had been employed on board previous to the shipping of the crew, continued on board till the master-master had inspected the ship's company (to answer for the complement of men required by Government), and were then discharged.

In a few days, having taken in all our stores, as a troopship from the King's Yard at Deptford, we received orders to proceed to Portsmouth. Accordingly, we hauled out of the Tier; when the master found it requisite to go to London on business, we therefore sheered the ship alongside a Frigate in Ordinary, and requested permission of the commanding officer (the cook's wife), to let us hang by the man-of-war for a tide, which was granted. This woman was the only person on board. A few hours after her husband (the cook), returned alongside drunk, and had broken his wooden leg on shore. This man abused us much for preventing his getting to the gangway, and threatened to turn our ship adrift as soon as he got on board. We endeavoured to pacify him by civility, and assisted in getting him into the ship, where the man and his wife settled all disputes. The next day we proceeded to Blackwall where we anchored, to return the stores our master had borrowed to pass the inspection of the Transport Board.

The next place we visited was Gravesend; here the crimp who had shipped us attended to receive his crimpage, and we received a month's advance. Nothing more being required here, we proceeded to the Downs and anchored opposite Deal. At this place a number of men reside, who are smugglers. Each of these has a particular signal, which being made by any vessel, the person on shore who is wanted used to bring off spirits, tea, etc., openly to supply the shipping. We embraced the first opportunity to leave this anchorage, and proceeded to Spithead, and was then ordered to anchor in Stokes Bay, the usual place of resort for unemployed transports. Here we lay for many weeks, and I used to go to Portsmouth market in the boat once or twice a week, the master's wife, his sister and two children being still on board, by which we got many a pull to Portsmouth in blowing weather, to supply their cravings. Our vessel being rather light of ballast, we were employed to bring on board shingle from the beach, which we spread over the water casks, stowed in the hold, making a clean and comfortable surface. The boat was hoisted up at night to prevent desertion. Two of the apprentices, notwithstanding, found the way to get clear off. Soon afterwards we procured two other boys in their stead.

About the 15th December 1782, we received orders to prepare for an expedition to Guernsey. Accordingly, the master's family took lodgings at his washer-woman's at Portsea, which was no sorrow to me. We then ran over to Cowes Road and anchored. Here we were joined by other transports for the same expedition. Whilst laying here I saw a poor, miserable, dirty prostitute, ducked from the yard-arm of one of the ships, two or three times, which was an unwarrantable and an unmanly action, whatever her crime might have been, as her life was much endangered by the fright. The agent for the direction (a Naval Lieutenant), having joined the fleet, we proceeded to Yarmouth Roads, Isle of Wight, to wait for a wind. Here we lay a week or two. While on my night watch here I have heard a flock of Solan geese on a calm night, making a noise like a pack of hounds. At this place one of our new boys ran from the boat on shore, and I was informed that about twenty boys had deserted from this ship in a short space, by the turbulent and cruel disposition of the master. I have seen him strike one with a large iron bolt about two feet long. Notwithstanding the weather was now very cold, we were still kept at work on deck from daylight to sunset. After breakfast we had an allowance of points, gaskets, etc., to make daily, though the cold benumbed our fingers that we could scarcely feel the plait in our hands.

The 31st December 1782, we sailed from Yarmouth with the expedition. The 2nd January 1783, we saw the island of Guernsey.

The 3rd January hoisted out the long boat, and prepared to receive the sick and convalescent men of the 96th Regiment of Foot, and the next day completed the embarkation, having on board 190 men. Having procured an old man for a pilot we sailed with other vessels for Jersey, it being a most formidable navigation of rocks, and small islands, awful to behold. We left Guernsey the 6th, and the next day arrived at Jersey, and anchored in St. Hiliers Road. On the same evening we landed the troops at St. Aubins (or the Tower).

On the 9th, we received on board, by our boats, 212 men of the 18th (or Royal Irish) Regiment of Foot, with their women and baggage. These men had to sleep in the same bedding used before by the sick of the former regiment. After the watch was set, one of our boys being poorly clothed, for a rainy night crept in amongst the knapsacks and having found a sergeant's coat, put it on. Soon after this the sergeant, missing his baggage, came on deck with a light, and approaching the spot, the boy fearing a discovery, slipped his lobster's shell and decamped to the other side of the boat, where he got clear without a drubbing. I think on the next night, when I had the first watch, and had put out the fires on deck, I discovered a soldier raking up the scattered cinders in the hearth, to kindle a small fire. I desired him to desist, on which he replied that his wife below had been just delivered of a child, and he wanted to boil something. This information I reported to our master, who permitted me to offer the soldier anything he might want for her comfort. This news he carried to the nursery, and on his return informed me that he would be obliged by receiving a little gin (probably for the good woman who attended, being the mother to one of the band). This article I delivered him, with liberty to make the fire. Every six soldiers, being allowed only four seamen's allowance of provisions, while embarked, four inches of candle was allowed to every six men on board, and having occasion to go below amongst the troops soon after, I found the place completely illuminated to the great annoyance of the poor woman, as they were also very noisy. I was told the child was to be named after the ship (Jason). This night's jollity amongst the soldiers was a great contrast to the following. During the next day we had rather rough weather, but towards evening the gale increased in strength. The wind was right in the bay, and about eight or nine at night, the *Fanny* Transport, to windward of the fleet, broke her anchor and fell on board the cruiser's cutter whose anchor gave way and both these vessels drifted down on us. To save the king's cutter from being sunk our cable was immediately cut, and we drifted from them. When we obtained a proper distance from these vessels our best bower anchor was dropped, and though this cable tier had been cleared before night, we could not give the vessel the cable, owing to the soldiers having spread some of their beds there unknown to us. Our vessel therefore drove into shoal water, near a large reef of rocks, over which the waves were running tremendously high, when our ship was brought up by the best bower. Our Guernsey pilot was in the greatest fright imaginable, so as to lose his English tongue. The army officers kept teasing our master with questions and foolish proposals during the hurricane, and he was himself in great terror, fearing that as we were in shoal water while the tide was high, that at low water we should beat to pieces against the ground and perhaps lose all our lives. The poor helpless soldiers were crawling about on their hands and knees, not being able to stand, as the vessel was tossed in a violent manner. Many of the troops placed themselves in the long-boat to secure a passage on shore should the vessel go to pieces. We fired many distress guns during the first half of the night, but it was impossible to obtain any assistance. About midnight a consultation was held when the tide was still high, what was to be done for the good of the whole, when it was determined to cut the cable and run at all adventures to gain the beach to save the lives of the people. The moon was shining bright at times through the flying clouds. Two seamen were ordered to loose the foresail, and we got a spring on the cable to cast the ship the right way, to avoid the horrible rocks near us. The men had cast off the yard-arm gaskets and the goose wings were loose, when some man cried out a lull. This was immediately noticed and confirmed by many who concluded the gale had passed its zenith. The sail was therefore ordered to be again furled, and the wind continued to moderate till daylight.

At daylight the band assembled to play a tune on the quarter-deck (I imagine from custom, or regimental orders), this aroused the fury of our master (who probably had not yet forgotten the danger of the night, and being still near the rocks), was astonished at this inconsideration. He therefore with the speaking trumpet in his hand began to lay it on the heads of the musicians with great violence, which soon dispersed the harmony. Having only two cables we were obliged to splice the one cut, which was performed as quickly as possible, and we sailed with the fleet for

Guernsey on the 12th and arrived there the following day.

On the 14th the troops walked on shore with the poor woman that had so recently lain in of a boy. About the 17th we had taken on board 211 men of the 83rd (or Royal Glasgow volunteers) Regiment of Foot, and sailed with the convoy for Portsmouth. On the 23rd two cutters came alongside for the troops and baggage, and conveyed them to the *Pigot* and *Haughton* East Indiamen lying at the Mother Bank. As this regiment was intended for foreign service, the number of women were limited in the embarkation at Guernsey to about six for each company, which caused great dissatisfaction amongst the men. One of the regiments for India lying at Portsmouth was very riotous, and compulsion was found requisite to force them afloat. On the 24th we moored our ship at Gosport, and the master's family returned on board. We now got an addition of another female, by exchanging our mate for another, the new one bringing his wife with him. Our old mate was rather too easy with the men, and was as happy as a prince when he had some beer to drink, and a good stock of tobacco. He had two papers of a pound each of shag lying about in his cabin. His quid was about the size of a pigeon's egg, which on going to rest he stuck up in the crevices of his bed place, but was not sufficiently prudent to resume it in the morning, and as those monstrosities increased in number from time to time they were left behind him as a decorating legacy in the cabin of his successor. Our new mate was a Scotchman, and a politician, by making a fair show where it was likely the master would cast an eye, but was short of that sincerity which was observable in his predecessor. He often amused himself on the violin.

I was now placed completely under petticoat government. My female captain, on her return to the ship, informed me that I was to content myself with a half-pound of brown sugar per week, with the benefit of the tea-leaves (when well drawn). I was now made her complete drudge, and had to fetch milk, beer, barm, etc., from Gosport, and to carry the bread to and from the bakehouse, clothes to and from washing beyond Portsmouth, and many other domestic affairs.

Somewhere about this period I received the intelligence of the death of my father, who had been to me a kind and an affectionate parent, though very reserved in communicating anything relative of his past life to his children. There was much of the gentleman to be discovered in his address and conversation, walked very upright from his having been in the army in his youth, and I believe him to have been an upright, honest man, though he did not profess to be a serious Christian. He had just sufficient money left to pay the expenses of his funeral and was, I hope, taken away in mercy before he was reduced to want.

A General Peace having taken place we were now ordered to prepare for receiving discharged men from the Navy and to convey them to their native places before they had squandered away their money. Accordingly a vane was fixed at the mast-head to signify that our ship was to take men to Leith in Scotland. As the seamen were paid off they resorted to the transports destined for different ports in Ireland, Scotland and Britain. After receiving 127 men,

SEAMEN OF THE 'EDGAR.'
(*From a print in the possession of* Mr. C. Le Grice of Trereife.)

chiefly from the *Edgar*[1] and *Elizabeth* line of battleships, we sailed on the 1st April 1783, for Leith. Those men being now free from restraint took the management of our ship in a great measure on themselves; that is, in taking in and making sail at their pleasure, and on our anchoring in the Downs they purchased a quantity of spirits with which they made very free, and this increased wantonness and disorder, and as they have a great antipathy to pursers and stewards I came in for a share of their malignity, and had the cheese that I had issued thrown back at my head, merely for its having suffered a little from decay, and it was not safe at all times for me to appear on deck, and I was afterwards informed by the steward of the *Fanny* transport that they had, or were intending to reeve a rope to hang him at the yard-arm! The Navy officers we had on board thought it prudent to join the men in their dances and merriment, for fear of what might otherwise happen. They purchased a large red, broad pendant of our master, on which they affixed the word *Edgar* and hoisted it at the main top-gallant masthead.

About this time several of the men being drunk, one of their party was killed by stifling him whilst in bed, by heaping other beds upon him in their mirth, and on the evening of the next day he was thrown overboard. This sad catastrophe threw some damp on their gaiety.

In the course of a week from our sailing we drew near the Firth of Forth, and having discovered the light on the

---

[1] The third *Edgar*, a 74-gun ship launched in 1779. In various actions, among others Copenhagen. Eventually renamed *Retribution*, and became a convict ship. – ED.

Isle of May in the evening, we plied off and on till day-light, when we ran up the Firth. As the weather was fine, several boats came alongside, which were immediately hired to land the men according to their wishes in different parts of the Forth. Therefore before we gained our anchor-age most of our cargo had been delivered. This being beef and pudding day, many a pudding, boiling in the coppers, was abandoned by its owners, and which fell to the share of our crew, who were allowed no flour, and our daily food from month to month was only beef and pease pudding, for dinner and supper. We dropped our anchor about noon above Newhaven in Leith Roads, and rigged our skiff with two spreet[1] sails to go on shore at Leith. The next morning the master and two of us left the ship, the wind blowing very fresh down the Forth which speedily landed us in the harbour, when I was dispatched to the market, and on inquiring for greenes, a garden woman to induce me to buy spinnach which she had on sale, told me that '*Ain* penny-worth of spinnach was better than *two* pennyworth of green kale.' We here visited a public-house, known by the name of Locky Curries, where we obtained an excellent bottle of London porter for fourpence, with bread and cheese in the bargain, it being customary in this country to the public-houses to give something to eat for nothing to those who pay for the drink. I found it so in many places both sides of the Forth. Having obtained our requisites here, we pre-pared for our return by reefing the sails, etc., our ship lying some miles off directly to windward. Having made sail, we found it very difficult to work out of the harbour,

[1] Sprit. – ED.

being very narrow, and had nearly swamped the boat in the attempt, but providentially we weathered the rocks and in less than two hours got alongside our vessel. I had always a dislike to open sailing boats, especially if they were ballasted with ponderous materials such as iron pigs or stones, but generally this ship's boats were ballasted with gang casks filled with water and lashed to the benches, or thwarts, so that if the boat should fill with water, she could not sink, and would float the crew as long as they could hold on.

Our master's wife having an inclination to see the city of Edinburgh, we took her on shore and from Leith she and her husband took coach for the metropolis of North Britain. As soon as they departed, I set off on foot for the same place, intending just to peep into the city and return to the boat immediately. On my way I entered into conversation with a wayfaring man respecting the place, who behaved very civil in describing the country, and even stepped out of his course to show me what is called the New Town. When having seen the register office, a grand Advocate's house, and a square, I hastened back to Leith, where I arrived long before our gentry. The houses on what is called Bunker's Hill, were eight or ten stories high, near Edinburgh bridge, and the servant women at Leith neither wore shoes nor stockings, which had a mean appearance.

One evening our crew assembled with two of their wives at the public-house, kept by Locky Curries, who had two daughters, and being at that time in my natural state, and an enemy to God, I saw no harm in being one of the party at a dance. I had been under the tuition of a French master at Helston, and was fond of this vanity. We drank whisky punch during the evening and had supper gratis! I observed the people of this place were fond of snuff; this article was kept in a cow's horn to which was sometimes chained a brass spoon, full of little holes, and a hare's foot. The former was called a pen, in which the tobacco was lifted to their nose, the holes emitted air to assist the drawing of it into the head, and what remained on their upper lip and face, was brushed off with the other instrument!

About the latter end of April we sailed with a fair wind, and reaching Tynemouth bar, we ran in and moored ship off South Shields. This place was so very full of smoke that it turned our bright (newly painted) deck and sides almost black. On the back of the town I was amazed to see the hills of ballast carted from the colliers on their return from London and other places, and which perhaps had been accumulating for several centuries. I was also much pleased in viewing the expertness of the pilots here in managing and dropping up on the tide, not single ships only but large tiers of vessels, fast to each other, controlled by the sails of one or two of the number. There are on this river a vast number of keels or barges employed in bringing coals from the pits to the vessels loading at North and South Shields, which makes the scene very lively. Having now taken in our coals, we sailed for Portsmouth, and arrived safe at Spithead about the third week in May.

Our ship was much haunted with rats; we therefore employed a rat catcher from Portsmouth who laid oatmeal balls containing poison in different parts of the vessel, and on my going down in the after hold, two or three hours after it had been deposited, I heard a most pitiful outcry from numbers of these animals, and killed one or two that were unable to escape from me. The stink from the dead in a little while was very disagreeable, and I think we found some buckets full of rats amongst the casks, which we threw overboard.

*　　*　　*　　*　　*　　*

4

He Sails to New York

WE being ready for sea about the middle of June, and after receiving our sealed orders we landed our female captain and sailed on the 22nd in company with the *Fanny* and *Diligence* transports, on the same service. Our orders were to be opened when we got to the westward of Scilly.

On the 25th being in mid-channel, at the top of high-water, the *James* brig of Sunderland had anchored to stop the flood, and they having offered to ride us by a towline, we accepted their civility, and our master went on board the *James*, where he procured six pieces of salt pork, having none laid in for our present expedition, though we had to traverse some thousands of miles on the Atlantic Ocean. The only provisions for our crew including the master's mess was salt beef, bread and pease, and many a breakfast have we made on bread and *cold* pease pudding during this voyage, as we were generally close pinched in the beef.

On the 30th June we fell in with a ship from Bordeaux to Waterford, with brandy, from whom we procured a hogshead of cognac, our master paying for it by a draft on the ship's owner. On opening our orders we found our destination to be New York, and our business was the evacuation of that place. Our master obtained a few quarts of split peas about this time from the *Fanny*, which with his six pieces of pork and some potatoes were well husbanded for cabin use. One evening, I having heated some pease soup in the dark on deck, for the master's supper, and being in attendance when he began to help himself, I was not a little surprised to perceive that he had lifted out of the soup something like a long leaf of cabbage, and knowing we had nothing of this kind on board, I soon discovered that after washing the saucepan at dinner, the cook had put into it the washed potato net and which had escaped my notice in the dark. This oversight procured me some abuse, but I had the satisfaction to receive the soup for myself in consequence of the blunder.

The *Fanny* transport being a crazy old ship sprang a leak about the 10th of July, and our master was desired to come on board her, to consult what was to be done, when it was determined that it was not safe for her to prosecute the voyage, and accordingly on the 15th she bore away for Great Britain. Having had some rough weather we had put two pigs below in the 'tween decks, one of which having discovered some oatmeal balls, laid to kill the rats, poisoned itself by eating them, and was thrown overboard. The wind blowing in general from the westward we made but slow progress, the first half of our passage ; and this had great influence on our master's temper, as it changed according to circumstances, like the wind. We were kept at work during the day in making twice laid rope, he having purchased a large quantity of junk, etc., at Portsmouth, for this purpose. One night the weather being moderate, about eleven o'clock I requested one of my shipmates to comb and tie my hair, for which purpose I sat under the bow of the boat. While we were at this work the master came forward to see what we were about, and being very superstitious, he flew into a great passion and gave us to understand that it was no wonder we experienced such a foul wind when such trash (as me) was combing his hair in the night.

One day carrying our top-gallant sails by the wind, against a head sea, one of the braces broke and the yard kept flying to and fro as the vessel plunged and rose to the waves. To remedy this disaster was a most dangerous service, and each person wished to shift it from himself, on which our blustering commander resorted to his usual mode of abuse. This roused my pride and I immediately undertook the service. When I began to go out on the yard with the brace, he perceiving the perilous situation I was in, became extremely frightened, and was now more desirous for me to come back than he was before to urge me on, but being determined to persevere, I paid no attention to his bawling and remonstrances, but accomplished the business at the risk of being jerked into the sea, at the expense of my life. What a mercy it is that an elect sinner cannot lose his life till he has experienced the grace of effectual calling.

In the longitude of 57° west, we spoke the *Argo* man-of-war, bound to England, and found by her (and our own experience afterwards), that at this time we were 10° ahead of the ship in our reckoning, and of course a sad mortification to our master, who I imagine was much better acquainted with the intricacies, and setting of the tides in the Swin Channel, than with plain traverse and current-sailing in the great Atlantic Ocean! We spoke several vessels from time to time but all their information was discouraging, viz. that we were much further from America than our captain expected. At last on the 23rd of August we got soundings in eighty fathoms.

On the 26th we saw Long Island, and the high land of

Neversink, and on the same day got within Sandy Hook, the *Diligence* having arrived long before us.

The 28th we began hoisting up our beer and provisions for a survey, when the master sent me to the men-of-war to solicit the attendance of their sailing-masters, to inspect the provisions. I first went to the *Diomede* of 44 guns, Commander Affleck, Mr. Nelson (afterwards Lord Nelson) being the first lieutenant and commanding officer on deck. Here I obtained the surveying officer, and then applied to the *Belisarius* frigate for another; these masters condemned our beer, cheese, oatmeal, etc., which were ordered to be thrown into the river. These orders we began to execute immediately, when our master invited the surveyors into the cabin, and as soon as they disappeared we kept the remainder for our own use, being often much troubled with short commons! After putting our ship into proper repair, we were ordered to the Haymarket Wharf.

On the 16th began to receive on board emigrants, or Loyalists', furniture, stock, etc., for St. John's River, in the Bay of Fundy, Nova Scotia.[1] The 23rd mustered the Loyalists in number 73.

The 24th we dropped down to Staten Island. The 28th received on board forty-eight soldiers, discharged from the 42nd Highland Regiment of Foot, intended to settle in Nova Scotia. Whilst lying here some of our crew were encouraged to go on shore and plunder the farms on Staten Island, and they brought on board a large quantity of apples from the Jersey side.

On the 30th we sailed from Sandy Hook for St. John's

[1] New Brunswick.

River. During our passage the soldiers and emigrants did not agree, the former stealing the goods of the latter.

About a fortnight after sailing, having got past the Bay of Fundy unknown to us, the moon having brightened the horizon a little, we were astonished by seeing land, with a sandy beach close to us. The ship was immediately tacked, all hands running on deck, and through mercy we escaped being immediately wrecked on Cape Sable. The Loyalists had several large dogs with them, which were tied on the forecastle. These animals did not like the seamen coming near them at night, being vicious; they were thrown down the hatchway to the care of their owners, and I believe one or two were wantonly thrown overboard.

On the 17th October we entered the Bay of Fundy, and on the 18th arrived in St. John's River. On entering this place we were highly gratified in beholding the numerous huts and houses scattered over the hills and rising grounds near the entrance of the river, all of which I believe had been erected since March last, and great numbers of new wigwams, framed and log houses were continually beginning as the Settlers arrived. On going on shore I found that though the houses appeared pleasantly situated, from the ship, all seemed in disorder on a nearer inspection, for want of a good plan at first. It was with the greatest difficulty any man could be found, there being no regular streets or lanes. These hills were covered with small trees on their first arrival, and they grew so close that it was difficult to pass between them; it was therefore requisite to fell them, but by carelessly leaving the stumps six inches or a foot above ground, a person ran the risk of breaking his leg, or cutting his shin in passing through the settlement during the day. At night few moved from their habitation, as it would be difficult to find it on their return. At the head of the first reach of the river, on a round hill, there appeared an old fortification built I suppose on the British taking possession. The soil appeared poor, being covered with moss, in which the swine delighted to rout.

We heard on our arrival that the bears had visited the settlement, but were driven away or killed. At this place the settlers were to have one year's provisions and a Lot in the town, and at a future period each single man was to obtain 150 acres, and a married man 200 acres of new or unsettled land in this country. As winter was now fast approaching our Loyalists were anxious to land to prepare their habitations as fast as possible; the weather being now very cold and often severe, we therefore landed them with their goods, wherever they requested it. An old pair with two daughters, not very robust, wished to be landed one afternoon and would not be persuaded to wait for the next morning. They were therefore put on shore under a cliff, with their furniture about them for shelter. The day following I perceived them in the same place, and thought the tide had visited their abode during the night. I therefore obtained leave to take a lad with me and a rope to their assistance, and we with great labour hauled their effects to the top of the cliffs, where we placed them in a circle to shelter the family from the wind.

Every shipment of emigrants from New York had a captain and lieutenants appointed from their own body, to transact the business of the shipment, etc. Our captain had conversed with the master of the ship concerning the mode of obtaining the land, and as our commander had some inclination to obtain an estate here, the refugee captain agreed to enter him on the settlers' list, if he wished it. I was now applied to by the master to see if I was willing to remain behind, and draw his lot of land, as well as 150 acres for myself, while he returned to England for his family, and finding I was not against it, provided he supplied me from the ship with such articles as I wanted, he agreed to leave with me boxes of glass, nails, rum, etc., for sale to supply my wants. One year's provisions I could also obtain from Government. Whilst our settlement was in agitation, the winter came on suddenly, and very severe with sleet and snow, which settled in large masses on our yards, and sails, and which fell from time to time in such heavy lumps as made it dangerous to stay on deck. This cooled the courage of our master, and made him give up the idea of obtaining an estate in this dreary province, and to tell the truth I was not sorry. Having occasion to call on our refugee captain, I proceeded to inquire him out, when passing through the extreme part of the buildings, a girl who had come here in our ship, called to me and requested I would visit her father in a wicker cottage, where I found him in bed and extremely ill, having got cold, the hovel not being yet thatched to keep out the weather; but having no future opportunity of visiting him, I know not whether he ever recovered and fear many must have perished from cold before they could protect themselves from the severity of the climate. Many of the first settlers had gone up the river to look for a suitable place to build on. One of these made a large raft with timber, on which he deposited his family and property and committed himself to the stream, and on which he was floating out of the river one evening, when we providentially discovered him and I went in company with two or three boats' crews to his assistance, and towed the raft to the shore.

Our carpenter was sent with another man to cut wood towards the settlement of the discharged soldiers, who were not permitted to mix with the refugees. One afternoon I was ordered into the boat to fetch the wood cut, our master being also with us. On our way we passed a deep laden boat with barrels of flour, conducted by two soldiers, one of which was very drunk. Our master on seeing their danger, advised them to be careful that they might not swamp the boat, but this advice they disregarded and laughed at his supposed folly. We therefore passed on to the shipping place of our wood. We had not been here long before a person informed us that a boat had sunk, when we discovered it was the boat we had been fearful about, and on looking saw one of the soldiers at a distance swimming. Our master said it was no matter, as they were saucy, and was disinclined to render assistance, but at last we prevailed on him to let us go. We pulled away towards them with the greatest alacrity. The first we approached was swimming on an oar, and seeing he was in a good way, we passed him with words of comfort, exhorting him to keep up his spirits till we picked up his comrade, who was hanging by the boat. This being effected, we took up the swimmer also, who informed us he was not much obliged for our kindness, as we had given his partner the preference. We therefore proceeded to land them, when they informed us that it was useless to save their lives, unless we also picked up their boat and flour. Captain A.   replied that as they had been saucy he would do no more, unless they paid for our trouble. This they agreed to, on which we picked up the flour and towed the boat on shore. Payment was demanded, but they endeavoured to shuffle it off, saying they had little or no money. But on finding our master disposed to seize a barrel of flour for our trouble, a guinea was produced, which our captain took care of, and we returned to load the boat with firewood, which was birch.

I had often heard of a wild-goose chase and had now an opportunity of realizing it. One evening after dark, a tufted goose of the wild breed got loose and flew into the river from our ship. We were immediately sent to search for it, which was difficult employ, the tufts of froth from the Falls being very numerous, and many of them appeared like the goose. A person on board made a goose squall which the one in the water answered, and this directed our search; we frequently got close to it, when it dived and escaped, but at last after a long and unpleasant chase, and drifting away on the ebb, we seized on our prey and had a good tug at the oars to regain our vessel.

While we lay here a seaman of ours on going on board the *Bridgwater* (a large transport), caught the small-pox. He was a handsome young man, and had them very numerous, which disfigured him so much and changed his fresh-coloured complexion to a dirty yellow, that no person could say it was the same man. We had no advice for him, and he was very averse to be governed in his diet. We endeavoured to keep him from salted provisions, but he would watch for an opportunity and get out of his hammock to carry off the meat when the way was clear, and notwithstanding this (as his time was in the Lord's hands), he recovered.

Two of the transports' boats, having been up the river one day, discovered a large mouse-deer in the water, which was wounded and pursued by hunters, but the boats overtook it and brought it to the ship as their prize. I saw part of it, viz. the antlers and a foot, from which I judged it must have been a large animal. I think the extreme of each horn must have been from three to four feet apart. Here our master wished to spend some time to avoid another expedition from New York, but the agent for transports drove us from our nest, and we got ready for sea. A widow woman Loyalist and her daughter took their passage with us, being alarmed at the dreary appearance of the country. I was informed that the tide rose to sixty feet at the head of the Bay of Fundy. What an astonishing height! The day we sailed we had a fair wind, and at night it blew very strong while we scudded under low sail. It was my turn to go below from eight to twelve at night, but the master requiring my attendance till about nine, my watch-mates were in bed when I got into the steerage. Here I perceived a great quantity of smoke, which increased and smelt very disagreeable as I approached my hammock. The second mate's hammock being in the same corner with mine I asked him what he thought of the smoke, which now proceeded from the bulk-head, that was at the foot of the mate's cabin. I therefore returned to the captain and informed him of our fears, and on opening the mate's cabin found it in the most alarming state. This man was in the habit of sticking his candle against his rum case of bottles, and having forgotten that he had left his light in his cabin did not return to it, but remained on his watch. As the door opened with me the fire began to glow, the wind being strong on deck. I called loudly and water was immediately handed down in buckets, and we well drenched the fiddler's cabin putting out the fire. His rum case was burnt on one side, and part of his feather bed.

When we were near the shoals of Nantucket we experienced a most tremendous gale of wind, and fearing the sea would drive in the cabin windows, I was ordered to fix in the dead lights or window shutters, but on going into the storeroom, and not finding them as I expected, I questioned the cabin boy about them. The poor woman being much frightened with the storm, was now further alarmed at the sound of *dead* lights, and as I was about chastising the boy for being saucy, she entreated me that I would not fight while we were in such danger. However, having found dead lights I fixed them in their places, and the old lady became more reconciled, now she understood their meaning.

About the third week in November, 1783, we arrived at New York and found the evacuation nearly completed, which gave our master great hopes of returning to Great Britain. We were now ordered to lie off Staten Island and to prepare for sea by filling our water, etc. It being my lot to follow this business in cold, frosty weather, dipping the water out of a small well, without any shelter and lightly clothed, my feet and hands suffered severely. We had also to be exposed on the masts and yards, in cold, frosty winds, with hail, sleet, etc., which often benumbed my hands so much as nearly to deprive me of feeling, and was therefore obliged often to hold fast by the bending of my arm to prevent falling in my descent. My head was covered with a blue Highland worsted bonnet which had no rim to keep the hail from my face, therefore it was fully exposed to all weathers. Whilst our master was regaling himself with the thoughts of Sunderland, lo! he was aroused from his trance by receiving orders to proceed to St. Augustine for the evacuation of the province of East Florida. This was like an electric shock to him, and his displeasure (as customary) was experienced in full measure by the crew.

Here our master laid in a few slops to sell to us, from which each man was supplied with a pair of red baize trousers, so that when we were aloft reefing the sails we appeared like a flock of flamingoes (a bird seen on the beach of the Bahama Islands, one of which that I saw was about four feet from the extremity of one wing, when spread, to the other). The seamen call them filimingoes.

*   *   *   *   *   *

G

5
He Sails to Florida

WE sailed from Sandy Hook the 13th December 1783, in company with the *Spring*, *Juno*, *Bonita*, and *Sykes* transports for St. Augustine, and soon after parted with all but the *Spring*. We experienced very turbulent weather during this passage to the southward. In one of the strong gales we perceived a meteor at the top of the mast, like a dull light in a lanthorn. Sometimes these meteors appear at all the mast heads and are seen at times running up by a rope till they arrive at the truck. Sailors in general, call these lights 'corps sants,' which I imagine is a term used by Popish seamen, and the meaning is that they suppose it to be the spirit or corpse of a saint. It is a received opinion that these lights appear at the height of the storm, and of course are not looked on as unwelcome visitants, though as sailors are generally superstitious I never knew one hardy enough to go near it, and strange stories are reported concerning them.

The *Spring* having made a signal of distress, we bore down to her and found she had sprung her main-yard and rudder, which retarded our progress. We found our caps on the main and foremast heads to be in a shattered condition, and immediately clapped on preventer ones by woolding rope, below the originals. One day after a heavy gale, the *Spring* being too near us, and it falling suddenly calm, our ship drifted and, being also attracted, we fell on board the *Spring*. The sea running very high at the time, threw us all into the greatest consternation, expecting the ships would dash each other to pieces. They appeared like wild bulls jumping and goring each other, tearing and breaking all before them. At length we passed a rope from the head of one ship to the stern of the other, and by pulling this rope one ship shot by the other, and a small breeze arising, they were kept from a repetition. These accidents frequently occur in fleets.

On the 9th we discovered St. Simona Head in Georgia, and the next morning found ourselves close in with St. Mary's bar. Having now entered the river, we rounded the shoal point of Amelia Island, and discovered a brig at anchor, which served as a guide for berthing our ship. We were informed that a king's schooner galley lay a little farther up the river, to whom we applied for advice, and our master found it requisite to go to St. Johnstown on the river of that name, from which a communication was carried on with St. Augustine, the Governor's residence. St. John's lay about forty miles off and the track was through marshes and drowned islands. The only inhabitants we found on Amelia Islands were an old man and his daughter, who I believe subsisted chiefly on oysters which covered the banks of the rivers and creeks. I have heard that the racoons are sometimes caught by the oysters that are fast to the bed, by thrusting in their paw in an open shell, which immediately closes on them.

Our carpenter was now sent to cut down a large live oak, of about eighteen or twenty inches diameter for the purpose of making new caps for the lower masts, and these caps we boiled in the coppers to season them for the purpose. The carpenter having learnt that there were some deer near us in a wood, he and the mate furnished themselves with muskets and ammunition and in the evening landed in hopes to bring on board a deer by the morning. But not being acquainted with the haunt of these animals, nor with the track in the woods, they got bewildered and returned to the ship at day-break with part of the carpenter's jacket torn off by the gunpowder exploding in his pocket, and this sickened them of hunting in future. I was given to understand that the method pursued by the native hunters to procure deer was as follows:

After acquainting themselves with the deer haunts, they endeavoured to get to leeward of them in the night, and then kindle a fire with pitch pine or turpentine sticks, which was in general placed in a long-handled frying-pan. This was carried on one of their shoulders and the light attracted the attention of the deer, whose eyes – from the reflection – appeared like two stars, at which the hunters always aimed and killed the animal. A deer exclusive of its skin and head, was to be purchased of the hunters for a dollar, or a pound of gunpowder, but the venison was far from being fat like the English, and the best method to dress it was in an iron pot on the fire, with fat pork, like roasted meat. Indeed, this was far superior to roasting it, except it had been first larded.

The tide now answering early, we procured a pilot for the inland navigation, from the galley, and set out on our first visit to St. John's in our four oared boat, Captain L – t of the *Spring* and our captain being with us. We got to the Narrows (a shoal creek) soon after daylight, and there being no room to row we had to set, or push, our boat through with our oars, though this creek had been considerably widened by the crew of a king's galley that had some time before gone this way. Having got past this creek, we sometimes passed close to bushes, woods, reeds and mud, and about mid-day arrived at Nassau Sound, an inlet from the sea, running between Amelia and Talbot Islands. On this latter island we landed to wait for the flood tide, and having dined on salted beef, close by an oyster bed, we rambled about on the sandy beach marked by the footsteps of wild horses. Our pilot informed us that these animals were numerous here. We had only discovered two or three huts hitherto, one of which was occupied by a robber and his family. About two o'clock we again pushed forward for Davis's Bluff, so called from a hunter and his wife residing here, and we arrived at the town about eight or nine at night. This day's work was one of the longest I had ever been in a boat, having been rowing from daylight to this time of night, with only a little respite at dinner, and had accomplished the distance of forty miles (so reputed).

Before this settlement we passed two king's galleys, the *Viper* and *Enterprise*; these vessels were rigged with latine yards, similar to the row galleys in the Mediterranean. Having dispatched the business at St. John's, we proceeded to the entrance of the river and found it shallower than St. Mary's, it being also a barred channel. We reached Davis's Bluff by dark, and the shipmasters retired for the night into the small hut, leaving the crew to shift for themselves. After we had landed our stores and secured the boat, we collected some dry wood and kindled a fire near the border of a large forest, round which we lay down and slept, but not very soundly, as we were roused by hearing some animal eating our quarter's beef. In the morning we proceeded to the ship.

As our work was now laborious, our master allowed us a

purser's pint[1] of rum per day divided in grog between us, amounting to about a quarter of a pint of grog for each. What liberality! The bread, oatmeal and flour we used, was the condemned provisions, the former full of weevils and the two latter sour. About once a week we had either venison or fresh beef for dinner and supper, breakfast being a Banian meal. The beef was lean, as the cattle were wild, and killed by shooting. From our ship I have seen the deer browsing in the marshes. Having hauled our ship to the beach, we gave her bottom a good cleaning, after which some of us were sent to cut wood and others to bring it on board, having a long distance to carry it on our shoulders through the marshes, on broken reeds. Having neither shoes nor stockings this galled my feet severely, as well as my shoulder, having nothing on it but a shirt or canvas frock. These marshes were swarming with mosquitoes and sand-flies, which made many a good meal on my blood, and the latter used to come on board the ship in clouds, about sunset, and their bite on hands and face was like the prick of a fine needle. We discovered some sassafras trees, the roots of which, with China root, we occasionally boiled for breakfast; the latter made the tea of a red colour and was used by the natives.

After laying here several weeks a fleet of transports arrived from England for the evacuation. We were now ordered to prepare for loading Ordnance stores; accordingly we got our water on deck, and started it, in which I perceived fish alive that we must have taken out of the well on Staten Island, some months before.

[1] Purser's pint = a short pint. – ED.

On the first day of March the surface of the river was almost covered with brown worms, very lively in their motions. Many of them took possession of the wood sheathing on our bottom and ate it to a honeycomb. Our master now, under a pretence of dunnaging the ship to keep the guns high in the hold, made us work hard in the woods in cutting, splitting and carrying through a marsh about forty dozen (I believe) of rough hickory hand-pikes. These he doubtless expected to make a good sale of in England, but alas! being ignorant of the season for cutting the wood, it was hewn in the spring when full of sap, they were therefore rotten long before we got to Great Britain. We also procured a large quantity of oak for firewood.

This being a hot country bordering on the Torrid Zone and by my wearing a Highland bonnet, my face was much exposed to the rays of the sun, which made it turn nearly to the colour of an Indian. The sandy paths on shore were sometimes so hot as to hurt the bottoms of my feet, and they were often wounded by landing on oyster beds, especially on the Tyger Island side of the harbour, which island was skirted with mud and oysters, and near which was a sand bank where we used to haul for fish with a borrowed net, and could half fill the boat in two or three hours with the following fish, viz., drum, trout, mullet, whiting, shrimps, sting rays, skate, sheeps head, bone fish, pearl fish, cat fish, and many others unknown by name. Once *only* we caught two fish of the torpedo species at the same haul: one was larger than the other, nearly fifteen inches long, and of the shape of a turbot; they had dark brown circles on their backs about an inch in diameter. When they were thrown out of the net, one of our crew took hold of one of them and received such a shock as to fling away the fish. This stroke he imagined had been given him by a man near him, which caused him to abuse his neighbour with threats to the astonishment of his shipmate, who had not touched him. Another person tried the fish and also received a lighter stroke, which became weaker from the torpedo as it expired. We carried them on board, but were afraid to eat them.

This province being now in an unsettled state, encouraged a number of poor hunters to rob and plunder the emigrants of their horses and negroes, which were sold to the Spaniards in West Florida. These banditti associated in gangs of twenty or thirty and were become formidable. A man named MacGirt was at the head of one company, and lived a few miles from hence. One day advice was received that a number of boats laden with plunder were expected down the river on their way to Georgia during the ensuing night, and as there was a navigable creek for them to turn off without coming near the galleys, it was thought advisable to waylay them. Accordingly two boats were ordered to be got ready with five men in each, armed (including myself).

Being provided with muskets, pistols and cutlasses, we set out at dark for the creek, a few miles up the river, and on arrival placed our boats close under the point of the creek marsh. Here we lay still and quiet, and every noise we heard from alligators which abounded in this river, or from fish leaping, made us look about. Our only chance, humanly speaking, for gaining a victory was by surprise, the robbers being all excellent marksmen, and their lives being at stake if taken, they would probably have fought hard, and 'tis likely overpower us by numbers. I sometimes got a nod or two while sitting on the thwart of the boat, surrounded with clouds of sand flies, and was not a little pleased to return to the *Viper* in whole skin.

In this country the hunters build their huts near a live oak tree, which not only casts a great shade, but is an indication of a spring of water. These men are lightly clothed with a large piece of coarse blue cloth, wrapped round each leg instead of stockings, and which guards their legs in their hunting excursions. Their shoes are made from a new hide in one piece, laced up before, which when dry is very hard, and these are called mawkisins. They are generally seen armed with their rifle gun. It was our custom for one man to be always on the watch on deck during the night, at which time one of the apprentices again ran from the ship. He took with him whatever he thought useful, without any regard to the owners, and also the beef watering for the next day's boiling. On gaining the shore he stole a canoe (being a noted thief, and formerly a collier in the county of Durham). Our master thought it useless to go after him, as he had taken a route unknown to us, but suppose he went towards Savannah in Georgia. We obtained a negro named York in his place. This man was sent to build a hut for his residence in a clear spot in the wood. He also built huts for keeping fowls and hogs during the night. To this place several captains sent their stock to feed during the day, and at night the poultry were penned up by York in their huts, but notwithstanding this precaution, the tiger cats, or some other animals, found means to steal away the fowls.

Two small hogs were kept on board on the lower deck, one

of which, having got on top of a tub of pitch sunk down into it, except his head, and as he was dead our cook had orders to clean him and it was roasted to regale some of our master's friends at dinner. A large quantity of frogs lived here in the marshes and made a great noise when rain was coming on.

Here our second mate went on board the *Love* transport on some business, and whilst in the cabin a huge bear fixed his claws in the back of his jacket and gave it a huge rent, to the great astonishment of the Caledonian.

The shipping at St. Mary's had now drawn a number of settlers to the beach to accommodate the sailors with grog, clothes, etc. One of these grog sellers, being in want of rum, had dispatched two negroes in a canoe to St. John's for that article, but as they were going through the Narrows two robbers came to them and ordered the slaves to land and follow, which they did, taking a bottle of oil from the canoe. In the course of their route on Amelia Island they came to a creek and one of the robbers entered the creek to see if it was fordable. Before this man had reached the opposite side, the other robber's back being towards the negro with the oil, he aimed a blow with the bottle at his head and brought him to the ground, and having given him his death wound, seized on his rifle and on firing at the other in the water, wounded him so that he could scarcely crawl up the bank, but he got away. The negroes, not being desirous to stay in such a dangerous vicinity, stripped the dead, cut off a scalp from his head and returned back to their master.

I saw the negroes on the borders of the wood with a hunter's gun, pouch, etc., and they informed me of the catastrophe, and handed me the scalp, the hair on which was red or carrotty and appeared inclined to curl. One of our crew had visited a hut near the place where the man was killed, and on going a little way into the wood discovered a vast quantity of goods hid amongst the bushes, doubtless the plunder of many houses. Another man from our ship had been on an expedition in quest of MacGirt's company, and had visited his hut where they found Mrs. MacGirt, but could not find the captain.

The day after the robber was killed; a party was dispatched to bury him; amongst the rest was a negro belonging to an emigrant family residing in our ship, and having executed their work, on his return brought with him some young racoons that he had found. These he gave to his wife, then suckling her child, who permitted the animals to draw her breast also, which coming to Captain A.'s knowledge he flew into a violent rage with the woman who was obliged to part with her additional nursery.

The captain, that great Hector, took the two small boys with him one day into the woods, he having a musket in his hands, and as they were passing through some brakes they heard the noise of tiger cats, or some other animals fighting, and instead of guarding the boys from harm, he left the gun with them and ran off as fast as if a gang of robbers had been at his heels. We obtained a wild turkey here which weighed fourteen pounds. It was shot by a native who had the art of calling them down by imitating their cry.

About this time the Spanish Fleet had arrived at Augustine to take possession of the province, and having landed their troops and stores, appeared off St. Mary's bar. The transports' boats were sent by the agent to their assistance, and we piloted about twelve ships into safety, for which we received a gratuity. I was on board the *Commodore*, a king's brig, the crew of which were filthy in the extreme. Some little time after their arrival, an affray took place at some of the grog shops on the beach, between the seamen of both nations, which ended in the death of a Spaniard. To prevent disputes in future, a creek was made the line of division to part the subjects of both nations when on shore, and this boundary cut us off from our well, our hickory wood and our wild herbs. The Spanish Fleet was now moored above the creek in the main river, and our ships collected towards the entrance. Sometimes we had to pass the Spaniards in taking our ladies an excursion, at which time they used to abuse us and insult the women with obscene language. Many of the men died here with a contagious disease, whilst the English remained free from it. One of my acquaintances dropped down dead suddenly, which was attributed to a stroke of the sun! This climate was subject to violent storms of wind, rain, thunder and lightning, and its dreadful effects were to be seen on the trees in the woods in being shattered to pieces.

This place was famous for water melons, pumpkins, apricots and plums. I was one day eating a piece of a roasted pumpkin, very hot, when a wanton chap dashed it against my face, part of which flew up my nostrils and scalded them severely. I had often heard of a bird in Virginia that used to cry *wipper Will* in the night, but here a bird of the same description used to cry *Jack Will's widow*! Great numbers of these in fine nights used to repeat this sound all night long. Here were red humming and nonparel birds, also a

variety of berries, such as mulberries, blackberries, huckle-
berries, etc. A great variety of pines grew in this vicinity fit
for lower or smaller masts and yards, and these forests were
free in a great measure from underwood, which made them
appear from their arched heads both grand and gloomy. I
was informed some wolves ranged through these vast woods
but never saw any. On one of the transport's boats returning
down the river, the crew were alarmed by a continued noise
under the boat's bottom, which was occasioned by the
thrumming noise of a drum fish, which they had no knowledge of. These fish I have heard when in the ship's hold. I
have also heard the augurs at work of a multitude of worms,
like carpenters boring, and before we sailed our sheathing
was coming off in flakes, being an entire honeycomb.

The ship having now her Ordnance stores on board and
having also taken on board the scantling and boards of a
house for Mr. A - t - b - s (our old gentleman passenger), we
prepared for sea.

*   *   *   *   *   *

6

He Sails to Nassau

THE 28th August 1784, we sailed from St. Mary's River for New Providence. We had lain before Amelia Island *thirty-three* weeks, long enough to have made *four* voyages to the Bahamas. Our bottom was now so ragged and foul that we could make but little progress in sailing, and the wind generally blew from the S.E. so that we were just a month on our passage. We arrived at Nassau in New Providence about the 25th September, and moored our ship opposite the Custom house for another long sleep.

This harbour was about 150 fathoms wide, and about three miles in length with a ridge of sand running lengthways in the middle on which was Shoalwater. The harbour was formed by Hog and Providence Islands and was a snug harbour. The Governor's house was on a round hill just at the back of the town and very pleasantly situated.

The water was so clear in the harbour that when calm in the morning, a shilling could be seen at the bottom, and all fish that were of a good size might be discovered. I have also seen a green turtle swimming here.

Here, instead of having fresh beef, our crew had green turtle once a week, out of which the family on board selected what they wanted, and I was often employed by them in chopping the lean of the turtle with fat pork ready for the ladies to make up in force-meat balls. For some months I was the running footman to this family, and as the daughters made up shirts and gowns for people, I had many a jaunt to the stores for cloth, silks, thread, etc., and to carry home the work, and being barefooted, my heels were often bruised and the feet injured on sharp rocks and small stones through the streets of Nassau. I had to fetch almost daily milk and bread from the shop of Mr. Room, and to fetch water from a well in the bushes much frequented by the most elegant green and gold humming-birds. The tropical fruits were to be had here in great plenty, though very dear.

A great variety of fish were to be caught with hook and line, but many of those were of a poisonous quality. The Margaret fish, about the size of an English bream, was most in esteem and often stewed for soup. I have seen here green fish with beaks like parrots and their eyes red. This place is noted for black men diving for conks and other things. At the entrance of the harbour on Hog Island was a negro hung on an oblique pole, for murder, and as his legs were near the ground, the waves in blowing weather used to wash him to and fro on the rocky point. This place was noted for small, fast sailing schooners, employed in the trade to the Spanish Main, and some of these returned with green turtle, some of which on landing were so emaciated by being kept many weeks out of the water in these vessels that I have seen holes in the joints of the shell arising from poverty. On the arrival of the turtle they are deposited in the wharves built on purpose to receive them, and being fed in these wells, and having plenty of pure salt water to range in they soon recover their flesh. When one is to be killed a man descends through a trap hatch, and having selected the size wanted, it is drawn up by a rope and sold to any comer at sixpence per lb.

Other schooners are cruising amongst the labyrinth of keys, shoals and islands in hopes of discovering vessels wrecked in this vicinity, or in the Gulf of Florida. But whether the crew of these craft are descendants of the pirates that formerly frequented the Island of Providence, I know not, but I believe many of them are not more honest and I have been informed that instead of warning ships when they have been in danger, they have frequently misled them by going through difficult channels or showing lights to make them alter their course and run on shore. The principal well for watering shipping here, 'tis said, was dug by order of a pirate, known by the name of Blackbeard, but the water is very brackish, being near the sea and amongst the rocks. The shore at low water where it is sandy is inhabited by a numerous quantity of small black crabs with one large claw besides the small ones. A large flat fish was seen in the harbour while we lay here, which was supposed to be the devil fish, having two horns, and I was informed that one of these at Charleston had run away with a small schooner by means of its horns.

Whilst we lay at Nassau the election for the House of Assembly took place, through the Bahama Islands, and great rancour was manifested between the contending parties, viz. the old inhabitants which were termed Conks, and the new Settlers termed Refugees. Andros Island, not being yet inhabited, was to return two members, both parties resorted to it for temporary residence before the election, and on their return a Refugee in the boat with me threw something at the head of a Conk in another boat which brought the crews into great danger from the violence of the contending parties.

Whilst at Nassau, a ship's boat was appointed to run against a shore boat for a wager, and our captain was solicited for a crew to row the former, which gained the victory. The Nassau boat was rowed by people belonging to the island craft, and which are generally termed wreckers by the sailors, their business being to hunt for wrecks in the Gulf of Florida, especially on the Martyrs' Reef near the peninsula. One of the officers of a regiment in garrison here, purchased a native boat in which he took great delight by sailing about the harbour, but not being a proficient in the management, she overset and sank, having iron shot for ballast, but his life was saved.

In the street one day I discovered two live guannas on sale, about 8 or 10 lbs. weight each, they appeared of the lizard species, their colour black, and their skin soft. Their mouths were sewn up to prevent their biting, and I was informed were eaten stewed and counted excellent food, but their appearance was certainly disgusting. After being in this harbour some months we landed the Ordnance stores at the fort, and after there had been a grand ball one evening on our quarter deck, with violins and French horns, to accommodate the company from the town, the agent shifted his pennant to the *Hope* (powder ship) laying above the town. We now began to prepare for heaving down our ship to get her new sheathed, the worms having nearly destroyed the old.

Mr. Russel, the shipbuilder at St. John's, had brought his property here in the *Live Oak* brig that he had built there, and finding a proper careening place at Hog Island, had now established a shipyard there. To this place we hauled our ship, and there being an old store there we began removing our ship's stores into it. I used to be locked in this place at night as a guard. I hung my hammock to the rafter beams, very high, and had to place casks on each other to get to my bed in the dark. The rats made a sad noise in the night which often disturbed my rest. The floor of this place was dirty and dusty, and it was also swarming with weevils and chigoes which paraded over me during the night, and many a chigoe burrowed in my flesh. These insects are brown like a flea, but nearly the size of a mite; they make their passage through the skin and there lay their eggs in a bag about the size of a pea. They are discovered by the part itching, and on inspection a small brown spot is discovered with a transparent circle round it, which is the extremity of the bag of nits. Great care is required to extract the whole of this bag by breaking the skin round the circle with a fine needle, and then lifting out the bag, but it is in general broken and, of course, some of the nits remain, to destroy which, sailors fill the holes with snuff, turpentine, pepper or some other strong ingredient. As I had neither shoes nor hose, my toes were often tied up with turpentine whilst we remained here, and were very sore. I have gone into this store in the day time for an article and on my return have washed the dust off my feet, at the same time discovering that several chigoes were in this short space sticking to my feet and legs like the ticks found in the grass in England.

Our ship being stripped and the main-mast being well secured by outriggers, whilst the carpenter was caulking the top sides, we began to heave her keel out, but the water found means to increase in the hold all day long, notwithstanding we were constantly at the pump.

Mr. A., now intending to give a rout in his newly erected

dwelling, I was dispatched in the morning from the careening place to procure the requisite refreshments. The domestics of this house were two old negroes. The man had a wooden leg and the woman was grey headed with age (almost in her dotage). When the air was cool she made her appearance in a green blanket which had a slit about the middle for her head to appear through, and this was then her cloak or mantle. These negroes being infirm and stupid, I often had to officiate in various departments in this day's attendance, and then, when dismissed, to return to Hog Island to be locked in the store for a few hours' rest.

Whilst the agent belonged to our ship we had to keep a black bear on board belonging to him. This animal used to go aloft and was often surly and troublesome. Sometimes when thirsty he would open the door under the drip stone to get at the water, and he and I had often disputes before I could get him to retire. He would grumble, scratch and bite, and I had to flog him well with a rope to make him quit his hold.

Our ship being now new sheathed, we moved the ship before the town of Nassau, to prepare for sea.

The inhabitants of Nassau were dissipated in the extreme, and from night revels many had injured their health. I saw little appearance of any religion, but heard that a man of colour frequently preached to the eastward of the town under a large spreading tree.

* * * * * *

7

He Returns to Florida and England

Having been here above seven months we received our sailing orders to return to St. Mary River, and left Nassau the 14th April 1785. We continued plying to windward till the 19th when we took our departure from Talon's Key, and about the 25th got in, over St. Mary's bar, and anchored within Amelia Island.

About a week after our arrival I had been sent with some hogsheads to fill with fresh water, at a well dug in the sand amongst the bushes on Amelia Island, and as it flowed slowly, we had to roll the casks over a loose sand hill, so we did not return to the ship till about three o'clock in the afternoon. At this time a storm was brooding in the western quarter which urged us to hoist on board the water quickly, that we might get below before the rain began, the thunder being loud, and the lightning vivid. We at length seated ourselves in the steerage, well in out of the hatchway. Soon after this the ship was struck with lightning at our mainmast head, which first drew out an iron bolt and then descended in a crooked direction, towards the deck, tearing the mast to shivers. It then came down the hatchway and struck several men and boys. When it struck me I thought a piece of fire ejecting a spark about the size of a duck's egg had knocked me down, and on recovering from the blow the first thing that occurred to me was that the lightning had got into the magazine under the lazarette, and as there was a cask of powder and cartridges that had been saved from barrels that had fallen to pieces just under the scuttle, I thought this barrel had blown up the ship. As I came more to my senses I saw the men about me in various postures, but

one after another began to speak as a man just awakened
from sleep. There was a great emanation of a sulphury
scent in our apartment and a sound of bells ringing in my
ears all the night after. The peals of thunder removing at a
distance and the sound becoming weaker, encouraged a man
to peep on deck where he discovered a multitude of splinters from the mast. The mate was in the cabin but was
ignorant of the disaster till we called him up. On searching
about we found the shears erected to get out the mizen
mast had also suffered and the cross-jack yard was become
useless. The side of the ship next the captain's state-room
had also suffered and the treenails were started. The bottle
containing the snake, caught a few days before, was shivered
in bits, and other things damaged in the cupboard. The
cook, who was sick in one of the cabins built for troops, we
found dead.

It is an old proverb that one trouble seldom comes alone,
and it was now verified by the return of our carpenter and
his companion, from Stricklands Bluff, before they had
accomplished their work. They had kindled a fire to dress
their victuals near their tent, and in their absence from it
the grass had led the fire to their habitation, which they
found on their return nearly consumed, and being now har-
bourless and without provision, they embraced the opportunity of a ship's boat that called there to return to the ship.
A coffin was now made and a grave dug in the bushes, when
we carried the cook on shore, and I read the burial service
at the interment, though I believe it did no good, either to
the dead or the living.

Many masts and spars being now wanted, our captain set

off with a gang to a forest on the south fork of St. Mary's River, where they cut a spar for a main-mast. After the branches were lopped off more men than our crew were found necessary to drag it out of the wood, and this was done by fixing a tackle or purchase from tree to tree, and placing rollers under the mast. After great labour and exertion it was brought to Amelia beach and there finished. We now were next employed in getting in the masts and rigging out the ship. This being accomplished we had orders to prepare to load for London, to our great joy.

Our master had now some intention of going in search of a hunter, on the Georgia side, who often brought deer to the shipping; we accordingly set out on the excursion early, and after ascending the river three or four miles, we discovered an alligator asleep in our direction, and by keeping quiet got so near as to strike it with an oar when he made a spring and immediately disappeared. We had little difficulty in finding the beaten track through the marsh, which led to Stricklands hut, or wig-wam, which was erected under the shade of a large spreading tree (probably a live oak). The hunter, his wife and another man we found here, and at a little distance from his residence I discovered a quantity of slices of meat on sticks which had been smoked, and proved to be the flesh of a bear lately shot. This place having been formerly settled we found an orchard of apricots, the trees bending down with their weight, and a vast quantity we carried by permission to the boat. A small patch of Indian corn was in ear, under which cucumbers, water melons, etc., were in plenty, and the melons were equal in my opinion both in size and flavour to those I have eaten at Lisbon.

The hunters, or crackers, are generally an indolent set of men unless urged by necessity to exert themselves. They will place a pumpkin to roast by the fire, and instead of waiting till it is perfectly dressed they cut off the part roasted, and then replace it at the fire, making irregular meals and sleeping at intervals.

As sailors when idle are generally plotting mischief, some of the men finding several wooden houses evacuated here, were determined to have a bonfire at night that the Spanish who had taken possession of the province might not obtain the benefit of those dwellings. Accordingly after dark the men separated in various directions to bring away doors, windows, shutters, etc., to the beach, and to demolish the small houses. A large fire was kindled under the bluff, which continued to be supplied with timber thrown down on the beach till the agent hearing of what was doing came amongst them, and even then he found it extremely difficult to stop the devastation, it being very dark, and whilst he was engaged with one party, another was feeding the fire, and a vessel of about 20 tons laying on the beach was also burnt.

In a day or two after this, we were informed that the Governor intended to proceed from St. Augustine to the Jericho plantation, on St. John's River, and there to embark in a boat. We therefore ascended the river fifteen or twenty miles, and landed from the squadron at the above plantation, which we found evacuated by its late proprietor. The morning after our arrival here, it being little wind and fine weather, the alligators were roaring like so many bulls as they floated on the ebb tide, and many of them were heard from a considerable distance. I perceived that they moved

their upper jaw when they opened their mouth to roar;
the noise all around us was like in some degree to the
lowing of cattle on a farm.

This morning some of the seamen set fire to a stable,
in which was a large quantity of leaves of Indian corn, used
as fodder for the cattle, and as it burned with great rapidity
it was consumed in a few minutes. They next burned a
new erected dwelling merely to obtain the nails and iron-
work. In the afternoon going over the plantation with a
musket, we discovered a small horned owl in a tree, which
we shot; the horns were two feathers, erect, one over each
eye, its plumage was a varigated brown, and little larger
than a thrush. After being here a day or two, the Governor
arrived and embarked.

We were now ordered to return to our ships, each boat
making the best of its way back. We just got alongside our
ship when the Governor arrived at St. Mary's and we had
the opportunity of seeing the *Cyrus's* yards manned to salute
him, as well as the firing of her guns. The Governor now
took up his residence in the *Cyrus*, armed ship, and on board
this ship I saw a number of Grecians with their families,
who had lately been inhabitants of this province, and perhaps were brought here to cultivate the growth of silk worms
(many mulberry trees being here), or else to cultivate vines.

On entering our ship, I perceived several ladies on deck,
and found they were three daughters of Colonel B –, whose
family, consisting of father, mother, three daughters and
three sons, had come by sea from Augustine with their
servants and baggage and intended to go to London in our
vessel. As our cabin was fitted up with bed places by

Government, originally for army officers and still at the disposal of the agent, our master was obliged to evacuate his dwelling and retire to his state room, and as this family was genteel and had come on board to his great mortification, he scarcely treated them with common civility. For his deficiency in politeness and attention I endeavoured to make up, and which was not altogether unnoticed by the mother and daughters.

We often used to pay visits to the apricot orchard where I used to fill my pillow-case with the fruit, from which stock I supplied Colonel B –'s sons, the eldest not being above twelve years old, and the ladies often came in for a share.

We were now going on with loading red bay logs, turpentine and staves for England, when many more passengers arrived on board, and as there was no room for them in the cabin, they struck a bargain with our master for the steerage, the habitation of our crew. We were therefore immediately ejected and retired to the forecastle, a place not sufficiently large to contain our hammocks. I was therefore obliged to sling mine in the cable-tier, a dark back-breaking situation. I seldom retired to my bed but slept many weeks either on deck for air, or else on a chest without any bedding. We had often tremendous storms of rain, thunder and lightning, which frequently wetted me to the skin. At those times I either let my shirt dry again on my back, or wrung out the water; but at last I found myself attacked by illness, attended with great languor and lowness of spirits, my skin also became yellow like jaundice, therefore suppose my complaint was bilious. The surgeon of the *Cyrus* was sent to visit me, but whether at the request of our master or Mrs. B – I know not, but he I think sent me a quart black bottle of medicine, and as he did not consider me as a very profitable patient, I do not recollect that he ever called on me the second time. Mrs. B –, with her eldest daughter, visited me in my hammock, and the latter sent me her smelling bottle, and I had some victuals sent by them from the table. In about a week (through mercy) I began to regain my spirits, and was soon able to do my work again.

About this time an Indian Chief, either of the Creek or Cherokee nations, had arrived at a place called the Township, on the south fork of St. Mary's River. The Governor hearing of his arrival sent some boats to bring him to the *Cyrus*. He passed with his two wives near our ship; they were dressed very tawdry and I believe painted. On getting alongside the armed ship the chief was afraid to go up the side till the Governor (his acquaintance) appeared to encourage him, when he entered the ship with courage. His business was to complain that the British had given away his country to the Spaniards without his consent. He promised to protect any of the old settlers that would remain in the province, but threatened immediate hostility against the Spaniards after the final departure of the British. In a day or two after he was sent back to the Township where a large escort of Indians were in waiting. The Indians were in the habit of visiting the Governor at Augustine to obtain presents, and I have seen one or two at St. John's. They had a large hole cut through under the gristle of their nose.

At the beach of Amelia Island, people often caught large

yellow bass, about the size of a cod, with hook and line: these were excellent fish, and turtle was sometimes found on the beach, one of which I saw, and I have been informed that eggs belonging to them are sometimes found in the sand.

On going alongside the *Bonita* transport, I saw a chain from her masthead led down into the water to conduct the lightning; it was about the size of the chains used in land measure, and had such a one been fixed at our mainmast, 'tis probable it would not have been shivered. I was informed that the fire has been seen in storms running down these chains in a continued succession, without any injury to the ship. Our ship being now laden, we prepared for sea, but to the best of my recollection we had not a single pound of any kind of provisions on board for the crew. On the 23rd of August 1785, we sailed for London, having been in St. Mary's River seventeen weeks. The master was well acquainted with our want of provisions, and as I had once received a good flogging with the bite of a large rope for asking for more meat for the crew, I was not very fond of risking a repetition; but as we were now commencing a passage of some thousand miles, I thought it prudent to represent our situation and to propose short allowance to take place immediately on the Government provisions. He now thought it advisable to adopt my proposal; our crew was accordingly put on an allowance of rice for breakfast, a small allowance of meat for dinner, and a small allowance of bread. The passengers had laid in a sea stock of pigs, fowls, etc., and our master and mate, being in the steerage mess with the passengers, fed well. One of our gentlemen had brought on board a barrel of salted mackerel, which on being opened was found rotten with age, the fish being broken in small pieces; this was given to us and which we ate undressed to savour our rice and bread.

As we drew near Newfoundland we experienced much fog and rain, which continued many days, and as I had little clothing and had been long in a warm climate, I suffered severely not being able to dry my jacket, or even my shirt, the weather being so wet. The foresail being directly over the scuttle descending our habitation conducted the wind down in such a torrent on our wet bodies that it made us tremble with the cold, and two or three of our small crew were laid by which was much felt, as our ship required often pumping. I have gone below wet, and for want of a change of clothes have been afraid to go to bed, dreading what I should experience in turning out of my bed, in a bath of sweat occasioned by going to sleep in a wet shirt, and then again putting on my wet jacket and trousers to keep my watch on deck. I have in preference to turning into my hammock, during my four hours below, sat down on a chest with my arms across shivering and shaking with the wind pouring down on my wet clothes. Our carpenter, cook, etc., had entirely deserted the deck, and our master fearing more would flinch from duty, stormed at the invalids and at length got them on deck again.

Near my bed two small white face monkeys were tied in bad weather, which were under my protection and belonged to the Colonel. These animals were very amusing;

one was named Jacko, the other Cæsar. They were fed with boiled rice and I observed they made it a general rule, when their food was set before them, first to fill both hands and then their cheek bag and lastly their stomach. What was deposited in their hands remained there till they cleared the plate. I have seen a person smoking tobacco near them, and though the smoke obliged them to close their eyes, yet they endeavoured to collect it with their hands and kept rubbing it into their hair on their bodies with greediness. I imagine from an instinct that it would rout the fleas. On giving them an onion they would regularly take off the different layers, rubbing each piece over their bodies, their eyes at the same time discharging water and half shut. The Colonel had also a racoon on board and each of the young ladies had a lap dog, procured from the Spaniards arrived at Augustine.

Soon after leaving the banks of Newfoundland, the middle finger of my right hand was attacked by a whitlow or pied, the pain of which broke my rest, and when it got to a head a passenger, who had been an overseer of negroes, cut it open with a razor, but it did not heal but continued to gather and discharge till we arrived at Portsmouth. One day, the ladies having appeared on deck, they sent a negress to inquire what was the matter with my hand and afterwards sent me some linen cloth and salve, but as I had to do duty aloft I frequently hurt it. When hauling on a rope one day on deck with one hand only, our master abused me severely and insisted on my using both hands, and he not only used his tongue but handled me very roughly also.

Having now gained the English Channel and passed

Plymouth, one morning as I came on deck I found our ship hauling in round St. Albans head, our master supposing it to be the Isle of Wight. I looked again and again at the place, but the view was quite unknown to me, and I declared it was not the place he supposed it to be, and on looking to the eastward he perceived the Wight, and as the wind was fair we entered the Needles about nine in the morning, and anchored to my great joy at Spithead about noon, some day the latter end of September 1785.

In the afternoon I was ordered to Portsmouth for fresh meat, when I called on a surgeon who informed me that the reason of my finger having been so long bad was that it had never been sufficiently cut open. He therefore with a scissors did the needful and charged me half a crown.

We now sailed for the river Thames and got safe to our moorings at the Redhouse, Deptford. Here the Jews soon found we had been long from England and consequently much wages was due and pressed hard for watches, etc., which they obtained from many, but I resisted their importunity.

My brother having sailed out of London some years, and as I knew his lodgings when at home, the day after arrival I went in quest of him and on application at the house I found to my great satisfaction he was then in London, and recently returned in the *Houghton* from Bengal, in which ship he had been midshipman and coxswain. Having left instructions where to find me I returned to the ship and in the afternoon my brother came on board when I gathered my few clothes together and took them on shore to his lodgings.

This ends when I was turned of twenty-one years of age.

Part two

8

He Becomes Mate in the Coasting Trade

I FOUND my brother a high-spirited young man, of good abilities. He informed me that he was now preparing to be examined to pass for a fourth mate for the ship *Earl Cornwallis* for Canton, without going through the degrees of sixth and fifth mates. Not having seen my brother a long while before this, I was determined to stay a few weeks with him and then pay a visit to my relations in Cornwall.

I now began to provide a good stock of clothes either to appear as a gentleman, or as a jack tar. I also laid in a stock of useful books, and remitted a Bank Post Bill of £20 to my uncle, to remain in his hands until my arrival in the west. My brother appeared to be possessed of all that spirit and generosity incident to the character of British seamen, and as he had nearly cleared the gains of his late voyage, he was ready to assist in reducing mine, and was so lavish of his money, that I have known him when intending to cross Tower Hill, to get a shilling exchanged for halfpence to supply the numerous mendicants. As this was a common custom with him, as soon as he was discovered on the hill you might see the lame, lazy and maimed all in motion, directing their course to a well-known benefactor. The tailor who made my clothes had a wife greatly afflicted with asthma; her day was spent in leaning over a chair back, and at night kneeling by her bedside with her day-clothes on, and I think she told me that she had not been in bed for some years. Her spirits appeared lively and she pronounced her words with the greatest rapidity.

My brother being a good pilot in London I put myself under his direction, and in one of our rambles, passing through St. James's Park I met Colonel B.'s lady and two of her daughters. The young ladies knew me immediately, but their mother only recollected being familiar with my features without being able to call me by name, and well she might be at a loss as I had exchanged my old sea clothes for a fashionable blue coat, ruffled shirt, etc., with my hair dressed and powdered.

As I did not like squandering away my money I only went once to Drury Lane Theatre, and then merely to see the King, Queen and family, and instead of frequenting a place of worship on Sundays to return thanks for the numberless mercies I had experienced during my voyage, I spent the Sabbath in wandering about and in paying visits.

I had lent my brother ten guineas besides treating him occasionally, but he was very desirous to obtain a further sum, which I resisted, and as I had little more money than what would serve till my arrival in the west I was determined to go to Falmouth by sea, and took my passage in the cabin of a trader, for a guinea. My brother followed me to the vessel and by entreaty procured from me a half-guinea more, which, as I never saw him after, remains unpaid.

After having been in London above a month I sailed for the Downs. In the Downs we experienced much blowing weather, and after trying to get round the South Foreland, we were forced to run for Ramsgate pier, and in going in broke the arm of one of our bower anchors. Here we lay against a narrow quay in a tier of vessels for a great while, and as all the vessels had fires *on deck*, I have seen the sparks

OLD FALMOUTH, FROM THE SOUTH.

(*From a print in the possession of* Mr. J. A. D. Bridger.)

of fire flying over the brig, and from the carelessness of our crew the scuttle was sometimes lifted off, where the gunpowder was kept. This being the case I was not very fond of staying on board in the daytime, and to avoid resorting to a public-house I used to wander about the fields on the Isle of Thanet. We at length sailed, and at last reached Falmouth, after being full five weeks on our passage. The captain charged me a shilling per day for my victuals during the whole time, though I assisted in working the vessel and though my clothes were much injured in my chest by wet. It would have been cheaper had I come by coach.

Having informed my friends in the west of my arrival, I stayed here a few days, and then rode to the town where I had been about seven years at school.[1] There I stayed a day or two with some of my old playfellows who wished me to stay to dance at the Assembly. I had been a considerable time in the borough at the dancing school in the days of my youth and vanity, under the tuition of Monsieur Thuillier (a Frenchman) and was very fond of this exercise, but I now declined. I now rode to my native place[2] at the western extremity of Britain, and found a welcome reception from my relations. My sister was a little girl when I had last seen her, but now she was a woman. At this place I received the most marked attention from all orders and degrees of people, from the mayor to the town crier, and from the Church minister to the sexton, most of the grown people having known me from my infancy.

[1] Helston.   [2] St. Ives.

Having dined with a gentleman here, after dinner, he produced a bottle of Jamaica rum to make some punch, which spirit had been presented to him by my father when master of the ship *General Wolfe*, which vessel was stranded in this bay *before my parents were married*, and which my friend had preserved till this time, to entertain me.

My brother had now prevailed on my Uncle W. to join him in a bond of £50, to provide necessaries for his voyage to China, for which place he sailed in the spring of 1786; but on his passage most of the officers of his ship being North Britain my brother and them did not agree. He therefore on arrival of the ship in China quitted her to go into the country vessel, after which I never heard what became of him correctly, therefore I imagine he soon after paid the debt of nature. I now obtained a few articles left by my father, viz., a silver watch, shoe, knee and stock buckles, his shaving apparatus, a few old sea charts, a quadrant made by Davis, and a hat. His clothes my brother had long since received.

My Uncle W., with whom my sister resided here, had sunk a great part of his money (gained when captain of a Guinea-man out of Liverpool) in shipping and the mines, he had still an estate in the eastern part of this county which might bring in about £70 per annum. The only life remaining was that of his only daughter and she was now in bad health. My uncle expecting her death sold this estate for about £200, after which his daughter lived about twenty years! !

As my uncle was a very moral, prudent man, I cannot account for his losses to anything so much as from the property being obtained in the slave trade. In January 1786 a *second* crop of apples as large as walnuts was gathered from a tree in a relation's orchard while I remained here. A cousin of mine, a native of this place, had been many years master of a brig in the coasting trade between Bristol and Liverpool, and his vessel had been lately run down and sunk by another brig in the Channel, part of the crew being drowned, while himself, a woman passenger, and several others got on board the other vessel and were preserved. He had just agreed in Bristol for building a new vessel, and was now come here on a visit. He proposed taking me as a chief, and only mate, in the new brig if I was willing, to which I assented. In some part of February 1786, we took our passage for Bristol in an old brig (the *Nancy*), and having got under sail, the pilot leaving us, discovered a hole under the brig's quarter which had been broken by another vessel in the great surf running in the pier. This was a very providential discovery as we were to encounter very rough gales in our passage, the brig being also ancient and decayed. We had now to wait in the bay while the pilot went on shore to procure some sheet lead to nail over the hole. This being effected we sailed and with great exertion got as far as Aberthaw, from which place we were forced to run for Ilfracombe, where we lay many days waiting for moderate weather, my cousin having set out by land from hence for Bristol.

The wind inclining to the south we sailed; soon after, it veered again to the eastward; the second evening we got near the Holmes. About midnight on the height of the flood we sheered in towards Woodspring and came to an anchor.

Soon after bringing up, the tide being very rapid, and having a man at the helm steering we found the anchor had started and continued to drag. The weather being very severe with an intense frost the pilot did not like to leave the cabin fire, and the captain could not get two men on deck which were benumbed with the cold. These two, with the man to helm, and the captain (four in all) made the whole crew. It was now found necessary to drop the other anchor, which was executed by myself and the captain, and we veered away the cable 'till both anchors brought her up. At daylight the brig was covered with ice and the cables very thick, the tide of flood also coming on it was determined to endeavour to get the anchors. The captain undertook to hold the cable whilst I had got a handspike at the windlass, which kept my hands a great deal from the wet; having secured the anchors and in attempting to work the windward the fore stay-sail blew away from the bolt rope, and the foretop-sail split on the leech, which obliged us to run for Minehead. On getting near the place we made a signal for a boat, but no one appearing we proceeded for Ilfracombe once more, our captain's finger having been frost bitten in the morning was turned very black. We got into the harbour before dark, having only about one meal of biscuits remaining on board. At this place I saw a large handsome brig launched at low water. She was lowered on one side and launched on her bilge; the launch was well executed and she ran off the ways nearly her length on the oar-weed laid for to receive her.

Having repaired our vessel we again sailed and reached Bristol in safety, and as I had been serviceable to the captain he would have no money for my passage. During the passage the captain was applied to for a chart that we might compute our distance from the headland, to which he replied that he believed there had never been such a thing on board the vessel, which I believe was full thirty years old. In this vessel he had sailed from his apprenticeship and knew the Bristol Channel thoroughly, but when blown out of his old track he was totally at a loss. He once sailed from Hayle for the Bristol Channel, and after having made a few tacks and supposing he was standing over to the coast of Wales he ran on shore in Mounts Bay.[1] But he made his exit in his old track, having built a new vessel, and in running for Swansea, struck on the Mixon sand, where the vessel went to pieces and he was drowned. He was a hardy little man and so very courageous that having broken his leg by a fall from a ladder, some time before, and after it had been set a considerable time, several splinters of bone used to work out. One day he informed me, that having discovered a splinter he was determned to extract it himself. Having prepared a razor or penknife he requested the mate to hold the candle, while he made an incision in his leg. The mate attending closely to the process fainted away, when the noble captain stopped short to assist his attendant by fetching a dram of brandy to revive him, and then went on with the operation.

On my arrival at Bristol I took lodgings where my relation lived, and found on inspecting the new vessel that she had little more than the lower foottocks[2] laid, and was not likely to be launched till June. I spent much of my time in

---

[1] The other side of Cornwall.   [2] Futtocks. — ED.

ranging round the country and in copying verses and
epitaphs into a book of 184 pages from the different re-
positories of the dead in this vicinity.

Having now got in the lower masts on the stocks, the brig
was launched, and though the hatchways were not finished
I commenced sleeping on board immediately, and believe
from this period to the end of April 1789, which was the
whole time I acted as chief mate in this brig, *Liverpool*, and
in the ship *Thetis* I never slept a single night on shore,
though within this time I had visited Liverpool, Almeria,
Marseilles, Sicily, Gibralter, Jamaica, London, and twice
Philadelphia.

In July 1786 we laid on the berth and loaded a general
cargo for Liverpool. In going down the Avon, our vessel
struck the ground, going through the clifts (or cleeves), but
did not stop. We, having reached Pill, moored there to wait
for a wind. All our crew was to be paid by the run, which
generally makes them think they have no right to work when
windbound, but I endeavoured to teach them that as they
ate the provisions of the vessel they were to do the work.
One of these men, who had been an old Guineaman, I detected in stealing a piece of beef from the harness tub, but
notwithstanding his dishonesty he afterwards found means
to get the command of a Guinea ship out of Liverpool.
This man had given me such an account of the iniquity
practised in the slave trade that I determined never to go
into that employ.

We were several weeks in getting to Liverpool where we
discharged our cargo. I boarded while here at a public-
house, where all the masters in three regular traders to

Bristol lodged when here. A mate of one of these vessels was now my companion, and the landlady to make the most of her money used to give us two milk with a little sugar in it for supper, and at our breakfast we were often finished of bread and butter. I have known her mother at 90 years of age kept so short of victuals as to steal a round of the loaf when the servant was out of the way and hide it, she being only a kitchen guest. After loading principally with rock salt we sailed for Bristol with a southerly wind, which towards evening blew very strong, and brought us under low sails, when, it was determined to go into Holyhead to cut the distance short, our master was determined to run within the Skerry Island, a channel very narrow, with dangerous reefs of rocks on both sides, and no leading mark at night to direct the course. I was a stranger to this place, but knew sufficient to vote against the attempt, but the master, as if infatuated, was positive. The night was gloomy, and as we entered the channel the water was much agitated like a pot boiling and foaming. Having reached the reef, running the length of half a mile of the Island of Anglesea, we ran bounce against it, the next wave lifted us above the rocks, and when we were on the middle of the reef we struck again, and the vessel swung round. All was immediately in confusion and the master had disappeared. Under a supposition that as we were not afloat the vessel would now sink in deep water I ran below for the axe to cut the boat loose from her lashings, and having given orders to a man to execute this, I ran to sound the pump, and to my great joy found she had not sprung a leak. We found now that we were drifting towards the

West Mouse which providentially we cleared and steered for Holyhead bay. In all our hurry the master had not shown himself, but on my going into the cabin I found him there, greatly terrified. We continued tacking in the bay till the tide answered, and then ran into Holyhead and moored. I have read somewhere that seamen are neither reckoned among the living nor the dead, their whole lives being spent in jeopardy. No sooner is one peril over, but another comes rolling on, like the waves of a full grown sea. In the Atlantic one fright after another undermines the most robust constitution and brings on apparent old age in the prime of life. No trouble softens their hard obdurate hearts, but as soon as the danger is past they return in the greatest avidity to practice wickedness and blaspheme their Maker and preserver. Our master with the great fright, had taken to his bed and required great persuasion to get him to exert himself. I think we were six weeks in going to Bristol, having visited also Milford and Ilfracombe by reason of the blowing weather and foul winds.

*　　*　　*　　*　　*　　*

9

He Sails to Philadelphia

ABOUT the beginning of the year 1787 my Uncle W., with whom my sister lived, was so far reduced as to be obliged to break up house-keeping and go to sea again, being now about seventy years of age. He obtained the situation of supercargo to Jamaica. His daughter and my sister were now obliged to go to Liverpool to reside awhile with his late wife's friends, he having married there. On our arrival at Liverpool I found my sister there. I had now much reason to dislike this berth which brought me in 40s. per month, and as I wished to go abroad in the foreign trade, Providence soon prepared me the means. The ship's husband[1] for the three Bristol traders here was largely concerned in shipping, who I shall call Mr. 10.10. He had now bought a vessel for the Philadelphia trade and I was informed that I might have the chief mate's berth if I wished it. I readily embraced the proposal, and as soon as she began to load I removed my bedding from the brig to the *Thetis*. The first night I slept on board the vessel I was much annoyed with a vast number of rats and was obliged to take my clothes into bed to prevent their being injured, being well acquainted with these animals in different ships and having had the horn buttons destroyed of my jacket. After taking on board a quantity of fine salt we levelled it, to stow other goods thereon, but on viewing the surface of the salt in the morning it was marked all over as if sheep had been treading it all night.

After being laden, we sailed for Philadelphia, about the

---

[1] 'The agent or broker who manages her accounts with regard to work performed, repairs, etc., under refit or loading.' – SMYTH.

1st April 1787. I soon found my captain, though a civil man and an excellent seaman, had nothing more of a gentleman about him than what was confined to his clothes; his whole delight was vulgarity in the extreme, and not only associated with the seamen but played at halfpence with the boys. Nothing particular occurred on our passage out, but experiencing very rough weather until we struck soundings on the American coast about the middle of May following. We now stood in for the land about 30 miles to the southward of the Delaware, when in a fog we threw the lead over and found only 14 fathoms of water, which made us try again, when we found about 8; we immediately tacked and providentially escaped being wrecked on Jink, a teek shoal, but not laid down in our chart although it lays several miles off the land. In about two days more we got a pilot and entered the Delaware; the land being low towards the sea, the first that appears are the tops of trees like a fleet of ships. Our pilot was a young man from whom I wished to draw information respecting the shoals in the Delaware Bay, but he gave me to understand that whatever he knew of these things was not to be communicated to a British subject.

We had a pleasant run with a fresh breeze up the river, and after passing the towns of Newcastle, Wilmington and Chester we arrived at Philadelphia, which extended on a bay in the river, in the shape of a crescent, the length of two miles.

Having hauled into a wharf, our salt was soon bargained for and we began to discharge. Having got some lettuces on board and recollecting that rats were fond of vegetables, I baited the trap with the leaves and caught eleven at once.

One evening, sitting alone writing in the cabin, I heard a rat at work in the locker, when having looked therein, I saw a rat with one eye shut, eating the cork of an oil jar. Soon after I heard him again. I therefore called the cabin boy and told him to hold the candle that I might kill the rat he heard in the locker, and in order to make the boy be more afraid of doing anything amiss, I gave him to understand that I could discover many things, and as a proof of it that I knew the said rat had but one eye. I then (with the poker) opened the locker and killed the rat, which I told the boy to examine, and he was not a little surprised at finding my report true.

I generally endeavoured to visit a place of worship on the Sabbath, not only from custom but in hopes my good deeds would help me finally to Heaven. One Sabbath in the morning I directed my steps to the Episcopal Church or St. Paul's (without a tower); while passing through the churchyard, I met a man with a little girl whose person I had known at Falmouth, and on mentioning my name he pressed me to dine with him that day. Two of my sisters had been put to board with his wife's mother at the time of my mother's death, and one of them died there with the small-pox in Falmouth. I found this house well-stowed with new mahogany furniture, for sale; even the parlour where we dined was crowded with tables, etc., heaped one on another, and for want of money could make no sale.

Tradesmen in general here being obliged to carry on a barter business, which was very unsatisfactory, and therefore my friend had determined to emigrate with his family to Kentucky, a frontier new settlement, bordering on the

Indian nations, which at this time was draining many inhabitants away from this city. The letters of introduction I had received at Ilfracombe I now presented, and not only procured me a dinner in a genteel family but also a general invitation.

Having delivered our cargo, our vessel was chartered to load mahogany and dyewood for Liverpool. Being now laden, we took on board a quantity of dollars privately, as the British agents, for want of procuring Bills on England, were obliged to make their returns in dollars. Having obtained a passenger belonging to Glasgow, we sailed from the wharf the beginning of July 1787. The 22nd sounded on the grand Bank of Newfoundland, hove too, and caught 10 codfish. The 23rd found our ship in the midst of vessels fishing at anchor. French ships are not allowed by the British to anchor on the Bank; they generally fish driving about, although I have seen them at anchor.

After leaving the Bank we discovered a field or island of ice drifting to the southward with the current, and although it was now the month of August, from its vast bulk under water, it is probable it would take many weeks more to dissolve, although apparently a stream of water was now falling from it. It would have been dangerous to have met it during the night.

The 10th August we got to the eastward of Cape Clear, and about the 13th arrived at Liverpool. On my taking leave of our passenger he made me a present of two handsome waistcoat pieces, for my attention to him during the passage. He was a martyr to the effects of his former improprieties and was often obliged to leave his bed at night and apply cold wet clothes to his shin bones to relieve the pain therein.

After our ship was put into good repair a quantity of copper bolts, presented as part of a cargo from Toulon, intended for building the French Navy, which was to be landed at Marseilles, these we agreed to load with Smith's coal to make up a cargo.

The 14th November, 1787, we sailed for Marseilles, and experienced very turbulent weather and contrary winds in getting to the southward. On the 23rd we saw a number of grampuses sporting themselves; they are a species of whale. Towards the latter end of November we experienced heavy thunder and lightning with incessant rain.

On the 5th December we passed Cape Trafalgar, and the day following we were near Gibraltar. The 9th being off Cape de Gate, and a Levanter, or strong easterly gale blowing, we ran into Almeria bay and anchored with the best bower in 20 fathoms in order to veer out all the new cable and give it a good washing and stretching. Many captains are so careful of their best cable as to preserve it dry as long as possible, and trusting to this, when they have let their best bower anchor go in a roadstead, have been much surprised to find the cable snap off before the ship was brought up, by its being dry rotten. But it was our custom to wet the cables often with salt water, even when crossing the western ocean, which by long experience I have found to preserve them from the injury of the dry rot, and from the fresh water draining from seamen's wet clothes after rain.

The 12th December we sailed for the eastward, and the

19th passed Cape Dragon and entered the Gulf of Lyons. This is a very blusterous and dangerous navigation, and in strong gales the sea runs short and irregular, which does much damage to shipping. As soon as we rounded Cape Dragon at intervals we were becalmed and at other times we were much annoyed with whirlwinds, formed first on the Pyrenean Mountains (that parts France from Spain), and then poured down into the gulf with accumulating violence. We have seen the sea all of a foam between us and the land, with these squalls, while our ship was without an air of wind. While the day continued by looking out sharply we did pretty well, but at midnight we were attacked by one of the squalls which, as fast as we secured one sail, another was required to be taken in, until we were reduced to a very low sail. At daylight we found ourselves very near the land, and the water much discoloured, but by carrying a good press of sail we entered the Port of Marseilles in the morning of the 20th, and in the course of five minutes' time from our entrance we found our ship land-locked in one of the snuggest harbours I had ever been in, being like a large floating dock, surrounded by houses. Having anchored, our master repaired to the Health Office, but as he had neglected to procure a Bill of Health at Liverpool, which is always demanded in the European side of the Mediterranean, we were ordered into quarantine at the entrance of the Mole. On Sunday, the 23rd, at daylight some officers came on board to smoke our crew, the whole of which was ordered into the steerage, where a fire was made, into which was thrown some drugs which made a great smoke. No light, fire, or smoking tobacco was allowed on board here, which was unpleasant some cold days, on which the gentlemen on shore wore muffs in the street.

The crews of the French vessels were badly fed. I do not recollect their having any meat, but fed on fish, and I have seen shell fish for their dinner known in England by the name of sea eggs.

When our boat arrived here her bottom was white painted, but on being hoisted out, the salt water in this Mole was so corrupt that it turned the paint black.

The person put on board to prevent smuggling was a soldier. One night, being inclined to desert his post, to avoid detection, he got one of our seamen to put on his top-coat and hat to walk the deck with, giving strict orders how to behave when the patrol passed the ship. He accordingly went and returned to the vessel undetected.

On one side of the Mole was the promenade, well filled on Sabbath afternoons with people of all ranks and degrees. My attention was attracted by a man with a table, on which was a small brass cannon, birds, etc. A goldfinch was now dressed like a soldier with a Grenadiers cap, a lighted match was then given to him, and at the word of command discharged the gun, and did not appear to mind the report, which was as great as from a duelling pistol. The man then addressed his audience informing them that he had on sale a preparation for killing vermin in the head. Many people were busy roasting chestnuts for sale, piping hot.

The Mall being now filled, I paraded amongst them and was not a little disgusted to behold the ladies, young and old, so strongly painted and their faces so disfigured that I scarcely saw a handsome woman amongst them. I was much pleased with the marble fountains here, being well executed in various forms and elegant figures. This is a noted place for cordials, also for artificial fruit and flowers. I purchased a plate of the former, well executed in marble, for about 5s., consisting of a peach, nectarine, lemon, apple, peas, and two figs.

Near our vessel at the head of the Mole the fishing boats landed their cargoes. I had, therefore, an opportunity of observing that the female dealers in this article were not at all deficient in loquacity and virulence from the sisterhood on our side of the water. Their language was neither French nor Italian, but a confused mixture of both languages.

The captain had lost his respectability entirely with the crew by familiarity, and I now found it necessary to keep a tight rein on them that they might feel who was their master. They were much inclined to visit the cordial shops on shore, to prevent which I kept them close at work from daylight till after dark, which made them lodge a complaint with the captain against me, but he thought it prudent to say little to me on the subject, especially as I not only did equal work with them through the day, but had to sit up for him (occasionally) to a late hour at night, especially when he was at the masquerade until two or three o'clock in the morning.

A young English gentleman of good family, and who had been travelling through France and Italy was now here, and understanding that our ship was intending to proceed to Sicily, engaged to take his passage with us, and sent on board seven hogsheads of red wine, as an adventure. As we now had a numerous quantity of rats on board (many of which probably came on board here, as the French ships were honeycombed with them) our captain was determined to suffocate them with charcoal. Having got our victuals for the day on deck we lighted our fires and then closed the hatchways which were opened again at sunset. Having to sleep below gave me a violent headache next day, but we got clear of all the rats except *one*.

Our passenger had continued hitherto on shore, for some private reasons, but was now fetched by our captain. We therefore got under way for Sicily, unknown to his landlord to whom I believe he was much in arrears.

Having now rounded Sardinia, we steered for the Island of Maritimo, near Trapanno, in Sicily. The wind being contrary and blowing strong, we did not get in with Sicily till the 18th, and then got on a lee shore, which obliged us to carry a press of sail until 3 p.m., at which time we weathered away Columbra, and brought to an anchor in Trapanno bay. The 19th. As the wind was strong we unbent the sails, struck our lower yards, and got the top-sail yards fore and aft in the tops, this being an open bay with little shelter. Our ship's company were now ordered on shore to the Health Office, leaving the ship to the mercy of the Sicilians. Great care was taken on our landing to prevent anyone touching our clothes, as the place was formerly nearly depopulated by the plague. In calling a man named Peacock they pronounced it Peacocko, but at Marseilles his name contracted to Pea'co. After due examination, we were admitted to Prattick, or free communication with the shore.

Our Captain now struck a bargain for a cargo of sea-salt,

at about 7s. 6d. per ton. The proprietor was a Sicilian Baron, and as our passenger (Mr. W – rr – l) was perfect in the Italian language, from long residence at Rome and other parts of Italy, the transaction was easily accomplished. Bad weather prevented us from working till the 21st, when we began to deliver our ballast into shore boats.

One afternoon Mr. W – l invited the Baron's lady and daughters on board, and our boat was dispatched for them at the time appointed; they brought several attendants with them, wearing long swords, and wished to have some punch, but our captain kept a miserable table and had no kind of spirit on board. Fortunately I had two gallons of brandy which I offered, and the punch was made. The whole company appeared voracious, eating quickly whatever was set before them; even the sugar was devoured, and there was no ceremony whilst eating between the principals and domestics. About sunset they were landed, but to the great disgrace of one of the daughters our tars discovered that she had many holes in her stockings.

The inhabitants of this place appeared indigent and slothful. Their bread was the sweetest I ever ate, and of a yellow colour. This being a noted place for cameos and intaglios, our passenger purchased a few of the former for about 4s. 6d. each, about the size to set in a ring for the finger and which were admirably well executed. Our captain purchased a pair of stone bracelets, and got an imitation of a locket done in the same materials, on which were figures of two of his children in hair. I was informed that a rougish English captain was once laying in this bay, and he, having discovered on shore a neglected heap of valuable marble ruins, made free to transport them to his ship, and as no one had authority here to stop his proceedings, a courier was dispatched to Palermo for instructions, and as several days elapsed before the messenger returned, the captain had finished the business and had departed from the island.

The 29th we unmoored and hoisted in the long-boat, and sailed on the 1st March 1788, for Philadelphia. Having a fresh gale from the S.E. we passed the island of Maritimo about 10 in the morning; this island was formerly a residence for Sicilian convicts. Before night the wind became contrary or, according to the sea term, 'right in our teeth.' The 16th March we experienced hail, rain, thunder, lightning, waterspouts and strong gales, and on some days were incommoded with whirlwinds. The 27th we reached Cape de Gatt, off which place the current always running into the Mediterranean begins to be sensibly felt, in foul westerly gales. This sea is frequented by many logger-headed turtle, which sleep on the surface in fine weather. Some of these were taken up by the boat, but from ignorance in not throwing away the fat, which is hurtful, many of our people were made sick.

The Italians are so expert in catching this animal that a man will swim to it when discovered asleep, and by taking hold of its shoulders and laying on its hind part, leaving the fins at liberty, the turtle will carry the man to the vessel, he steering its course.

The 6th April 1788, we anchored in Gibraltar bay. Soon after the Health Officer came alongside, and for fear of catching the plague received our Bill of Health in a split stick.

A strong Levanter was now blowing, and Mount Calp, above the town, was enveloped in clouds. We had from ignorance anchored where the remains of the Duc da Crillon's celebrated armada was deposited, in the year 1782, which did our cable no good. The Moors, who generally supply this garrison with provisions, were at this time in open hostility, which made the passing through the Straits dangerous, and as we were unarmed, our captain came to a resolution that should a Barbary Corsair approach us (as we passed Tangier), to endeavour to give her our stem, or run over her, as there was a strong breeze suitable for that purpose. The 7th April having obtained our refreshments we sailed for Gibraltar and were given to understand that the *Southampton* frigate was cruising to the southwards of Cape Spartel to watch the motions of the Moors, which gave us some hopes of escaping from those infidels. The wind continued fair for several days which gave us a good run to the westward.

I will now give a short account of Mr. W–rr–l (our passenger) received on board at Marseilles. He was a young man of good family, about 26 years of age, and finished his education at Cambridge. But instead of improving the acquirements obtained there for his eternal interest he, like many more at that seat of learning, spent his precious hours with profligate companions in midnight scenes of riot and dissipation. How he spent his time after he left the University I know not, but his father resided not far from Bedford Square in London, and probably he lived with him. When he had left the Cliffs of Dover he had a lady of rank under his protection with whom he travelled through France and

THE TOWN AND ROCK OF GIBRALTAR FROM THE BAY.

Italy, but she, being displeased with his conduct in a certain place, parted from him and settled in the City of Florence. At Rome he carried on an intrigue with a young lady of noble family, having got a key made to let himself into the palace at night, but this affair being discovered the lady was placed in a nunnery. He afterwards dressed himself in woman's clothes and endeavoured to gain admittance. Having rung a bell a lay Sister presented herself at the grate, with whom he conversed with ease, but when the Lady Abbess made her appearance he became intimidated and could not recollect the Italian language. His failure in this soon laid open his person and business to the Abbess, who told him that should he attempt to gain admission the second time, she would have him secured; he therefore withdrew in confusion. After this he was informed that the brother of the lady intended to assassinate him, and was advised to quit Rome, which he did. He passed on to Naples and then to Sicily where he visited Mount Etna, a description of which he related to me, but it is not to be compared with Brydone's representation. He on leaving this island, returned to Italy, but his father's dishonouring his drafts, he repaired to Marseilles with what view I know not, but believe he was very short of money when he agreed for his passge. He possessed a number of valuable prints and curiosities laid in during his travels in Italy, and had two sets of coat buttons made of two sorts of lava. He had also laid out some money in Italian books, especially in the works of the Italian dramatic author, Metastasio, which he would sometimes read to me in English. It was his intention on arrival in America (should he fail of employment) to proceed to the Indian Nations, but for what purpose I could not learn, but Providence had designed that his talents should be otherwise employed.[1]

On our passage to America our sails were often out of repair, and as I was the principal sewer of canvas, I was kept much at work both in the tops and on deck, in mending and shifting cloths in the sails. Our captain spent much of his time in card playing with the crew, both day and night, in which Mr. W – often joined, but they never could prevail on me to associate familiarly with the seamen, as I was well aware that by so doing I should lose my respectability. The captain also played at heads and tails with halfpence, an apprentice boy being his chief companion, and whatever he gained at gambling from the crew appeared at their debit in his account book, as money advanced, and this was the conduct of a man apparently verging on the age of fifty.

The 28th April we hoisted out the boat and secured a turtle asleep, which weighed 76 lbs., and on the same day caught a dolphin. Many days we experienced severe gales with heavy rain, thunder and lightning, and on the 24th May got soundings in 36 fathoms. The next day saw Cape May and received a pilot on board. The 26th we got into the Delaware, and in two days more reached Philadelphia. The gambling being carried on after the pilot came on board caused him to remark privately to me that (though he was a man in years) he never saw a captain so degrade himself before. As we passed by the wharves, being hailed, we replied we came from Trapanny, but as no one knew such a place they imagined we meant Tripoli and began to fear the

[1] When I last heard of Mr. W – rr – l, about the year 1792, he had a practice as a physician in Virginia, which brought in about £500 per annum.

plague, and after the captain landed, he was ordered by the Health Officer to remove the ship below the town to lay quarantine – but we were soon permitted to haul to a wharf.

The Delaware River is famous for sturgeon; many we saw leaping out of the water on our passage from the sea. Some of them will weigh many hundreds, and a ship builder here informed me that he once saw a fishhawk pounce on a sturgeon, and fix his claws so firm in the back of the fish that he was drawn under water. Small fish, such as perch, dace, etc., were so plentiful alongside the wharves that women with a basket, baited at bottom with any animal substance and let down to the bottom of the wharves might catch any quantity wanted.

The seven hogsheads of wine belonging to Mr. W – l were now landed, two of which were given to our captain instead of money for his passage.

One day I observed an old gentleman in the street who attracted my attention by having round his neck what I concluded to be a gold chain, and was afterwards given to understand that he was no other than the celebrated Benjamin Franklin, late Ambassador for the United States to the Court of Versailles.

The second mate of our ship was a middle-aged man, married in Whitehaven, with a family grown up. He had been many years master of a vessel in the coal trade from that port, but turning out a tippler he lost his vessel and credit. A woman having often called on board here with shoes for sale, I was not a little surprised one day at being informed that our second mate had taken her to wife and had left our ship. A few days after this one of our crew saw the wife hawking about her husband's old Greenland boots for sale.

Having delivered our salt and no eligible freight presenting for Europe, our ship was chartered by Mr. P. B. to load flour and lumber, for Kingston, Jamaica.

10

He Sails to Kingston, Jamaica

THE beginning of July 1788, we left Philadelphia, but did not leave the Capes of Delaware until the 7th, the wind being strong from the southward. We experienced much bad weather after sailing, and was led far to the eastward before we could shape a southerly course. The squalls were so frequent and heavy with rain, thunder and lightning, that we were often obliged to clew up our sails to prevent their being blown from the yards. At three in the afternoon of the 2nd August, we saw the Island of Grand-Turk, and before sunset entered the passage between it and the great Corcos.

On the 3rd we saw Hispaniola and Fortudas, and on the 4th passed Cape Nichola Mole. On the 5th, at night, we were nearly overset by a violent squall, and as the hurricane season was now set in we were not a little alarmed till it abated, as our ship was totally unfit for carrying a press of sail. On the 7th passed the Island of Navassa, and saw the Blue Mountains in Jamaica; the 8th, got a pilot, and in the evening passed Port Royal, and anchored off Greenwich. The 9th arrived at Kingston, and hauled to Mr. Isaac Blight's[1] wharf, to whom our cargo was consigned. We found very few vessels here, as the hurricane season was set in; the men-of-war had quitted Port Royal and were now at anchor before this town, with yards and topmasts struck. His R.H. the Duke of C–c commanded one of the frigates. Whilst our vessel was discharging the cargo, I made inquiry about my old master Mr. Byrne, who formerly persuaded me to

[1] Isaac Blight, afterwards a ship breaker at Greenland Dock, London, and killed by his clerk, Richard Patch, who was executed for the murder.

desert my ship to be his clerk, but I found he was dead and the woman of colour (Mary Morris) who formerly lived with him was now in gaol for debt, and I saw the negress belonging to her whom I knew, now advertised in the newspaper for sale.

One Sabbath afternoon, instead of keeping the day holy and visiting a place of worship, I undertook to conduct my captain to Spring Path, the great burial-ground for negroes, where those still living generally dance to music of their own invention, such as a jawbone of some animal with a stick rubbed up and down the teeth, a tin box with small pebbles or shot therein, a hollow piece of a tree with a piece of skin spread thereon; in short, anything that would make a noise would suit their purpose to dance to. Whilst passing near this scene of riot a negress ran after us calling Massa Capen, who informed us that her mistress wanted to see us. We thought she was mistaken in our persons, but on looking where she directed us, we discovered our washerwoman (a Sambo)[1] inviting us to her dwelling, which we entered and seated ourselves. She soon produced some punch, and on seeing a cake-woman in the street, called her and asked us to treat herself and companions with cakes, which was complied with. This woman, dressed in a large brown beaver hat, with several rows thereon of silver lace and buckles, which I think could not be very far short of the value of two guineas and a half; but what she prided herself most in was out of sight, namely, a quantity of fine muslin and other petticoats which she was desirous of displaying, and accordingly showed that she had on either five or seven.

[1] A Sambo is the child of a Mulatto and a black: two-thirds negro blood. – ED.

A few days after this a white man was exhibited in the pillory for decoying negroes from their owners. Round him (in a principal street) a vast number of women of colour were assembled in most expensive dresses, but they were soon defiled and many ruined by the rotten eggs thrown. Few were aimed at the pillory, the greatest part being levelled at the ladies' fine beavers, which made them squall and decamp as fast as possible. In the afternoons a number of negresses carry about candles on boards upon their heads for sale, and as hard candles are most saleable, they are directed to call or cry 'Here candles, here candle, burn like a wax, hard like a stone,' but sometimes forgetting their lesson, they cry 'hard like a wax, burn like a stone!'

We had lain the ship on the ground whilst discharging at Mr. Blight's wharf and the fresh sea breezes had caused her to wallow in the surf, so as to make her leaky, which was unpleasant at the commencement of lading; but as we were daily in fear of a hurricane from a northerly wind sometimes blowing, and heavy white clouds often hanging over the Blue Mountains, edged with the colour of a rainbow, our captain was determined to persevere in leaving the island as soon as possible. On the 25th I was directed to proceed with the ship to Port Royal, whilst our captain remained in Kingston to settle with the consignees. In the evening he came on board and soon after dark a tremendous fire burst out suddenly at Kingston which illuminated our ship and the objects around although at five miles distance. Two or three stores were consumed by the carelessness of a negro in stealing rum which he set on fire. The 26th, early in the morning at gun-fire (before which no vessel is permitted to leave Port

Royal), we sailed for Old Harbour and the same afternoon our longboat fetched on board some hogsheads of sugar. As we proceeded with our lading our leak kept increasing so that we had to pump every two hours, and at last every hour.

The captain and myself had some conversation respecting the state of the ship, when we concluded to proceed to sea. Accordingly we endeavoured to keep the men in good humour, and sailed from Old Harbour for London the 15th September 1788, intending to run into one of the ports in the United States, should we find it requisite. The 16th departed from Negril point. The 18th saw the grand Cayman. The weather was unsettled for several days with much thunder and lightning. The 25th at daylight found ourselves very near a low island, belonging to the labyrinth of the Jardines de Reyna on the south coast of Cuba. The 30th saw the Dolphin head not far from the Havannah and to our great astonishment saw the double-headed Shot keys on the 2nd October by which we found the current was running very strong to the east.

The captain and myself were strangers to the Gulf of Florida, for though I had often been at Jamaica in the packets, we always beat to windward, and went through one or other of the passages of the Bahama Islands. The 4th saw the grand Bahama Islands and also saw a fish as long as a ship's boat spring out of the sea, which made the water foam.

Our pump was kept constantly at work by one man, who was obliged to clear all the water before he was relieved. We had now two seamen sick (who continued below from duty till we arrived in the Downs, and then they found their way on deck again). While we were running through the Gulf our captain sold some rum to the seamen, on which they got drunk, which caused me double labour till they were sober again. On the 6th October we cleared the Gulf. On the 12th, having bad weather, we sprung our bowsprit, which our captain repaired with an oak fish, having no carpenter on board; but, indeed, such man was unnecessary, as our captain was not only one of the most complete and expert seamen I had ever met with, but also an excellent mechanic, being very ingenious. He could make masts and yards, mend a frying-pan, or manage a ship with any man, and I have seen him make good cabinet work, for which purpose he kept various tools. The 16th saw some waterspouts and had rain, thunder and lightning with heavy squalls. Finding our ship did not make more water while we ranged along the American coast, we ventured to run towards Newfoundland. The 22nd, at night, the northern lights appeared very vivid. Having a fair wind when we reached the Grand Bank, we pushed on for England, but when we reefed the topsails it was requisite for the captain to take the wheel and myself ply the pump, we were so weakly manned. About the 10th November we were greatly rejoiced at getting soundings, and the first land we saw, I think, was the Island of Aldernay, off which place we picked up almost a new bowsprit but not large enough for our ship.

Having got the pilot on board at Deal and some fresh provisions, we sailed for the river. Our pilot, seeing our cat frolicsome, who doubtless smelled the land, and was running in and out on the bowsprit, became exasperated against the poor animal; he being superstitious concluded her gambols denoted a heavy gale of wind, which actually came on and we rode out the storm in Margate Roads, but I do not think the manœuvres of the cat were in any way connected with it. We got safe as far as Gravesend, the second week in November 1788, where we received on board two Custom-house Officers and two Excise men to watch each other. The next day, through rich mercy, we moored our ship in London river at the Guinea chain.

Our two seamen who had declined duty ever since we left the Gulf of Florida, could now visit the deck again, and as they could at all times clear their victuals, I have since, on reviewing their conduct in my mind, concluded that their disease was a nervous affection.

We had not been many hours at the Chain before something was sucked in the leak, which suddenly stopped our pump. The merchants who took our cargo had never received such a one before, many of the hogsheads of sugar being nearly a ton weight, and I kept a good look out to prevent plunderage on board; we indeed detected a man at work in the hold with false trousers, the bottom of which was tied round his legs, and had therein about 12 or 14lbs. of sugar which was taken from him.

I employed my old tailor to make me some clothes, who informed me that my brother was unable to pay the whole amount of his bill before he sailed for China, which I was sorry to hear, he having been liberally supplied with money; however, as I was then in hopes to have seen him again in Britain, I discharged the debt.

Our cargo being delivered, it was our intention to load for

Liverpool; accordingly a lighter came alongside with hogsheads of whiting to stiffen the ship for removing to a wharf.
Our cabin being cleared of the sugar was literally black
where painted from the stench of the drainage of the sugar
mixing with the salt bilge water which was stinking much
before we left Jamaica, and must have been very unwholesome, as the paint in the cabin first turned black and then
a silver or shining surface appeared thereon. Having taken
in our whiting we transported our ship to Drummonds
Ways to search for the leak, where we cleaned the bottom
from barnacles and caulked the open seams; but as the ice
was forming in the river we hurried to get to the wharf.

Towards evening we endeavoured to heave in to Staunton's
wharf, but a quantity of ice prevented us from getting the
vessel square and it was found absolutely requisite to heave
off her bow to let the accumulating ice float away with the
tide. It was now very dark, and though we had many watermen on board, only one could be prevailed on to run the
warp out, the flakes of ice being so large and the cold so
intense. But as I saw clearly that the ship was in the greatest
peril I jumped into the boat with a waterman and we carried
a warp out through the ice to a solitary brig at Pickle her-
ring[1] swinging chain (all the other vessels having hauled to
the shore). The man on the watch was very much against
my making fast the warp, but by smooth words and hard
arguments I got him to make it fast and remained to guard
it, whilst the captain and our crew hove off the bow of the
ship.

The next day all the crews of the shipping on the Thames

---

[1] 'Pickle-harin, a sea-sprite, borrowed from the Teutonic.' – SMYTH.

were busy securing them from the ice, by laying down ponderous anchors in the streets, some of which had six or eight bower cables fast to them and the navigation was closed for many weeks. As far as I can now recollect, I think the wind continued to the eastward for about ten weeks after our arrival here; therefore, it was a very great mercy considering our leaky condition that we arrived before the easterly wind commenced. I believe many frigates were sent by Government to supply homeward bound vessels with water and provisions in the chops of the Channel. The ice soon became so compact as to bear the discharging of cargoes on it and a regular intercourse was carried on between the opposite sides of the river over the ice, especially between Tower stairs and Horsley Down. Tents were erected in various parts on the river with colours flying, etc., to encourage riot and revelling. One day the ice separated on the flood tide into many islands, when I saw a very interesting scene near London Bridge in tents, people, vessels, etc., floating towards the arches, and I actually saw a brig and sloop lashed together go through the centre arch, carrying away their masts and pushing down a great many of the pillars on top, with many amazing heavy stones. Whilst we were laying at the wharf the captain and myself visited two places of public resort, viz., Allhallows Church, to hear Mr. Wesley preach. The other place was Covent Garden Theatre; to this place I went to worship the Prince of this world, even the Devil, and to countenance immorality, profaneness and dissipation; but this was in the days of my ignorance, before heavenly light began its dawn on my mind.

A VIEW OF THE THAMES FROM ROTHERHITHE STAIRS DURING THE GREAT FROST, 1789.

Our captain's brother (an old tippling seaman) now joined our ship and was appointed second mate. Soon after this a brig ahead of us by inattention was suffered to ground under our ship's bowsprit, the mate of which to save his vessel from injury was very busy in damaging ours with an iron crowbar, and would not desist when repeatedly requested. Finding words would not do I ran out on our bow-sprit to resist him, where we entered on blows, and finding I had the advantage of him he seized hold of my hair, which was then worn long at the side, and tore most of it out by the roots. Our second mate coming to my assistance, he retired, but it was providential that we did not both fall on the ice during our battle. My hair on the other side was not obliged to be cut short to correspond.

Having procured a stock of coals, our crew at night made a cinder fire in the steerage in an iron pot, and after closing the hatches retired to sleep. In the morning when I turned out, my head was aching, but was ignorant of the cause. I then called the crew and opened their hatchway, but not seeing the men appear as usual, I found they were ill, being almost suffocated by the sulphurous vapour of their fire.

One morning two men appeared on board to pay their respects to me, one of whom informed me that he had been an officer in the ship with my brother to Bengal, and having heard of my being in London had come in quest of me. They invited me to their lodgings and offered to introduce me to a lady of some property, but not approving of their loose conversation I declined their great civility. Hearing that a gentleman of my acquaintance was confined in the King's Bench for debt, I paid him a visit (he having married a relation of mine). I found him in a room near the top of the prison with two or three more debtors, who, in order to raise their spirits, had employed a hairdresser to play the violin to them. We got away from the wharf sometime in February 1789.

On our passage through the shipping we saw several vessels sunk by the ice. Our captain having been brought up in the coal trade, thought himself sufficiently acquainted with the river to warrant his declining taking a pilot, but he was mistaken and we gounded on a point on the ebb; but with much trouble we got her afloat again before midnight. We lay several weeks off Deal, experiencing many heavy gales from the south and west, in one of which the sea ran so high that I saw the very keel of an outward-bound East India ship, rising to a wave.

Our second mate, taking the advantage of his relationship, was often on the sculk, neither keeping watch in turn with the crew nor assisting in turn with me, although it is not every old seaman knows how to keep the cable from getting round the stock or upper flew of the anchor in a roadstead. Many die from old age in the sea service that never attain to this knowledge, and numbers of ship masters are also stupidly ignorant of this branch of seamanship, especially those not accustomed to the British coasting trade in tide ways.

We at last got clear of the Downs, and beat to the westward as far as Falmouth, when towards night we endeavoured to shelter there, but when close to the Castle, in great expectation of visiting some of my old friends, the wind suddenly backed to the eastward and finding we could weather the Manacle rocks that night, we tacked and stood off again, and in a few days arrived at Liverpool.

*   *   *   *   *   *

11

He Becomes a Master

I WAS soon informed that the master of the *Mayflower* had been promoted to a vessel in the foreign trade and this brig had been reserved for me in the Bristol trade. The brig having been locked up for several weeks before my taking to her, the poor cat, being forgotten, had perished, and on my feeling something hairy in one of the lockers, I dragged it out to find that it was the skin and bones of a cat, the flesh having been eaten off by her old opponents the rats.

I was now given to understand that as the Bristol traders generally lay on the berth in Bristol many months for goods, making little more than two voyages in the year, that the profits would not afford to pay a mate, therefore none would be allowed.

Having laden a cargo of fishery salt and procured four men to work the ship by the run, I sailed for Bristol.

When we had delivered our cargo I laid on the berth to load for Liverpool, and as the Welshmen opposed us much it was requisite for me to cruise the city for goods. I therefore hired a trusty old man at about half a guinea per week to stay on board and give answers while I was absent. He was no seaman but professed quackery and did not like going aloft, and this was my chief assistant. After my return from procuring goods day by day, which were chiefly British spirits, I had to turn to in the hold and stow them. Soon after, I received orders to proceed immediately by coach to Liverpool to take the command of the *John* in the Philadelphia trade, which was good news for me.

Having taken my place in the mail for Birmingham I arrived there at nine the next morning, and according to orders waited on several manufacturers who were in the habit of sending goods to America, to solicit their favours for the *John* (a constant trader to Philadelphia), but could not obtain a single package, as the vessel, though only about three years old, was in very bad credit as a slow sailer, always making long passages.

I finished my business here in time to save the 12 o'clock coach for Liverpool, having two ladies (a mother and daughter) for my companions, we soon became sociable. We slept that night at Newcastle-under-Lyme, at a most wretched inn, both for neglect and imposition; but above all, the bed or bedding must have been damp, which gave me a violent cold and great pain in my breast and which I believe continued till I sailed.

Near Warrington a partridge sprang up on one side of the road leaving her brood to the mercy of the coachman, who stopped and, having put seven or nine young ones into his hat, handed them to the ladies, who took possession of two birds, which, as soon as we gave them crumbs of bread, ate heartily, like young chicken.

On my arrival at Liverpool, I found the *John* newly painted, rigged and ready to receive on board a cargo; her cabin was fitted up with great elegance for passengers; the decorations were composed of plaster of paris and gilded. All the bed places had curtains of a blue running chintz pattern with white fringe, and the whole was extremely neat and clean which pleased me much. A new chief mate had been shipped prior to my arrival, strongly recommended. I was now enabled to sleep in a comfortable bed on shore till ready for sea, which appeared a great luxury. My wages while mate of the *Thetis* was three pounds per month, and on being shipmaster, was raised to five pounds per month, but I do not think during the whole time I commanded a vessel (except my last voyage) that I ever made more in wages and perquisites than barely seventy-five pounds per annum. From this income I had to assist three of my relations.

I could save nothing, and out of my *wages* of sixty pounds per annum I had always to pay for my board whilst at home in Liverpool. This was a miserable income for the duty, anxiety and responsibility of a shipmaster.

The vessel having taken in a cargo of salt, coals and bales, we sailed from Liverpool for America the 17th July 1789. The 23rd near Tuscar, a strong gale came on from the northward, which soon made me acquainted that I was now on board a very badly constructed vessel, not having sufficient bearings at the bow to prevent her from plunging forecastle under when sailing on a wind. The 16th discovered that the fid of the fore topmast was broken and the mast sprung, which we secured. The 29th at daylight found a ship near us becalmed, whose boat came alongside to solicit for provisions; she was from Ria-bona in Jamaica for London. We spared what we could with convenience, and though I made a present of some of my cabin stores, the vulgar swearing captain paid for the provisions in *light* gold coin. The same day found the fid of our main topmast broke, and secured the mast with lashings. September 2nd got soundings in 73 fathoms, fine white sand on the Grand Bank of Newfoundland. The 6th spoke the American brig *Neptune* 57 days from the Downs for New York and we had been 51 days from Liverpool. The 9th we had run the

Neptune hull down astern. The 17th saw a quantity of birds, chiefly what is known to seamen by the name of Mother Carey's chicken, hovering near the water in a direct line across our ship. When looking to windward we discovered a dead whale, the oil from which they were feeding on. The 18th saw a sloop laying to, on the whale fishery. The 19th got soundings in 30 fathoms, and the same day in 15 fathoms received a Delaware pilot on board and saw the land near Five Miles Beach. The 20th September saw Cape May and anchored on the ebb in 8 fathoms near the Over Falls. On the flood made sail and turned to windward in Delaware Bay, and as the wind continued contrary we had to anchor on the ebb tides, till we arrived on the 22nd at Philadelphia, and moored the vessel at Arch Street wharf. On each side of the Delaware River below this city there are many marshes with reeds growing therein, which at this season of the year were in seed and fed vast quantities of small reed birds, on which they get so fat as to be esteemed a dainty like the wheatear in England or the ortolan in Flanders.

As soon as I had a little time I made inquiry about Mr. W – rr – l (the passenger) who came with me the year before in the ship *Thetis* from Marseilles. I found him at an apothecary's studying physic, dressed in the habit of a Quaker, with a large hat. As soon as I gave my name he seemed rejoiced to see an old friend and immediately locked his study, taking me with him to his lodgings in another street to get tea. He informed me that he was not only practising physic, but was Editor of the *Columbian Magazine* and was then busy translating the life of Frederic the Great from the French.

After our vessel was discharged, having liberty from my owners to embrace a freight for any part most eligible, I agreed to take a cargo of wheat and flour to Barcelona in Spain.

Our bark was very deeply laden and we left the wharf the 12th November. This season of the year here is generally clear of clouds and squalls, but very cold, especially with the winds that sweep over the lakes of Canada to this part. The next flood tide we brought up opposite Chester, an inconsiderable town in the Delaware State; the next place we passed was Wilmington on the same side. This town was built on an eminence (apparently of timber) and though the buildings were low and irregular it had a pretty appearance from the ship. I saw in the Philadelphia newspaper an advertisement of a man who kept a store here, and it being a curiosity I committed it to memory. It ran thus :

> Cloths midling coarse and superfine,
>   Figs, raisins, sugar-candy;
> Sago and rice, pepper allspice,
>   Madeira wine and brandy.
>
> Good corduroys for men and boys,
>   Excellent Irish linen;
> Jeans and jeannets and velverets
>   And cloth of Joan's spinning.
>
> Cloves, ginger, prunes and silver spoons,
>   Both wax and tallow candles;
> Bottles and corks and knives and forks,
>   With horn and ivory handles.

Starch, mustard, snuff, all cheap enough,
  Gloves, ribbands, gauze and laces,
Good castile soap, all kinds of rope,
  Bed-cords, plough-lines and traces.

Brass warming pans, and ladies fans,
  Queen's ware and pewter plates,
Half gallon jugs and earthen mugs,
  Assorted well in crates.

Neat coverlids for feather beds,
  And clarified honey;
Good callicoes and cotton hose
  All cheap for ready money.

Sweet muscadine and fyall wine,
  Venetian red and umber;
Brass curtain rings and many things
  Too tedious here to number.

The 14th November we passed the town of Newcastle, which is not very large. One of the houses had the year of its erection placed on it in large figures, which signified that it had been standing more than a century. We anchored next in the bay, below the town, and the next day reached Reedy Island, a winter rendezvous for outward bound vessels waiting for a fair wind.

* * * * * *

12

He visits Barcelona and Yvaci

THE 17th the wind being strong at north-west, we sailed in company with 30 vessels soon after daylight. We experienced much bad weather, and had to lay to several times; we also split many sails, and as the vessel was very deeply laden the sea used to make a free passage over her. For several days we had much labour with the pump, particularly on one tack, which made us conclude the leak was in her top-side. On our passage a flying fish, nearly as large as a mackerel, flew on board which I preserved. On the 25th December saw the Barbary shore, and before dark entered the Straits. Soon after a fog came on and the wind so squally and variable that we scarcely knew whether we were on the Spanish or Barbary side of the Gut, for as we endeavoured to keep close to a weather shore, by the frequent changes of wind we were as often on a lee shore. At last it cleared a little when we found we had providentially escaped running on a low flat island at the foot of Mount Abyla, or Apeshill, on the Moorish side, and soon after saw the hill of Gibraltar, which I scarcely need say gave me great pleasure.

The 5th January, 1790, passed Cape St. Martin, and saw the Island of Yvica,[1] and soon afterwards had a foul wind and bad weather which kept us five days in sight of the Island of Mount Columbretta. The 16th I was much gratified with a fine sight of the mountains of Monserado in the kingdom of Catalonia, the large summit of which is formed

[1] This, I presume, is the island of Iviza, about sixty miles west of Cape St. Martin. Hereafter the author spells it Yvaca. – ED.

with spires, similar to a cluster of spar stones in England, but more peaked. It is about 14 miles in circumference, and 30 miles from Barcelona, inhabited by monks and hermits. The 17th saw Mount Jovi. About midnight I was alarmed by the mate calling out 'that the vessel was on shore.' I ran immediately on deck and asked the reason of his not throwing the lead. He replied that he had just done so but could find no bottom. I then looked over the side and discovered we were in the midst of a luminous circle of small fishes, which the mate was not aware of, and which had made him think we had struck the ground. As the day dawned a long cloud of white smoke appeared on the land which we soon found arose from the city of Barcelona. As the wind was very feeble, we hoisted out the boat to tow the vessel, and about 3 p.m. anchored in Barcelona Road. We got into the Straits in 38 days and were 24 more before we arrived here. A Spanish boat came off and informed me that I must be content to remain in the road till we had lightered the vessel as there was not sufficient depth of water for her to go over the bar.

To expedite our delivery I immediately took my papers and proceeded in our boat for the Mole, but on approaching the bar found the waves running high, and the surf very dangerous, but seeing a small vessel going in we followed her, and our crew had to row with all their might to prevent the rolling surf from oversetting our yaul.

This roadstead is open to the east and south, and the water deep, but the greatest danger arises from the numberless anchors lost here. Whilst we remained two out of the four vessels in the roads had their cables cut through and the other brig had hers damaged. The mud dredged daily in the Mole is brought out in well vessels and let out by means of a hatch in the bottom in the road.

The 21st we sent seven boats laden on shore at the head of the Mole, where the Spanish boats laden are accustomed to be drawn up on dry land by horses. The corn was thrown from the boats on mats, and the Government required that for the first three days the poor might purchase (not exceeding a specified quantity for each person) at the rate the bulk of the cargo was sold at, which is a good regulation and lessens the evil of monopoly.

Our men on the beach informed me that not only the Spaniards were apt to steal, but the horses would approach the wheat softly, and taking a mouthful, would immediately run off to eat it. I detected a man sitting on the corn and playing with it, but observing him narrowly from a distant spot I perceived that he was in the act of stowing it in his trousers tucked into his shoes. I approached him behind and having laid my hickory stick across his shoulders he jumped up, at the same time pulling his trousers, discharged the grain to prevent proof of the theft.

The city of Barcelona is well built; the houses lofty, and often the outsides have various figures painted in colours on a white ground; such as flower-pots, vases, urns, men, women, animals, etc., in ridiculous attitudes, and I have seen many of the scenes represented by Cervantes in *Don Quixote* portrayed on a house. The walls round the city are high and sufficiently wide on top for two or three carriages abreast, with slopes to ascend them. Many fine brass cannon are mounted thereon, there being a foundry for such in the city.

There are a number of strong gates, two towards the port. People enter at one of these and go out at the other; the gates are shut while the porters go to dinner. I saw the Governor (O. Riley) in his carriage on the walls with two dragoons mounted as his precursors, and the different guards turn out on their appearance.

The exchange or meeting of merchants is held in an open square, the Governor's palace making one of the sides, and I once saw a black petticoat spread to dry in the sun, on a balcony rail, on the first floor of the said palace! When the clock strikes twelve on the great bell of the cathedral, which sounds loud and solemn, it is customary for all the inhabitants to repeat their Pater Nosters. Those at work or walking in the streets, take off their hats and stand still till the prayer is finished and the clock ceases striking. The whole is repeated again at sunset.

Many of the British residents here appear in the streets with their hair full dressed without hats, except a hat for ceremony under the arm, according to the French fashion.

Having received orders from the vessel's owners to load sea salt at the most eligible part of the Mediterranean and to proceed with the same as quick as possible to Philadelphia, we began to take on board our ballast.

I never was in a place where I received more civility and attention than this. I only dined on board twice, having sometimes from two to four different invitations in a day from the British merchants. A gentleman with whom I had no connection in the way of business invited me often to dine, sup, and to go with him to the opera. At this theatre the seats in the pit have arms; several of the front rows are let in single seats by the year. Such seat is lifted up at quitting it on the performing nights, and locked fast to the back by the occupier. There were several sentinels under arms in the place, and I perceived that the Fathers of the Inquisition had a spacious stall to gratify their sensuality. The piece was a comic opera by Italians, but I think I was never more disgusted at any public performance, and the actors were obliged frequently to make an abrupt application to the prompter, who sat on the edge of the stage with his back to the audience, and I think his feet and legs must have hung down in a hole. He made many motions with the book in his hand and the whole appeared so ridiculous that I never went afterwards.

There were about ten thousand troops in this garrison, mostly Walloon, or foreign guards, as the Catalans were not thought the most faithful subjects. The Officers of the army by the King's orders were to have free admission to all private balls, therefore the citizens are often annoyed with the intrusions of these pragmatical gentry. There was much intrigue carried on amongst high and low, and the morals corrupted in general. The Merchants' Tables were well served with two or three courses, and the livery servants well dressed. A decanter of water stood on one side of each of the guests on the table and a decanter of small red wine on the other, with a tumbler for each to help himself without trouble. After the dessert, one or at most two glasses of a good bodied wine was drunk, then a cup of coffee, and sometimes the repast ended with a small glass of French cordial.

One of the Consuls (a Spaniard) with whom I dined twice

or thrice had a spacious palace, and being remarkably civil, conducted me through a great part of it, nor did he omit taking me abruptly into a large bed chamber where his daughters were sitting, who appeared rather surprised at my visit. On leaving this house I passed a number of Ecclesiastics singing or rather bawling at the door of a dwelling in which some one was sick. I had to avoid the host twice while in this place to prevent my kneeling in the street, as the soldiers who attend sometimes ill-treat strangers that will not conform to this way of adoration.

The suburbs of this city next the harbour named Barcelonetta, was built on ground recovered from the sea, by throwing the earth and stones washed down from the mountains on the spot. In the front of this little uniform town (inhabited by mechanics and seafaring men) the sailmakers worked at their business in the open air, which is generally clear and fine, for though I was here in January I think there had been no rain for six weeks, and I have seen one of the planets at high noon, from the clearness of the atmosphere. Women are mostly employed on the sails.

Two of the British captains walking behind a priest on the walls made very free with his person, using obscene words. After listening to their conversation some time the priest turned round and mildly reproved the sea captains, informing them in English that he would have them be careful of their words in public, for it was not every man in the habit of a priest that was a Spaniard.

Having remitted what I could to my owners by a draft on London, I procured 400 or 500 gold dollars to carry with me to Yvaci, to purchase the salt, as silver is not allowed to be

M

exported from Barcelona. I was put under the protection
of many saints when I sailed, such as the Virgin Mary,
St. Ramundi, St. Francis and others, whose figures and
names were at the head of my Bill of Health procured
here.

On the 10th February 1790, we sailed for Yvaci. At the
entrance of the harbour I was met by a boat with ladies and
gentlemen therein playing music, who congratulated me on
my arrival, and tacking about led the van to the anchorage.
Having anchored in this snug harbour in four fathoms, I
proceeded in our boat to the landing place to look for the
Health Officer, the musical party accompanying me. The
Health Officer now questioned me in Spanish about our
crew, and whether any Turks had visited us on our passage.
The crew were now called over and those that had not florid
complexions were examined, being directed to extend their
arms whilst the doctor pressed their sides and armpits to
ascertain that they had not the plague.

On inviting the company into the cabin, some cigars being
on the table, were immediately pounced on by these ravenous
gentry. After they had ate and drank, I went on shore with
them and found the Vice-Consul on the Mole waiting for
me, who informed me that a British captain had lost an
earthen pint and a silver spoon by means of the island
visitors.

The next day Mr. Wills (the Vice-Consul) and myself set
off on foot for the salt pond, taking with us some hard-boiled
eggs and a pork sausage of his providing. As we passed
through the country I perceived the enclosures for barley
were very stony, which I imagined was the effect of indolence,

but I was given to understand that the number of small stones strewed over the ground kept it moist from the rays of the sun, which otherwise would parch it up. The natives appeared very poor and the country women wore large cues, suspended from the crown hair and bound with white tape, the inside being stiffened with a piece of wood and ending below their middle in hair from mules' tails.

Having reached the Salt Pond, I found a certain depth of water is let in from the sea, which in the course of the summer dries up and leaves about five inches deep of sea salt. A particular day is appointed for farmers to attend who rake it, and carry it on mules to the rising ground, where it is heaped up in the shape of soldiers' tents. Each person then deposits a certificate under a stone near the top ridge to certify that he raked that heap. The heaps are of various tints, some reddish, others white, grey and brown.

One man was reading a licence to eat eggs in Lent. These papers were now issuing from the Pope's agent, at elevenpence sterling each, which doubtless brought in a large Revenue from the Papists in the different kingdoms. On our return to town we stopped at a farmhouse to get our sausage warmed and eat our dinner. The salt supplied us at our meal had garlic mixed therewith. Our hostess furnished a dessert of small figs and almonds, for which a trifling sum of money was considered as a sufficient remuneration. I saw a number of goldfinches flying about, the plumage of which appeared far more brilliant than those of England.

We met a barber surgeon on an ass who was probably called into the country to bleed a patient, and Mr. W — gave me to understand that as money was a scarce article, he was obliged to receive payment in a fowl or some other produce of the farm.

The women's dress was generally dark jackets and petti-coats, some without sleeves. On the Sabbath I saw the people carrying their rush-bottomed chairs to church to sit on. The latine-rigged craft belonging to this place are employed in smuggling salt into France and Italy. Two of these vessels returned whilst I was here, and having made good voyages there was great rejoicing; even the ecclesi-astics paraded in procession on this happy occasion, and doubtless shared in the profits. I saw several windmills near this city with six vanes instead of four. Seeing a large con-course of people one evening in the suburbs, I had the curiosity to join them to know the reason, and found a new cart with a mule standing by it, harnessed. Not at all accustomed to see such a machine, whenever they attempted to lower the shafts on its back it got into a most violent rage, using its heels in every direction; at last it ran off with the vehicle, clearing its way through the crowd, and I was glad to shelter myself within a house door. I imagine this was the first cart that had appeared on the Island. The numerous asses here kept up almost a continual braying at night, which we could distinctly hear on board when in bed. They are fed in a great measure on the leaves of cauliflower which grow to a great size. Mr. W – s informed me that he had seen or heard of the flower weighing 24 lbs. I never saw any so large but I ordered a dozen with the roots for to take to sea, three of which on a man's shoulders was a good burden with the leaves on.

The 26th we finished loading the salt. My Bill of Health received at Barcelona was returned to me endorsed so that I was not put under the protection of any new saints.

*   *   *   *   *   *

13

He Sails to Philadelphia Again

THE 1st March 1790, the wind being fair, we got under sail. The 7th entered the Gut, and on the 8th, with a strong Levanter passed Cape Trafalgar. The sixth day after leaving the Straits we had run 950 miles to the westward.

The 20th we saw a large bird of the Booby kind, and the following day saw a sand bird, both of which I imagine were natives of the Azores. From April 7th to the 10th we found the current running swiftly to the northward, and on the latter day experienced a strong gale with violent squalls, rain, thunder, and very fierce lightning, the waves running mountains high in the greatest confusion, and so dangerous that it was difficult to determine which way to lay the vessel's head to prevent foundering.

The 19th the wind being strong at the south-east, shifted suddenly to the north-west, when our vessel plunged so violently under water as to break the sprit sail yard in the thickest part. After this accident we spoke the brig *Ruby* of Dundee, from Havre for Philadelphia. The next day being moderate her boat came to us for some provisions as the crew were much in want. As this brig sailed much faster than our vessel, and the captain signifying his intention of pushing forward, I gave him a letter for my merchants to signify that I was not far off. This vessel soon ran us hull down, but on the 28th, while we were carrying a press of sail in foggy weather, we were not a little surprised at passing the *Ruby*, she being under low sails. I imagine as the captain's reckoning was out he was fearful to run for the land in thick weather.

On 1st May we sprung our main yard in the slings, but

having no carpenter on board we turned too and fished it tolerably well. On the 7th got soundings in 25 fathoms, red sand with black specks. The 8th May saw Cape Henlopen and entered the Delaware, having been sixty-nine days from Yvaci.

The 11th May 1790, we moored at Smith's Wharf, Philadelphia. My merchants here could not get their price for our salt; we were therefore ordered to Kensington above the city, where we obtained a store for our salt at a much cheaper rate than in Philadelphia. Near this place lay a very long steamboat, which I have seen stemming the tide at the rate of about four miles an hour. The steam worked paddles under each quarter, which pushed it along, but I was informed the friction was so great that the works often wanted repairs. Many fires broke out in the city at different times in stables and places, but as they were found in general to belong to Cornfactors who were now standing out to oblige their corn porters to be content with their accustomed wages, it was supposed that the houses had been wilfully set on fire.

I had an opportunity of witnessing the alacrity manifested by the inhabitants at these fires, and indeed dispatch is highly requisite, as the houses are generally covered with thin boards called shingles, made of cedar or cypress. Each housekeeper is obliged to keep in readiness two leather buckets, a tow-handled basket and a bag to use at fires.

I once attended at the door of the Senate to get a sight of the President on opening the Session. I placed myself on the steps of the house. He soon afterwards arrived in an old coach, formerly belonging to Governor Penn (as I was informed). The two secretaries were in the General's chariot, and both carriages were a dark cream colour, apparently newly painted. The police officers (I believe) were the only attendants, the President disliking unnecessary state. He wore black velvet with a silk bag to his hair, and so much like the pictures of him that I had seen in England, that I could easily have selected him from a thousand men. The Senate was well crowded by the time I arrived at the top of the stairs, but I got near the door to hear part of the speech, and remained at the lower door till the President[1] appeared again. He stood a minute on the steps to thank the officers for their attendance, and then dismissed them from further ceremony. I think I never saw him but once, but the chariot conducting Lady Washington was often to be seen in the streets.

I visited the House of Representatives to hear the debates occasionally, to which there was free admission, and do not recollect ever seeing a single porter at the door nor the gallery more than half filled. One morning about 11 o'clock, I was there at the time of prayer, performed by a Dissenting minister, and at that time, few indeed attended in the Gallery, the populace paying far more attention to their farms and their merchandise than to politics and debates.

Near where our vessel lay at Kensington was a large spreading tree with dark green leaves, like the live oak. A friend of mine paced the diameter of the shade and supposed it to be nearly a hundred feet across; it was a pleasant sight in the great heat prevailing here in summer. A great quantity of fireflies are to be seen here in summer. The

[1] Washington.

females sitting at their doors for air after dark, catch them and place the insects on their hair, where they stay glowing a considerable time before they take wing. One evening, walking with a party, an insect of the beetle species flew into a lady's bosom and bit her severely; she screamed loudly, and ran off to her dwelling to strip. After our salt was landed we moved the vessel to Mr. Warder's Wharf in the Northern Liberties, to take on board pig-iron, tar, red cedar, staves, etc., for Liverpool.

Whilst at this wharf for two or three days in the month of May a vast number of small, cream-coloured butterflies were to be seen resting on walls and houses with which people on the wharf baited fish hooks to catch perch and other small fish, which seized the bait greedily. On inquiry I found it was a water fly, which appeared annually for the space of three days and then disappeared. 'Tis probable it is one of the same species as the Ephem'ron seen on the Rhine in Germany.

I had some conversation here with a shipbuilder who had been the master of a vessel during the American contest with England. This man in his youth had seen a raft ship built in America, when it was customary to send such to England, where they were broken up to sell the materials employed in their construction. I understood they were solidly built without planks and had no occasion for pumps. They were shaped fit for sailing with masts and sails like other ships and had a kind of cabin for sheltering the crew, being nothing more than a raft of timber bound together with wood and iron and the float very large. We lay here some time for want of suitable goods to load us, and during

our detention news arrived that there was great probability
of a war between the Spaniards and the English relative to
the settlement of Nootka Sound.[1] The vessels laying here
belonging to the Dons began to arm, and a report was in
circulation that they meant to intercept all the British
vessels on their leaving this port which considerably alarmed
us, as we actually saw their guns on board. The *Alert* being
now ready for Liverpool, and the master fearing two Spanish
armed schooners ready for sea also, went slyly to the Coffee
House and entered a notice in the Intelligence Book there,
that two British frigates had been seen off the Capes of
Delaware, and trusting this would have its intended effect on
the Spaniards, sailed immediately, leaving me to look out for
myself; but the armed vessels, in a few days after, departed
also, leaving me at an uncertainty whether they meant to
proceed immediately on their voyage or waylay me.

By going from hence to Barcelona, last voyage, instead of
returning to Britain, our seamen's articles were become
void, and according to custom, they were instigated by the
landlords here to give me some trouble. Some of our men
had left the vessel, intending to take away their chests at
night, tied a stone to the dog's neck and drowned him. This
kept me on the watch at night, and when I heard any of
them creeping softly on board, I used to jump out of bed and,
slipping a flannel gown on, attended to their motions in the

---

[1] Nootka Sound, on the west coast of Vancouver Island. Spain laid claim to
the sound and dispatched a force to eject the British settlers. The British
Government commissioned a fleet under Lord Howe and demanded restitu-
tion. Spain came to terms on October 28, 1791, agreeing to evacuate Nootka
and compensate the settlers. – ED.

companion. Others employed attorneys and I was obliged to pay them their wages and had trouble enough to get men in their room, as American ships gave more wages. I do not know anything so disagreeable to ship-masters as sailor-hunting, for as they are generally half drunk, they do not care what trouble they give, and may be justly compared for obstinacy to the wild ass of the wilderness. The houses they board at and the brothels they frequent here have scarcely any furniture, and are the most filthy places of this description that I ever met with in any country. The sailors chests are placed round the room and serve both for seats and beds, and in summer are the residence of innumerable hosts of flies, which creep into their punch glasses, being attracted by the sugar. Indeed, these house-flies are very troublesome both in all dwellings and churches in the warm weather. In the latter I have been bit by numbers on my face and, during the service, have been obliged to keep my handkerchief in motion to drive them off, while others were piercing my legs almost continually. Mirrors in the dwellings are at this season covered with black gauze, and at the time of dinner a servant is employed with a whisk to drive them off the face and dishes. As those insects are apt to dirt the goods in shop windows a young man of genius has full employment in painting the different species on sale on the inside of the glass.

I was acquainted with an old lady who remembered the rabbits running about in the spot where one of the central streets is now built in this city.

I shall now speak of my departure, which took place the 8th of July, having procured a passenger for Liverpool, whom I took at a low rate to obtain him. He was an Agent sent to America by the British manufacturers and he was so extremely parsimonious as to save the twine and paper wherewith his goods were packed, to carry again to England in his baggage. This man laid in a most miserable sea store, but as few passengers went from hence to Liverpool, I was glad to catch him, though he was truly a stingy bachelor and a complete character known by the name of Miss Molly.

The 8th July, 1790. As soon as I secured the men on board, I sent the vessel to Chester to wait for me. The 9th, Mr. Roberts, the passenger, and myself took places in the Baltimore stage for Chester and just as we left town the carriage broke down, which detained us some time. These stages, known here by the name of coaches, are longer than a coach, having four seats, each for two people, all with their faces towards the horses. The upper panels are all open with leathers rolled up, to let down in bad weather, and as the country is to be seen in every direction, they have much the advantage of the stages in England during the summer, but not in the winter. We crossed the Schulkill River on a floating bridge, which parts in the middle when vessels pass. I had often heard that Mrs. Whithers at Chester kept the best house for entertaining company in this State. We therefore determined to dine there and were not disappointed in our expectations. Our vessel appearing as soon as we had dined, we went on board.

The 12th we anchored in Holdkill Roads, the wind being contrary. The pilot was now going to leave us, and as I had never seen Lewistown, where the pilots generally reside within Cape Henlopen, Mr. R. and myself landed with him on the beach of the Cape. After walking about half a mile, partly through the bushes, we came to a muddy creek over which we were ferried in a small boat and entered the town, if such an insignificant place is worthy of that appellation, though I believe it has a Court house. Our pilot conducted us to an inn, which we entered, but seeing nothing attracting and much disgusting, we left it to walk through this straggling place, the houses being small and the inhabitants far beneath a state of mediocrity. We saw one decent building which we learnt belonged to a gentleman who had been a colonel in the army. This gentleman we afterwards met and after some conversation he invited us to take tea with his family, which we accepted. On entering a pleasant, white-limed parlour, we observed bunches of asparagus hung up here and there near the ceiling to attract the flies from dirting the nice white walls, and being fresh and green with red berries, had a cool and neat appearance. Towards dusk we took our leave and found our way to the beach where our boat was, but no appearance of the crew. After calling some time we went amongst the bushes and found a little hut where they had been regaling themselves with their beloved grog. We got them away and after some labour launched the boat and arrived safe on board.

The 14th the wind veering towards the south, we got under sail; but as we approached the sea we found a great swell setting in, and as the wind was getting again to the east we returned and anchored till the 17th, and then sailed with the wind at north-west.

The 20th. Took our anchors from the bows and secured them on the forecastle, and this was my general custom in this vessel in crossing the Atlantic, as she plunged so much in the sea that the stocks would be washed loose if left on the bows. This day we observed two vessels in the southern quarters standing towards us, and afterwards observing they were schooner rigged we conluded them to be the Spaniards who had left the Delaware before us, and this idea was so prevalent that double cloths were put on to secure them from plunder, but these vessels passed us to the northward without speaking us, and this gave us unutterable satisfaction.

The 21st we had a strong gale, the heavy sea occasioned by it broke in our quarter boards.

The 30th. Sounded on the bank in 40 fathoms, Saw several vessels, spoke a French brig fishing. At noon saw several vessels on the fishery at anchor.

The 31st saw two sails at anchor. Very foggy weather with rain, which obliged us to keep a good look out to keep clear of the fishermen at anchor. At 8 a.m. sounded in 90 fathoms, coarse gravel, which indicated that we were now on the east edge of the Bank. One of the French brigs we spoke was driving, the other was at anchor, contrary to the conditions of the treaty between the two nations and our ships of war often obliged the French to lift their anchor when brought up on the great Bank. After leaving soundings we had many easterly winds, and did not enter the Irish channel till the 20th August, and on the same day got soundings in 73 fathoms white sand, with black and red specks. Perhaps it may not be amiss to advise all shipmasters coming from the western ocean and bound to the south of Ireland, or St. George's channel, to run in the latitude of

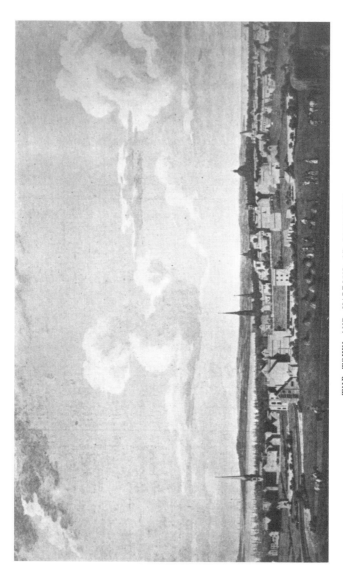

THE TOWN AND HARBOUR OF LIVERPOOL.

50° 50' N. and to be careful of a northerly current, and when they have struck soundings in this latitude, not exceeding 60 fathoms, they may be sure they are advancing on the Nymph Bank and are then to the eastward of Cape Clear, and may haul to the northward and make the Irish land at pleasure. Many vessels run for the west of Ireland and at night or in foggy weather get embayed, to the great risk of lives and property, but by adopting my method they may run in safety, attending to the lead occasionally.

The 22nd August, 1790. Passed Holyhead and got safe on the 23rd into George's dock basin, after thirty-six days' passage.

My owners had been appraised of my arrival by signal, which gives information long before the vessel enters the river, and before she can be seen from the town. This is managed on a hill in Cheshire opposite Liverpool, on which the merchants have each flagstaffs. On this eminence there is also a lighthouse kept by an old seaman who had been (I think) fourteen voyages to Africa in the slave trade. This man and his wife manage all the signals. When a Liverpool vessel approaches the north-west buoy at the entrance of the dangerous sands and shoals lying without the mouth of the Mersey a signal is made by the vessel that she belongs to such a merchant. The man residing at Bidston Lighthouse hoists the flag on that merchant's pole, and at the same time displaying a blackboard on one of three poles erected on the lighthouse, certifies whether the vessel making her signal is either a snow, brig or ship.

I learned from my owners that after I had left the port they had purchased a ship of about 400 tons. The new ship had been sent to New York and was returning with flour, staves, etc., she had got so near to Liverpool as to make her signal with a pilot on board, and having entered the channel near the north-west buoy, had anchored to stop the ebb tide, the day was remarkably fine. One of the underwriters had actually erased her name from his book, as being safe arrived, before he sat down to dinner, but having finished his meal he cast his eyes again on Bidston hill, and to his great surprise saw a signal for a vessel being on shore in the Rock channel. The next ebb washed away the sand under her middle and she burst in pieces, a total wreck. What uncertain property ships are! A puff of wind or a trifling mistake and they are no more. The pilot of this ship had been suspended twelve months for misconduct, during this time a spit had increased from one of the shoals which he was not aware of and on this he wrecked the vessel

Mr. 10.10. had purchased a ship at Lancaster in lieu of the one lost, and she was now arrived here. Her name was the *Brothers*, a three-decked ship, well-known on the Jamaica trade as a letter of marque in the American War, and was intended for the Quebec trade. I now got our vessel into the graving dock to caulk and coat her bottom, and whilst the shipwrights were at work a hole was discovered very low down, apparently bored by an augur from the inside while building, and there was nothing but a chip about the thickness of a barley corn pitched over. In this hazardous condition this vessel had crossed the Atlantic a number of times. Sailors may well say 'I can't die till my time comes.'

It will be recollected that I went to Bristol with Captain 5.16. when he was ill. That sickness ended his life, and his son 19. J. 16., then a youth, was made master of the vessel for to assist his mother and family (a steady mate was also continued in her), This young man I shall frequently have to mention, both as a friend and enemy, in future years.

Mr. 19. J. 16. had spent much of his time in Liverpool, and as his vessel lay frequently many months in the year in the docks there, he had a general acquaintance with gay families, which by degrees drew me also into the fashionable circle, to attend on females, to the play and routs, and one Sabbath evening at a tea party, I was much hurt and astonished to hear a lady of the house, at the pianoforte, sing the Scotch song of 'Sweet Lullaby,' me being a strict churchman on Sundays. Conceiving this conduct a gross violation of the Sabbath, I soon took my leave of the party, and retired to my lodgings. The remembrance of this improper company, or acquaintance, made me more circumspect in future, and believe I never went more than twice to a play after this, during my future life.

*   *   *   *   *   *

14

He Makes a Winter Passage from Liverpool to New York

I WAS ordered to prepare the vessel for to take salt and coals in, for Philadelphia. I shipped a new mate, who appeared more calculated for industry than the one I discharged, but he had little in his behaviour to recommend him, being the son of a rough farmer from the Lancashire hills, and had served his apprenticeship in the West Indian trade from Lancaster.

A few days after he commenced sleeping on board, in returning to the vessel from his supper, the press-gang laid hold of him and lodged him in the rendezvous. I had retired to bed in my lodgings when a messenger from the mate obliged me to dress again, and I paid him a visit, but could not prevail on the officer to release him until next day.

As the seamen were now obliged to secret themselves from the press-gang, I had many a weary step after them, but having obtained all but two of the crew I sent the vessel into the river by way of securing those I had shipped. Towards the close of Sunday I obtained a promise from two men at an ale-house of the lower order that they would go with me, but as they had not spent all their money, lately received from an African voyage, their landlord treated me with insult and endeavoured to throw obstacles in the way to prevent their shipment; but having got on their right side, I was determined to keep close to them. The next day I hired a boat in readiness and paid them an early visit, but as seamen are a wavering set of people, I had to follow them from place to place during the forenoon, and

at last, just at the top of high water, I was under the necessity of taking two women of their acquaintance into the
boat with them, they little knowing that the vessel was at
that moment under sail in the river. As soon as I got
alongside, their chests were handed on board, and as the
men entered the deck the boat was ordered away and we
proceeded to sea.

On the 12th at 6 a.m. we were obliged to hand the topsails, and at 10 a.m. the wind blew so violent at W.S.W.
with a heavy sea running, that we thought it prudent to
reef the foresail. Accordingly the mate and crew were on
the yard at work, when a wave struck our vessel on her
beam ends, and all the spars in the crutches with the
quarter rail and some stanchions gave way and buried me
under the wreck. As the man at the helm had now no tiller
rope to windward (he had been knocked away to leeward
with the tiller, and I heard him groan), there was no one on
deck but this man and me, but providentially the hen-coop
received the greatest weight of the spars, or else I might
have been crushed to death. I was soon relieved from my
disagreeable situation, and we set about the repairs as well
as we could, not having a carpenter, but determined not to
run to Liverpool again as it was expected a hot press was
going to take place, without any regard to Protections.
The gale continued in general the 13th and 14th and the
vessel was very leaky, with one of the pumps useless, it
having burst, therefore was obliged to veer ship often to
pump out the water. On the 15th some of our seamen's
hands had lost pieces of skin, and had wounds on their
palms nearly as large as a sixpence. This arose from their

want of work whilst hiding so long from the press-gang. About noon this day we ran for Ramsay Bay and anchored in ten fathoms, well sheltered.

The 16th, the wind being moderate in the morning from the westward, we sailed, but the weather threatening caused us to return again. Towards night the wind blew strong at S.S.E. We got our top-gallant mast on deck and gave the vessel about two-thirds of the cable. At midnight we were riding very uneasy, even pitching bows and bowsprit under water, and the spray of the sea flying the whole length of the vessel wetting us completely. As there was great danger of our cable parting and the lives of the crew (humanly speaking) being in jeopardy, I made a proposal that in case of parting the cable, to run the vessel farther in shore, to get a little more shelter from the sea and then let go the other anchor, and should this also be lost then to run her on shore on the beach. My mate thought it more advisable to run to the northward through a narrow channel in a dark night without having any guide whatever to direct us; which being a most simple scheme was rejected by all. In an hour after the wind veered on the point, which made the vessel ride easy, and we continued till the 19th, repairing our damage, and having put a plaster on the split part of the pump, it again became useful. We sailed this day with a westerly wind which again veered to S.W. the 20th passed Holyhead.

The 23rd had only reached Bardsey Island, the wind being contrary with rain. This night the moon was totally eclipsed. The 24th saw Arklow mountain in Ireland; the 25th, saw Strumble Head in Wales. The 26th, passed

Tusker with the wind at S.S.E. and S.E.; and on the 29th, after a good run to the westward, the wind got the northward and in squalls blew very strong with rain at the same time, a cross sea running, the vessel shipped much water.

The 12th November. Saw two men-of-war standing to the eastward, supposed them to be returning (as usual) from the Newfoundland station at this season of the year.

The 30th November we had only gained the longitude of 43° 17' W. though we had been now fifty days from Liverpool. I therefore thought it prudent for the whole crew (myself included) to submit to an allowance of bread in good time, and accordingly weighed each man 5lbs. to last the ensuing week, and then nailed fast the bread room.

The 4th December we saw many gulls and diving birds, which indicated that we were approaching near the Newfoundland bank.

The 8th, got soundings in 40 fathoms, pebbles with broken shells.

The 9th, we caught six cod fish, they were remarkably lean and had little in their maw-bag but pebble stones.

The 22nd, the squalls were so violent that we took in all our low sails and laid too under three hammocks spread on the main shrouds, the sea running mountains high and very long.

The 23rd, the wind was like a hurricane from the westward, and whilst laying too, at 1 p.m. a heavy wave fell on board before the larboard gangway, which washed our boats out of the chocks, and stove the long-boat, burst in the steerage hatchway, crushed the hencoops in pieces, broke the cabin sky-light, and finally carried away our lee quarter boards, but providentially swept no men overboard, they having secured themselves. We immediately set all to work and lashed the boats to the scuppers and nailed some canvas over the hatchway. The vessel now laying in the trough of the sea every minute we expected she would founder, the waves being as high as our mast heads. At 2 p.m. loosed the foresail and veered round on the other tack. As the rail, or rough tree was broken, we got in the spritsail yard to replace it. At 8 a.m. the wind being moderate we got the boats again in the chocks.

The 24th, we found more damage done by the sea, viz., the gallows stanchion was broken, the main spring stay was stranded, and other things much injured which we were now employed in repairing.

On the 11th January, 1791, being then in the longitude of 68° 8′ W., I thought it prudent to make a farther reduction in the allowance of bread to 4lbs. per man for a week. We had now been ninety-two days from Liverpool and still no appearance of a fair wind, or any (continued) moderate weather.

On the 15th we found our vessel getting more leaky.

The 16th we caught a pilot fish the companion of a shark.

The 18th January. I reduced the weekly allowance of bread to 3¼ lbs. for each man, with a pound of beef per day.

The 20th, saw some wreck of a vessel.

The 23rd, we had rough weather, and the sea full grown. Our vessel laying too. About mid-day a sea struck the vessel fore and aft her whole length, which shattered the channel bends, broke the remaining rough tree and its stanchions, threw the boats again across the deck and stove the long-boat (the second time), split the covering board of the gun-wale, broke the larboard gallows stanchion, and two stanchions on the quarter deck, and opened several seams so that I had to fix canvas spouts to lead the water across my bed from the side. I was in great anxiety respecting our stored salt cargo, for if the water had got to it, it would have melted and the vessel would have overset. We got some benefit even out of this disaster, viz., the broken timber to cook our victuals in the cabin, being almost without firing, and at night when we were not laying too, we steered by the stars. The few candles remaining I preserved for coming in with the land. Whilst we were repairing our damage the gale mercifully abated, and the sea mountains began to subside. We again lashed our boats to the scuppers, where they remained fastened across the deck.

The 25th seeing streams of weeds, straw reed, etc., N.E. and S.W. I concluded we were verging on the Gulf Stream, originating in the Bay of Mexico, from the easterly trade winds continually pressing a large body of water into that gulf. This day I reduced the weekly allowance of bread to 3 lbs.

As I had been accustomed to scent the pine trees when drawing near the American coast with the wind from the land, I was now confident of our near approach to that continent.

On the 30th, when I retired to rest I gave particular orders about heaving the lead without stopping the vessel's progress. At midnight tried for soundings with 40 fathoms of line without effect. At 2 a.m. threw the lead again, which when hauled in the officer applied the tallow to his tongue to feel for sand but found none. One of the men also tried the tallow and found sand on one edge of the grease, which occasioned a further trial which proved we were in 17 fathoms, coarse sand, and I have little need to say that this discovery gave us infinite satisfaction, though our troubles were not yet over. I knew by the intense cold we had experienced just before, and from the opinion of the Americans we had spoken to, that the Delaware was closed with the ice. Therefore according to orders I kept the vessel N.E. before a heavy sea running, to try for New York, and got our cables bent. At daylight we saw a number of wild fowl.

The 31st January, 1791, the wind flew round from S.W. to N.N.W. and blew strong, so that we were obliged again to take in our sails and lay too. The vessel shipping much water which turned to ice on our deck and cordage, and we had much snow and sleet. At 4 a.m. sounded in 40 fathoms and were afterwards driven off soundings.

The 1st February we had a strong cold gale with a heavy sea, but towards noon, being more moderate, we set our foresail and topsails.

The 2nd, we were obliged to take in our topsails and the vessel was plunging bows under in a turbulent sea, the wind being squally with dark clouds and snow.

The 3rd, we recovered the soundings, the wind being northerly and so cold that our deck was covered with ice.

The 4th, we had a southerly wind which enabled us to stand to the northward, and I do not think I was off the deck more than ten minutes all this day, so eager was I to spread and reduce the sails as occasion required.

The 5th, we had strong gales with cold rain. At 11 a.m. the long-looked-for land appeared in view. It was Long Island and, being in 15 fathoms, we stood to the westward. At noon saw the high land of Never-sink on the Jersey shore. At 3 o'clock we saw the lighthouse on Sandy Hook, but no pilot appearing I was determined to push the vessel in, as the wind was now blowing strong from the eastward. Having calculated the time of tide from H. Moore's *Practical Navigator*, I made for the Hook, under a supposition that it was now a quarter flood, but on getting into shoal water I found so much sea as to alarm me, it being occasioned by the ebb tide running against the wind, the book being erroneous as much as four hours in the time of high water, and from which error I had nearly lost the vessel. We immediately hauled on a wind and soon had the satisfaction of discovering a fast-sailing pilot boat coming round the Hook, which quickly came alongside and confirmed me that it was now the last quarter ebb. When the tide made, we ran in and anchored two miles above the Hook. The wind was now at north-west, and our sails and rigging covered with ice.

On Sunday the 6th of February, 1791, at seven in the morning, we got under sail, all hands being now at full allowance of provisions, and in high spirits. We got up the top-gallant yard and set studding sails both sides for a wonder! At eleven got through the Narrows, but as the wind was light when above Staten Island, and the ice coming down on us in a large field (though broken), we were obliged to drop our anchor to prevent being driven away with it. I went below for something and was astonished at the noise it made against the bottom. In about an hour after, a breeze springing up, we lifted our anchor and at five in the afternoon moored at the wharf below Beckman's slip in the East River, New York, after a passage of 119 days, or seventeen weeks, the marine grass growing on our sides as high as the gunwale.

On this passage I entered with a full determination to persevere, through storms of wind, hail, rain and snow. Sometimes I had the satisfaction of seeing a weather-beaten barque pursuing the same route, but they sailing faster and not being so low in the water, all left me in the rear. As we seldom had a moderate day the sea generally ran high, so that we could not lay our side to it for fear of being swamped. Eight days following we were obliged to lay too and during the passage we were laying too on forty-eight days. We melted ice to supply our drink, and as we were often unable to cook on deck, a small quantity of salted provisions was boiled in the cabin, till the coals got nearly expended, when we were obliged to nurse our firing. Many a long, dark, melancholy winter's night I passed in the cabin, and believe I never went to bed but once during the passage wholly undressed. Sometimes my bed was so wet that I had to coil myself round like a dog on one corner of it, but notwithstanding these disagreeables I continued firm in my resolution not to run to the southward.

On our approaching the American continent, vessels leaving the land endeavoured to avoid us, supposing we were in want of provisions, and one in particular I hailed till I was hoarse without getting a satisfactory answer, she making off from us as fast as possible. During fourteen dark dreary weeks of winter my views were bounded by the alternate succession of growing hills and bursting billows with hail and sleet and snow. When retired at night no ruddy fire nor beaming candle cheered the dismal gloom, but in gross darkness soothed to sleep by whistling winds and roaring seas. The long dark hours were spent in deep solemnity, save when the seaman tuned his ballads of past fought battles or the Chick Lane ghost.

I think (notwithstanding my allowance was the same as the men), I had on our arrival, nearly six pounds of biscuits in my bag, and our remaining stock was about 190 lbs., so that we could have reached the Caribee Islands had we been ultimately blown off the coast, and obliged to run for them as vessels frequently do in winter. My hair was such a length about my face that my old acquaintances could not help remarking the great alteration in my appearance.

Our cargo was soon disposed of, but when we opened the hatchway, instead of the salt touching the hatches as when we sailed, it had been so shaken on the passage that it had shrunk greatly into a solid mass, so as to require iron instruments to reduce it to its original grain.

On my arrival here I gave thanks to my Almighty preserver at the Episcopal Church of St. George, where I heard Bishop Seabury preach. Captain M –, who traded between Philadelphia and Jamaica, was now loading here and gave me a particular and general invitation to his wife's mother to spend my evenings. At this house I found a number of respectable and well-behaved females, who treated me with

the greatest hospitality. My consignee was an Englishman
at whose table a plate was always ready. This gentleman
was fond of hunting and fowling, and I was informed that
in shooting eighteen times he killed seventeen grouse, he
was such an excellent marksman. He had an English
hunting horse which he was inclined to try in a sledge on
the snow, though the animal was restive. However, I agreed
to accompany him and we were well pelted with snow and
dirt from the horse's heels during our excursion.

When the thaw took place the streets in some places were
impassable, and I was informed that a dirty sailor, seeing a
well-dressed lady stopped by the water, without any ceremony lifted her up and wading to the opposite side landed
her safely, but instead of being thanked for his civility she
told him he was an impudent fellow. On hearing this he
again caught her up saying, 'As you are not pleased I'll
take you back again,' and accordingly carried her to the
place where he first found her.

On Sabbath days during my stay here I generally attended
worship at the Dutch Reformed Church, the service being in
English. The ladies in general after being seated in their
pews received from their servants small stoves to warm their
feet. They were square wooden boxes with holes on the
top and an iron handle to hold it by. At the side was a slide
to open for putting in the fire in a small earthen or iron cup,
and to prevent smoke the live coals from a wood fire were
generally used. A lady in the seat with me was so civil
as to push her stove towards me, but not being accustomed
to such indulgence I immediately returned it. These stoves
are also used during the severity of the winter by the females

SOUTH PROSPECT OF THE CITY OF NEW YORK.

in their dwelling, each person having one. I think these machines would be very serviceable in the cold damp churches in England, especially to delicate people who often injure their constitutions by going from a warm carpeted parlour to sit for hours together in a church with the wet running from the walls and pillars.

In this city I became acquainted with a merchant of Kingston, Jamaica, who was just arrived in this city from Canada by a route across the frozen lakes, and part of the way I believe the sledge was drawn by dogs trained to draw like horses.

Our vessel being now laden with oak timber, ashes, staves, etc., we prepared for sea. I procured one passenger for England, but he beat me down to ten pounds, out of which five guineas went to the ship-owners, but he was to lay in a sufficient sea store of necessaries.

Before I sailed I heard of the loss of an American brig at Egg Harbour, having been twenty-two weeks on her passage from Liverpool, and at last was either ran or drove on shore on the coast. The crew were reduced to three potatoes per diem. Whatever our troubles had been, we now found they were light when compared with the crew of this vessel.

On the 20th March, 1791, we made sail in company with my friend Captain M – for Jamaica and the *New Success* for Granada, the wind being strong, with much snow. On turning out Mr. S – 's stores from the hampers, to my surprise instead of finding a good stock of tea, sugar, wine, beer, hams etc., I found a large quantity of turnips, which he had provided as an antiscorbutic, but whatever effects this root might have on the scurvy, I found it inefficacious for curing the itch, as Mr. S – was well covered with this disease. Amongst the hampers taken on board I found one containing excellent porter, which the merchant had sent for my use. The *Paragon* Snow,[1] loaded with wheat, had sailed for Liverpool a day or two before us.

The 22nd the gale was so strong at S.W., we were obliged to lay too. The 25th we had very stormy weather, the sun having a large ring round it by day and the moon was also encircled at night. We had mostly bad weather till the 1st April, on which day when laying too a heavy sea struck us, and broke the starboard quarter boards. Having been for several days in the Gulf Stream the heavy waves ran cross, which caused the vessel to be deluged with water, the wind being contrary from the Eastward. From the 7th to the 11th we saw numerous wild ducks and such birds as frequent the Banks of Newfoundland.

My passenger was now rubbing to eradicate the itch, I having supplied him with mercurial ointment from our medicine chest. Since our leaving the land, I had confined him to one set of utensils, which he was to keep clean himself to prevent the cabin boy from catching the disease. The 24th running in the latitude of 50° 50′ N. we got soundings in 98 fathoms, fine brown sand, and had been exactly five weeks from New York.

The 25th sounded in the different depths of 73, 65 and 64 fathoms, and then saw the Irish land. The 26th a foul wind

---

[1] A Snow is, for all rough purposes, a brig. Differs only from a brig in that the boom mainsail is hooped to a try-sail mast, or horse, instead of to the mainmast. – ED.

blowing strong, occasioned the vessel to plunge the forecastle under water. We did not pass Tusker till the 29th. The 30th saw Holyhead and continued beating against a strong gale till the 5th May, the Head being in sight six days. This day the wind shifted in the morning, from the eastward to the southward, and we got a Liverpool pilot out of the boat No. 5. About noon we anchored near the north-east buoy on Hayle Bank. We had been forty-six days from New York, one-half of which we had been mostly beating against an easterly wind. On looking into my liquor case, expecting to find nearly a gallon of cherry brandy there, which I had purchased at New York, I was much surprised to find but little left, and questioning the boy was informed that the passenger had drank it from time to time, when I was engaged on deck. This was a great mortification.

After the ebb tide had made two or three hours, a number of my friends came on board from Liverpool. Mr. 10.10's late wife's father, was a shipmaster and had arrived from a voyage and anchored to stop tide near the spot where our vessel now lay, many of his friends from Liverpool had come on board to congratulate him on his safe arrival (as my acquaintances had now done) a gale of wind came on, the vessel was wrecked and I believe the whole on board were drowned. I learned from a friend that one of the Underwriters had been so alarmed with our long passage out that he had reinsured at twenty per cent, though he was only to receive two and a half for his risk from the owners. Having now entered the river in safety we anchored before the town and the next morning ran into Georges dock.

I found the *Paragon* was not arrived, though she sailed before us; I was not sorry for this, as the master was a non-such in his own estimation and the disappointment might tend to lessen his pride, which was at all times insufferable.

* * * * * *

15

He Sails to Philadelphia for the last Time

I WAS then ordered to load for Philadelphia with liberty to take a freight from thence to any part of Europe. We again loaded salt and coals and the beginning of July 1791 we left the dock and as the wind was strong to the westward anchored at the Magazine, where we joined the ship *Elizabeth*, now commanded by captain P – k (formerly of the *Thetis* and *Cyclope*) belonging to the same employ and bound to Philadelphia also. We lay here wind-bound a considerable time, and one day on the weather tide the sea burst in our two middle cabin windows.

The 11th we got under sail, the ebb having made strong before the pilot reached the vessel. However, as he concluded there was sufficient depth, we attempted the Rock Channel, and soon after we passed the Perch the vessel stuck fast in the channel, but in a minute or two, the tide scoured away the sand so that we floated off, and after trailing over the ground for a considerable distance we got into deep water. As we had now a contrary wind blowing fresh we had to beat out. In executing this our pilot gave the vessel many strokes on the North bank, but through mercy we did not stop. Having discharged our pilot we made the best of our sails to overtake the *Elizabeth*, but as Captain P – found his vessel sailed much faster he was not disposed to wait, and by night she was hull down to windward. I now concluded that the *Elizabeth* would reach America long before us, though the race is not always gained by the swift.

On the 13th we passed the Smalls with a northerly wind and took our departure from the land. From the 22nd to the 27th we had very rough weather, at times shipping

much water. The 7th August the vessel was plunging forecastle under in a heavy sea from W.N.W.

The 17th the sea was much covered with feathers, which
indicated our approaching Newfoundland banks. This day
we also saw a white butterfly. One of our men caught a bird
of the woodpecker species. It had long yellow legs with
sharp claws, its breast was green like a parrot and its back a
greenish brown, on the top of its head it had no feathers, but
an oval light blue skin, the eyes red and lively. I tried it
with soaked biscuit of which it ate heartily. This encouraged me to provide it a cage but when any person put their
fingers near it would peck them with violence. Its body was
about the size of a thrush.

The 21st was very stormy and variable, round the compass,
part of the time we were scudding under bare poles. The
28th we spoke a schooner belonging to Nantucket on the
whale fishery. The 30th a sand bird kept hovering round
the vessel. On the American coast 'tis common to see land
birds at sea, such as cranes, owls, hawks, etc., which are
drove off in hard gales, or fly off in foggy weather. I have
seen owls of a most beautiful plumage. At night the birds
settle on the masts to rest, which being observed by the
boys are caught when asleep. A Welsh sailor caught a
hawk and was persuaded by a lad to feed him with bread
from his mouth, but was severely bitten in the attempt.

On the 1st September the wind blew strong at south-west
which caused such a sea as to make the vessel plunge forecastle under. We had also much rain and lightning. The
7th was very fine weather and we saw a white butterfly,
This day I discovered a line of froth tending N.b.W. S.b.E.

which I imagine was the edge of the Gulf Stream. The 10th got soundings in 24 fathoms brown sand.

The 11th September, 1791, we anchored off Market Street wharf, Philadelphia. According to the custom of the port, we peeked the yards and ran in the jib-boom, etc. On my landing, to my great surprise, was informed that the *Elizabeth* had not yet made her appearance, but she arrived in three days after us, and on her hauling to the wharf I went on board, and could see the mortification exhibited in Captain P – 's countenance. On asking where he had been so long, he replied, ' to the southward, catching Dolphins,' having run down the trade winds.

As the salt retailers would not give the price demanded for our cargo, we hauled to Peter Knight's wharf in the northern liberties, and there stored our salt. A friend of mine here, who wished me to become a citizen of the United States, now contracted for building a live oak and red cedar ship, which, if salted in, the timbers have been known to run thirty years. The hemp intended for the outfit was to be of the growth of Virginia.

The coals we had on board were sold to a curious character known by the name of the Absent Man. In his rambles he had once called at a friend's house, the family being at tea he was invited to partake, and after he had sat awhile he suddenly arose and said that he had quite forgotten that he was to be married that evening and hurried out of the house. I was also informed that one summer day having returned to his dwelling very warm, he hung up his hat and wig in the hall but soon after recollecting that he had omitted calling on a person, he proceeded up front street with the sun on his back. A friend accosted him enquiring the reason that he had neither hat nor wig on his head, he could not conceive the reason!

Myself and crew were invited to attend the funeral of a cook of a Scotch ship who was drowned at the wharf in the night. He was carried on the seamen's shoulders with the ship's colours over him to the Potters' field, but on our arrival found the grave too short and had to send to the digger to make it longer. On his arrival he reflected on the ship's carpenter for making the coffin longer than was necessary, and continued in an ill humour while he was doing the needful. When the body was lowered into the grave the Scotch captain took off his hat, which was followed by the company and made me expect an exhortation from the old gentleman, but he covered himself again and the seamen filled up the grave when we parted.

One morning, walking before breakfast with a Bristol shipmaster that had been acquainted with me in Spain, we called on board a British ship at a wharf, and understanding the captain was in bed we went into the cabin to rouse him, he having turned out and whilst dressing himself in the cabin I thought I discovered the curtain in the state-room moving, and, being suspicious of this married man, I had the curiosity to look further and discovered a strumpet in the bed. I also detected his mate afterwards with a female on board, and on going on board another married man's vessel I found two ladies of ill fame at dinner, after testifying my disapprobation to both masters I left their ships. One of these captains afterwards pressed me to dine with him. When I enquired whether he had landed the woman I had seen on board, he gave me to understand he had. I therefore promised to visit him at the time, and on walking towards the ship I saw a person run to give notice of my approach, and on entering the cabin saw the woman dressed very fine preparing for the table, on which I turned round and departed, not wishing to countenance such proceedings.

I generally attended the Episcopal churches on the Sabbath, and often heard Bishop White preach.

Two Quakers having talked to me about Pindar's works, I had an inclination to read them, especially as the author was well known to me, when he practised as a physician in the West of England, and attended my step-mother in her last illness. One of the above gentlemen accordingly conducted me to the city library to procure the said books for me, and informed me that if I wished to read any books in future the librarian would furnish me with them to read in the room only. I found the place spacious with a sort of false gallery to regulate the upper shelves, I was informed that this brick building was built by tradesmen each taking as many shares as the amount of his work came to, which were afterwards disposed of to the citizens. There was a niche over the outside door for a statue, then executing (I believe) in Italy, to represent Dr. Franklin.

I went into the House of Assembly for the State, and heard an able man addressing the President, but do not think there was more than a half dozen attending that did not belong to the Assembly. At the Court of Nisi prius it was the same, scarcely any attending from curiosity. The Court of Oyer and Terminen was crowded, but I obtained a place in the Gallery to hear the trial of four convicts who had broken prison and murdered a cattle drover. They were all condemned and executed afterwards on the common. The convicts in the gaol are employed so many hours in the day cleaning the roads and streets, sometimes they are chained to a wheel-barrow or cart, and at other times to each other. Their livery is red and blue, and their heads are shaved. At the Supreme Court I heard a counsellor plead who was also a merchant and a partner in a store, and would supply anyone with needles, pins, etc., after he had returned from the Courts. The crier was adjoining the Court when he made a mistake and instead of saying 'Save the Congress' he said 'Save the King,' which caused a laugh amongst the lawyers. I found afterwards that he had been Crier of the Court many years before the revolution and had not gone to bed sober for nearly twenty years.

Whilst I was here the election took place for Sheriffs, Representatives and Assembly men, by ticket. All citizens being voters. The electors prepared three papers with a name written on each, these were folded up and endorsed with the words Sheriff, etc., the voter then proceeded to the Court-house, and having discovered the window for his district, by the name being above it, he presented himself to the person in waiting at the window. His name was then looked for in the books and, being found eligible, his three tickets were received and dropped into three boxes according to their superscriptions, no one knowing whom he voted for. He then returned to his business, so that there was neither noise nor bustle.

My merchant intending to visit his plantation about fifteen miles from Philadelphia, invited me to accompany him. Accordingly we set off in his coachee after dinner, taking a large rock fish with us to recruit the next day's provisions at the farm. It was a fine day and our route laying through Germantown, I found it to consist of straggling houses to the extent of two miles. I perceived that the roads were much inferior to those in England. During our journey I got a sight of the Alligany mountains, which I little expected to see, being accustomed only to the sea-coast, which is low. After sunset we arrived at the plantation and found the farmer getting in his maize or Indian corn. The fire in the kitchen was now increased and some mush (Indian meal), was boiled to eat with milk, on which, with a hot herb pie, we supped. My companion slept with me, and soon after daylight I was preparing to dress myself to look about the farm, but my bedfellow began relating that he had lived in this house during the American War, and being considered a Tory, one day a commissary from the army brought waggons to carry away his corn, hay, etc., but having invited the man into his house, he began to enquire about several officers in the American army, saying they were his friends, at the same time urging him to take refreshment, which the officer seemed desirous of, and after taking a glass or two his ideas were altered in respect of his host being a Tory, and he would take nothing from him.

After breakfast I was taken around the plantation, which was extensive, and on the border of an old American army encampment, I saw an oak tree in the wood which I believe would bear squaring about seventy feet in length. The fence of the estate was post and rail, the posts were white cedar, as being durable. After dinner we returned to the city. I have seen on an estate in the vicinity of the town as fine a field of clover, and as fine fat oxen, as I ever remember to have seen in England.

The vessels trading from New Providence to this place were generally consigned to my merchants, I therefore had an opportunity of seeing many people from Nassau whom I knew when laying there so long in the transport. I was introduced to a lady dining at my merchant's as Mrs. R — in whom I recognized a shopkeeper who had often sold me a variety of articles. This lady had come to Philadelphia to get a Mullato boy inoculated for the small-pox. This boy, of whom she was so fond, and on whose account she had taken this voyage, was her husband's child by a negress slave, she having none of her own. The ladies and children I observed about this time in Philadelphia had much the appearance of having the smallpox, and some of their faces were much disfigured, but on enquiry found it was the effect of mosquito bites.

I visited Gray's gardens across the river Schuykil, twice, the first time with a party in a coach, and though no demand was made for our entrance (which omission I cannot account for), yet the expense of the visit cost us £3 12s. The second visit to this imitation of Vauxhall was in company with a gentleman of the city, and though we paid the entrance money, yet it only cost us about 6s. on the whole.

We passed over a floating bridge to the gardens, about sunset, which were situated on a high bank overlooking the river. The ground was not extensive but well diversified, many of the trees appeared originals and were changing the tints to their summer coats of various greens to brown, yellow, red, etc., which had a beautiful appearance after the illumination took place. The bridge across the river Schuylkil, and a miniature ship on the river (which had been built when I was here in the year 1787, for the procession that paraded through the city when the Federal delegates met) were illuminated and had a pretty effect when viewed from the gardens. Many rural scenes were exhibited during the evening, and the fall of water at a mill was discovered by the light of a fire kindled near it. The singing was not praiseworthy, nor were the fireworks equal to what I have seen in England, the word Washington burst out suddenly in a blaze of light, but was short lived. The first night I visited the place we had supper, and the reason of the great expense arose from one of the company ordering so many dishes, many of which were untouched. Two ladies being present prevented me from pointing out the impropriety of his conduct.

After laying by the wharf many weeks I at last heard of two freights, one for St. Andero in the Bay of Biscay, the other was a cargo of maize for Malaga, which article I agreed to take.

The people from some parts of this State, on visiting Philadelphia, to contract for produce, often at the end of their bargain make this provision, that they will fulfil the agreement unless they catch the ague, which they dread from its frequency in the marsh lands.

We transported our vessel now to the south end of the city, to load our cargo from Mr. L., the Spanish consul, the Indian corn was intended to feed hogs and consigned to Don Bartholomew Molina of Malaga.

Perhaps as I am now going to leave Philadelphia for ever, it will not be amiss to say something of the city. The length of the place runs in a parallel curve with the harbour about two miles; the low street next the fresh-water river Delaware, where the sailors generally resort, is called Water Street. The next parallel is Front Street, then Second, Third, etc. These are crossed at right angles by other streets, generally named from a tree, leaving squares for dwellings, churches, public buildings, etc., the stables, small gardens, etc., being in the centre or rear of the dwellings. The streets have many bushy trees, and also pumps of excellent water, which is so cold in summer that many incautious people get their deaths in drinking it. Shops in the warm season are open at five in the morning. People retire early to bed and few are to be seen after nine at night. The markets are well supplied, and venison and bear meat are to be found occasionally. Whoever may purchase the inferior articles, the labouring people will have the best, whose wives attend the market with light wheel barrows for the purpose.

Hearing the yellow fever had made its first appearance at one of the sailor houses in Water Street, I got my ship's company on board as soon as possible, but they were a motley set. Our cargo being laden of Indian corn, rice, etc., I found the vessel very deep for a winter's passage.

When I departed from this city on the 26th November, 1791, where I had so many valuable friends and acquaintances, and in which place I had spent so many happy hours, I little thought this was the last time I was ever to see this continent. For had I returned, it was probable (humanly speaking) that I should have arranged matters at home, not

ARCH STREET FERRY, PHILADELPHIA.

only to sail for Philadelphia in future, but also to marry there, having at this very time a wife in view, with an independent fortune, but providence meant to dispose of me otherwise.

Part three

He Visits Malaga, Alicante, Carthagena and Newry .

THE evening before I sailed from Philadelphia, having previously secured the sailors' clothes in the cabin, my mate was so inconsiderate as to deliver some of the articles, unknown to me, to the men, who had received a month's advance. This encouraged one or two to run, and obliged me to send the vessel off, keeping the boat to follow her, and having had a long, wild-goose chase through the day, I left the wharf in the evening with the men, and overtook the vessel near Mud Fort.

The 2nd December we experienced strong gales with heavy rain, from the southern quarter, which occasioned a high cross sea, so that the vessel was much agitated, and laboursome. The 8th and 9th we had rough weather, the sea making a free passage over the vessel, which washed away our larboard quarter boards. The 12th saw a Spanish ship steering our course. The 13th lost sight of the ship astern. The 14th we had very bad weather, which deluged us with water, it making a free passage over the deck. The 15th found the vessel very leaky, while laying to. The 16th the wind was strong, with rain, thunder and lightning. From this time to the 2nd of January, 1792, we had much bad weather. This day we spoke the Spanish ship we had seen often hitherto. She was from the Havannah for Cadiz. The 4th we were becalmed, but the waves running high caused the vessel to wallow in the trough of the sea, rough-trees in. The 7th we had a strong gale with a heavy sea, which made the vessel very laboursome, so that our leak .

increased. We had experienced much southerly winds hitherto, which brought us in sight of the Island of St. Michael, this day; which we could not weather. Seeing this island I was convinced that the day before, we must have passed near the spot where a volcano had once arisen out of the sea and after existing a few years, had again sunk and disappeared about the year 1712. The 8th at mid-day I came to a resolution to run between St. Michael and Tercera, to the northward, to have good sea room, but could not get a sight of the Whale rock. The 9th the wind blowing strong from S.S.E. caused us to lay to. We also lay to on the 14th and on this day saw several ships under low sails, which we imagined were British West India-men bound to the southward. The 16th we had a strong gale from the westward with heavy squalls and rain, the sea making a free passage over the whole length of the vessel and one wave struck the mainsail and split it. Saw a Portuguese brig laying to under a close reefed main top-sail.

The 19th we had hazy weather with the wind from the southward, so that we got near the Spanish 64-gun ship *St. Philip* before we discovered her. She obliged us to heave to and sent her launch alongside, with fourteen men, some of which were Marines armed, the sight of which made me conclude that a war had commenced, and that we were now captured. The officer on coming on deck, demanded my papers and ordered the hatchway to be opened. I endeavoured to persuade him (in the best Spanish I was master of) that it was highly improper to open the hatchway as the sea was then rolling over the deck, but he told me it must be done, as they were suspicious of the English sending gunpowder to the Moors, with whom the Spaniards were then at war. We accordingly complied and he pushed his sword into the corn, at the same time the sea went down the hatchway and damaged the grain. He then went down into the cabin and took several letters (written by others) out of his pocket. The wafers being wet, he opened some from curiosity, which having read, he closed again and requested that I would put them into the post office on my arrival in Malaga.

The 20th January we got a sight of Cape St. Vincent, or rather the monastery thereon, it being foggy, so that this white edifice was better seen than the land. This day we saw a great number of gannets. On the 22nd we saw the coast of Barbary. The 23rd at 8 a.m. we were abreast of Gibraltar, having been fifty-four days from the Capes of Delaware.

Our ship's company being very lazy and deficient in their duty, had given me a great deal of trouble on the passage, and had treated the commands of the mate with great contempt. I was well assured that one of them had been a convict, his head being bare when he shipped, but he said it was occasioned by illness. After we sailed a number of stolen articles were found in his possession. I was now obliged to threaten some with a prison, if they did not treat the mate with becoming respect.

As I have not yet mentioned anything relative to my treatment of seamen, I will now do it. First with regard to their provisions. I always endeavoured to get the best quality, and laid no restrictions on the quantity, unless I found some wasted, and then two or three days' short allowance

P

taught them its value. In addition to the usual articles of bread, beef, pork, peas and flour, I procured a hundred-weight of cheese to supply the crew when the weather would not permit boiling meat on the deck. I also allowed them oatmeal, or Indian meal, with treacle for breakfast. When the weather was severe and their clothes wet I gave them each a dram, and a bottle of rum on Saturday nights, provided their behaviour merited it. Secondly, after being the humble servant to the crew during their shipment on shore, I conversed little with them at sea, issuing my orders through the medium of the mate, which kept up his respectability, and as I neither made use of swearing, nor allowed any, the mate had instructions from me to discountenance all improper language, by giving additional work to those who made use of profane words, and also plenty of work to those who manifested a disposition to shrink from duty. I allowed no unnecessary work on the Sabbath, and encouraged the boys to read their Bibles and sometimes lent mine when wanted. I allowed no one to chastise the boys but myself, and in case of sea-sickness indulged them, having experienced very cruel treatment myself when a boy. Sick men I also treated with humanity, and even when I thought them otherwise, often winked at it, fearing my penetration might deceive me. When I issued orders in working the ship I was generally obeyed with promptitude, but at times when the person did not move so quick as I wished, I speedily passed him and performed the work myself, giving a reprimand.

Having been brought up to labour, I could not stand idle and see others hauling at the ropes when additional strength was required, this always kept my hands hard in the palms, and encouraged the men in their work. Industrious able seamen, I kept from too much labour, and when such a man was at the helm at night and no others in sight, I occasionally gave him a glass of grog to certify that his behaviour was not unnoticed. This treatment always kept me popular with brave seamen, but backward lazy people seldom offered themselves the second voyage.

On the 24th January, 1792, we got a sight of Malaga. The 25th at daylight we got a breeze and at eight o'clock in the morning anchored at the entrance of Malaga Mole. I immediately landed with my papers and letters, having a large parcel sealed in my hands; this parcel was plucked from me by a man with a blue cloak (who I afterwards found was the broker). He beckoned to me to follow him, and he conducted me to Don Bartholomew Molina's, to whom our Indian corn was consigned, who treated me with great state and coolness, and gave me no invitation to eat or drink. The 9th February, as I could procure no freight from hence, we began to take in ballast.

The foundation of the Mole is composed of ponderous rocks, taken from the foot of a mountain adjoining, and rolled on each other in an irregular way, on which the super-structure of squared stones is laid, and I believe is mostly the work of convicts.

My letters had introduced me to four merchants' tables, I found their dwellings built with a court or quadrangle in the middle. As I do not recollect seeing any houses of this construction in Barcelona, I imagine they originated with the Moors. The rooms for sitting were large, and as it was now winter, a new mat made of grass, or what is rather called bass, of dyed colours was spread over the tiled floor which scented like new hay.

At another merchant's table I found a family, who I imagine from their behaviour, took me to be a rough ignorant seaman and consequently a stranger to etiquette and good manners, and being accustomed in the course of trade to give some of this class a good dinner occasionally, they overlooked my courtesy towards them. The sops in my soup were so united with long human hairs that I found it difficult to single them. After I had done eating fish, a mutton chop was handed me on the same plate, on which I fixed my eyes with astonishment, which being observed, a clean plate was ordered.

At another house, which appeared the most opulent, I was always invited to dine on the Sabbath, with many other British shipmasters. The masters of Danes, Swedes, etc., were invited on a weekday. At this table many ecclesiastics and other Spaniards were present, who generally sat at the head part of the table. The English were seated at the other end, where a British partner of the house presided. Nearly opposite me, at the end of the Spanish department here, I once saw a priest who paid little attention to anything but the dinner. He stooped forward to smell to a dish that was near him and when the bread was handed he turned over and over the greatest number of pieces to select several for his own use. The wine was of two kinds, a light new quality for the Spaniards and a stout old strong bodied article for the shipmasters which the merchant called the Grenadier. Across the lower end of the room there were glass doors, the panes of which being quick-silvered I was not a little surprised, on looking that way, to see another party (as I thought) at dinner in another room with livery servants also in attendance.

There is a public walk here with marble seats to retire to when weary, but as they are often occupied by beggars and filthy people who sleep on them in the sun, they occasionally on departure desert some of their family, which lay hold of the next person that seats himself.

One afternoon being alone on shore I had the curiosity to ascend the mountain that commands the town, on which the Moors had expended an immense sum of money to fortify it. The works were now in ruins and had long been the resort of thieves and murderers who lurked in caves and bye places during the day and visited the city at night. This I was not aware of, but continued my route, till I got near the summit, from whence I had a fine sight of the town, country and sea, but having seen several ill-looking men, sitting and sauntering about, I thought it prudent to return; having my stout hickory stick in my hand, the sight of this, perhaps, prevented an attack on my person. Near the bottom of the fortification I perceived a cross or two painted on the stones, which in Spain informs the passenger that it was the spot where a murder had been committed. Near this place, I overtook two dirty soldiers, and was surprised at hearing them converse in English, but found they belonged to the Irish Brigade quartered in Malaga. On reaching the town, I called at my merchant's counting house, where I related my afternoon's excursion, which surprised them, when I was informed of the danger I had escaped, and that I had run a risk of both robbery and murder. I was farther informed that it was supposed nearly two hundred men, then in the town, had escaped punishment for murders by feeing the officers of justice.

An execution for murder occurred while I was here. The man was a convict in gaol, where he quarrelled with a fellow prisoner and killed him. I waylaid the procession in the morning, having previously viewed the gallows on the beach, where a regiment of foot were in attendance. The criminal was drawn in a hurdle by an ass on which a man rode without a shirt, who was to be flogged. The sides of the matted hurdle were supported in the hands of the magistrates or other respectable men, fully dressed in black. A large concourse of ecclesiastics, police officers and troops were in the parade. After the whole had passed I returned to my business, not being desirous to see the execution, but towards four o'clock, my curiosity led me to the spot, where I found the man hanging, and as there was no throng of people I drew near the gallows. The man was clothed in white flannel. Before him on the ground was a table on which a crucifix was placed, I think of silver with lighted wax candles, but whether the latter were intended to enlighten the sun, or enliven the dead, I know not. I also understood that every shopkeeper was obliged to contribute towards his dress and every carpenter towards the gallows. That after condemnation his cell was hung with red cloth, and every thing that he desired to eat or drink was provided for him; cordials were also given him by gentlemen to the place of execution. This condescention was a lesson of charity and intended to promote humility.

An American sloop arrived here, with flour from Philadelphia for sale. I cannot say how far up the Mediterranean
his original destination was, but being alarmed with the idea
of being an Algerine slave, as the Americans had not yet
procured peace by a present to the Dey, and seeing a latine
rigged vessel, he hastened here.

Having been much troubled with a decayed tooth for
several days I determined to have it extracted, for which
purpose I called at the merchant's counting house and a
barber surgeon was sent for, who secured my head under his
arm and over the back of the chair. Being determined to
accomplish his undertaking he grasped the jawbone with
his instrument and not only drew the tooth, but splintered
the bone, a piece of which I shewed him.

The 11th February the *Zebra* British sloop of war arrived
here from Alicant, and soon after the bald-headed convict
having an expectation that I would turn him over to the
King's ship went on board her and entered. In the afternoon a pert midshipman came on board to demand the
man's wages, but as he behaved with great insolence I dismissed him with a reproof. The next morning the young
officer called again, with a lieutenant, both in full dress with
gold-laced hats. The lieutenant wished to know the reason
I had not complied with the demand of his companion. I
replied that he had treated me with such insolence as I
had not deserved, and which I then detailed, to which the
lieutenant hinted that there was a way for me to receive
satisfaction, meaning that I might challenge the boy, which
was sufficient to provoke a smile, being now in the country
of which Don Quixote was a native. I informed the officer

that it was my intention to send two more men to his ship. He replied that he did not know they would be received and departed from me. As I knew it was customary for Naval officers to treat masters of merchant with hauteur and contempt, I was determined not to ask a favour. I therefore waited on the Consul and informed him that I had two ill-behaved men on board which I wished to get clear of, and that I might esteem it a favour, if he would request the captain of the *Zebra* to take them from me. Accordingly an application was made, and a boat came for them, with a very civil master's mate, and that he might lose nothing by his politeness I invited him to sup with me at night on a roast duck. I thought this would also act as a silent lecture to his messmate.

On Sunday evening I was much grieved at hearing that a valuable Mulatto sailor belonging to me had got drunk and entered on board the *Zebra*. I therefore shipped four new men, for those I had lost. I was informed that two of the officers of the *Zebra* had been on shore practising with a pistol at a mark.

Mr. K – having offered to conduct me through the large cathedral I went with him, but as he could not converse in English I could get little information. I think it is as large as St. Paul's in London, with two towers, one of which is unfinished. The outside is encrusted with marble and ornamented. After our entry we proceeded to the choir and were let in by a singing boy, it being locked up. I saw some of the largest books I ever met with, heaped up in an irregular manner round the reading desk, which was on the wings of a bird. I saw a pretty stained window, the light

it emitted on the ceiling was red like blood. I was informed
no one is allowed to turn their backs to the high Altar.
The Bishop's palace adjoins, but its appearance had nothing
worth notice. This prelate's income is said to be more
than £15,000 per annum.

The walls round Malaga are ancient and crowded with
dwellings. The entering ports were without gates, which
I imagine had been removed from decay. As I was passing
near the Custom house, I saw many men assembled together
in a circle, and on looking over their shoulders I perceived
my cabin boy in the centre exhibiting an American game-
cock for sale. British cocks will sell for near a guinea here,
at particular seasons. This boy was the son of a church
rector in England, and I believe had brought two cocks
from America for sale. The wine is brought from the
mountains in black goatskins on mules to the vaults; where
large quantities of eggs are used in refining it. I drank
some pale rough wine here, which was made near the place
of the sherry, by which name it was called, though unlike it.
I was introduced by an Irish gentleman to the officers of the
Irish Brigade, who appeared to be a rough unpolished
people, poorly paid. As I was in discourse one day with a
Genoese at the entering port, a woman seized my hand and
began talking at a great rate, I looked to the man for an
explanation and was informed she was a gipsy, telling my
fortune, whom I immediately dismissed. I saw a large
heap of remarkably red oranges piled in the street for sale,
which came from the Barbary shore.

The 16th February, 1792, we completed our ballast, and
having procured letters of introduction I sailed on the 23rd

a-freight hunting. The 27th we anchored in Alicant Bay in eight fathoms and found thirty vessels at anchor. Having engaged to load brandy and barilla at this place and Carthegena, for Newry and Belfast in Ireland, we got under sail to get nearer to the Mole. There were several Swedish vessels laying up here, being afraid to proceed to sea on account of their nation being at war with the Algerians. I now went on shore and called on the British Consul, who advised me to retain my Mediterranean pass, as the Algerians occasionally boarded vessels in this open bay.

One of the churches was shut up for several weeks to remove the remains of the people buried under the floor; and being nearly full I was annoyed with the scent as I passed near it. What a ridiculous plan to remove the dead after once being interred!

On entering the city one morning I was not a little surprised at seeing an open coffin with a dead old man, having a long black beard, laying therein. According to custom wax lighted candles were placed near him, with a pewter plate to receive contributions to pay the ecclesiastics for burying him. Some time after the funeral passed me, the attendants singing. Having some call to another part of the town, as I passed a church, I saw a Spanish sailor sitting opposite weeping and lamenting aloud for the loss of his father. This man I saw afterwards returning to his vessel with the bedclothes that had been in the coffin, as the coffins are not buried, but serve to carry others, the bodies being interred with quick lime.

This city had fine walls for walking on. The mountain was directly behind the town, and on the point of a rock on the summit stood an old castle so near the cliff that it was unpleasant to contemplate on, being likely to fall at some future period, probably on dwellings below. There were many palm trees without the city, but the female trees would bear no dates without a male tree being planted near it. All through the country saffron is sold in the market in large baskets by weight. I discovered in this city Mr. W. I–, the merchant to whom I consigned the vessel when at Barcelona. He was now banished from that city for a year, by order of the King, for sending a challenge to an army officer. I paid him a visit one morning and spared him a gallon of rum out of my stock. I heard some time after that he had fallen in a duel. What a propensity there is in human nature, to make use of the things fetched from far and dearly purchased. In the West Indies shipmasters drink Geneva and brandy in water, instead of the native article of rum. On the contrary I saw them here, in a wine and brandy country, resorting to the tavern to drink hot rum punch, which spirit the tavern keeper must procure from a British vessel.

The soldiers' sentry boxes here have sometimes a cross stuck on their top; to one of these crosses I saw a woman on her knees praying.

On the 11th at 6 p.m. we entered the harbour of Carthagena. This day two Spanish ships of the line sailed. Before their anchors were lifted their topsails were furled with small grass cords and the yards hoisted up. As soon as the anchor started, in sheeting home the topsails the cords or grass ropes broke and the sails were spread in a minute, which I think is a good method; but they made an intolerable noise on board, quite unlike the practice of the British Navy. We found several French vessels here, the captains of whom paid so much attention to the British that their new tri-coloured flag was displayed when they perceived the English ships going or coming, and on shore saluted us as brethren in the bonds of liberty.

I found the people of this city much alarmed by the tricks of a juggler from Britain, and there was some fear that the inquisition intended taking him under their discipline. My merchant here informed me that he had hung some prints round his room characterising some scenes in the novel of *Tom Jones* which had been noticed by an inquisitor and this gentleman received an order to remove them. At his table I dined in company with a Spanish admiral who informed me, that when a boy he had run from a Spanish vessel and shipped himself in an English vessel employed in their Newfoundland trade from Bristol, in which vessel he had learned the English language. He mentioned the name of an earthenware man in Bristol who had once or twice given him a dinner of very fat bacon, which had nearly turned his stomach.

The Spanish Marines are entirely governed by the naval officer, who I saw one evening exercising the men on parade. When the clock began to strike six, the whole line of troops took off their hats to say their prayers, as customary.

I found out a tavern kept by a native of Minorca, who spoke English, named Vincent, where I dined with another shipmaster twice or thrice. He had two spacious rooms, one within the other, the floors which were up one pair of stairs were paved with brown tiles, as customary through Spain, but for want of sweeping often and washing, a numerous host of fleas paraded there, and bit his customers. Eight of these insects I have seen at once on my cotton hose, trying to bleed me. Vincent acted as interpreter for the English and used to supply me with goats' milk for my breakfast on board. One day he informed me that it was an annual custom on that day for the inhabitants of the city to climb an adjoining mountain on their hands and knees, either by way of penance or to worship a saint on the summit, but as I was engaged about the cargo I did not attend the ceremony. My merchant here being unwell was laying on a sofa one morning when I paid him a visit. The priest, or confessor was in the room, and as both were Irish the conversation was carried on in English. I found the ecclesiastic had been attached to the late armament or expedition to Oran on the Barbary Shore, and dealt in the marvellous. I listened with attention, but though I was certain he was lying (being in a Popish country), I thought best to confine my answers in expressing my surprise only. He was relating what wonders were performed by the image of a saint at the siege; and that when he was sitting with his companion silently in a room, their souls would migrate from one body to the other, so that they understood each others' thoughts. I think I heard also about a soul ascending the wall of a house and perhaps I should have heard much more had not the master of the house pointed out the improbability of the facts related.[1]

[1] I once heard of two British tars, rambling into a church (I think) in Italy at a time when prayers were made for the souls in purgatory; the light being mostly excluded, the seamen were surprised at seeing the souls moving over

On the high rocks and mountains in the vicinity of this place large crosses were erected to admonish seamen to their devotion. The 26th we finished our lading of brandy and barilla and I had procured six thousand reeds for weavers' use, on my own account, being the first Adventure I had ever engaged in since I was a boy. I obtained two passengers from hence who were merchants. Mr. M – and Mr. B –. On the 27th we hoisted in our long boat and prepared for sea.

On the 28th March, 1792, we sailed from Carthagena with a light easterly breeze. The 30th the wind came round to the westward and blew strong in squalls which brought us under close-reefed topsails, and the sea was rough, which made Mr. M – very sick, and by straining violently he brought up blood, which alarmed him so much that he entreated me to land him at Almeria, which I was unwilling to do, as I had passed that place some leagues. The 31st we had strong gales and as we were gaining little ground, to oblige Mr. M –, who had teased me for many hours to put him on shore, I bore up in the afternoon for Almeria Road, which we did not reach till after dark, and as the anchorage was near the cliff we were obliged to run under low sail and keep the lead going to find bottom. We at length got ground and in a cast or two twelve fathoms, when we anchored. Point Adera bearing W.S.W., so that we were a little sheltered from the wind. Most of the night the wind became variable, which made me busy in keeping the cable from fouling the anchor. At last the dawn made its appearance, when I

the floor, one of which passing a seaman he seized on it unobserved and departed, but on getting into daylight he found it nothing more than a crab with a piece of coloured silk on its back, to deceive the superstitious.

hurried Mr. M – and his baggage into the boat, his friend
and myself accompanying him. We got to the beach before
good daylight, where we lay on our oars. At last a man appeared who was requested to call on a merchant in the town
and inform him that such a friend wanted to land. When
this man returned we found the merchant had been confined
to his dwelling by the King's order for smuggling, and
therefore sent another person to muster the Health Officers.
At last the person wanted made his appearance, but kept at
an awful distance whilst one of our men jumped on shore
with the Bill of Health, which he was ordered to lay on the
ground, and on retiring it was inspected and the usual
questions being answered we landed and proceeded to the
merchant's house. As we entered the porch a large curtain .
hung against the wall, covering a painting in a gilt frame,
which I believe represented the Virgin Mary, though I never
heard of her being the Patroness of smugglers!

I found the Spanish gentleman glad to see Mr. M –, and a
cup of thick chocolate with sweet cakes was handed to each.
As there was every appearance of a strong levanter by the
time we had breakfasted I was anxious to get on board, but
as Mr. M – had ordered mutton, bread and vegetables for
us, we waited near an hour for them and on my departure
Mr. M –, from the fulness of joy in his heart at being again
on shore, caught me in his arms and expressed his great
obligation, ordering Mr. B – to pay the passage money for
both on our arrival in Ireland. We now hurried on board
leaving Mr. M – to pay the port charges, but the easterly
wind had commenced its operations before we reached the
vessel, which I found dragging, or had brought home the

anchor for want of the mate veering away more cable. We soon hoisted in the boat and made sail at 8 a.m. As we passed the point of Adera we discovered a galliot on shore, near the watch-tower on the low land, she having taken the tower for her consort in the night.

The 2nd April at 8 p.m. we passed Gibraltar with a strong breeze and soon got clear of Cape Trafalgar. About the 20th, I imagine, we got soundings in the Channel, having been led a long way to the westward with north and east winds, but as my Journal after this period is imperfect I must now go by memory. We had moderate weather as we ranged along the Nymph Bank, and saw many fishing boats, and though we had the quarantine flag flying, they attempted to run alongside, but were repulsed. Near Tusker we had a fresh gale from the southward. After we had run all night we had thick rainy weather the next forenoon, but at Meridian we saw the Mountains of Morne, and soon after the entrance of Newry Harbour. Towards night we stood off the land and was brought under courses. I passed a very anxious night, and the sea ran very high and often broke on board with great violence, but through mercy it moderated towards morning and we got a pilot. This day we killed the last of our Spanish sheep which the passenger had provided.

In the afternoon I landed for the first time on Irish ground about the latter end of April, 1792. About sunset I procured a horse and a gentleman took Mr. B – in his gig to the town. We then proceeded to the house of the consignee of the cargo. We were engaged to dine this day with the merchant, who gave us a good dinner and each a good bed at night. We rose early and walked about the town and country. I saw a large linen hall going to decay for want of being more resorted to. There was a fine basin of water skirted with large spreading trees, in which was a Yarmouth brig that had come through the canal locks from the river. As this was the spring of the year and we had come from a parched land, the scenery on the skirts of the town appeared delightful, there being so many flowers and blossoms in every direction spreading their beauties to the sun, whilst the floating zephyr conveyed their aromatic scents to the early traveller. The birds also cheered and charmed us with their variety and melody, that we appeared to be in a paradise, but on our return to breakfast, I found sufficient reason to convince me that I still dwelt in a land of fallen creatures, by searching in the pocket of my great coat hanging in the gentleman's lobby, for a handkerchief I had left there, when alas it was gone, and this assured me that there exists a thief even in Ireland.

I returned this day to Warren's Point, the road lying by the side of the river and at high water is a pleasant ride. In a day or two after Mr. B – brought some acquaintances on board just before dinner and they were not displeased at seeing a roasted leg of the Spanish sheep for their entertainment. I had purchased a parcel of oranges with branches for hanging them up at Carthagena, which I had intended for some friends, and I had now removed them from sight, but Mr. B – had taken the liberty of promising them to the consignee's daughters, I was therefore reluctantly obliged to give them up, but I think the liberty taken was unhandsome.

Q

Whilst I was lying here, I invited a few of the inhabitants to take tea with me, but for want of knowing friends from enemies I happened to have two females on board who had the imprudence to renew an old quarrel, and carried it to such lengths that I was obliged to exert my authority to restore peace.

The town of Newry swarmed with beggars and I observed their lame were placed on a hand barrow and laid before the next neighbour's door, who removed each person to the next house either giving alms or not, and in this manner the cripples were transported through the town, and sought for and fetched home at night with their collections by their particular friends. Whilst I continued to use the Newry road the lanes and highways were often crowded with emigrants for America, which was far from a pleasant sight. One morning when I was preparing for Newry my negro cook presented himself in the cabin. He was a Portuguese black and a native of Anamaboo, whom I had shipped in America. He informed me that he wanted money. I asked him for what purpose. He replied to get married and buy clothes. On demanding the lady's name I was informed 'His name Rosy'; under a supposition that he was not in earnest I gave him 10s. 6d., which he said was sufficient, but when I returned to the vessel at night, in hauling her off the quay I missed the cook and was informed he was gone to bed sick, a girl at a public-house having been coquetting with the poor fellow who had expended his money in ribbands for her to his great mortification and disappointment.

My Adventure of Spanish reeds I sold to the consignee

of the cargo, who treated me with great hospitality, but I little thought I was to pay smartly for my good fare. On settling with my consignee, who with his family appeared genteel and respectable, I was not a little surprised at his petitioning me to give him two pounds or guineas from the money I was to receive from him. I represented the unreasonableness of his demand, but the poor merchant backed his claim with so many pitiful reasons that I was ashamed to stand out, not knowing but this man (setting aside appearances) might want the money more than I did, I yielded to his solicitations, and therefore was more money out of pocket (besides the handkerchief), than if I had always resorted to an inn in my visits to this place.

About the beginning of June I sailed in the morning for Belfast, having paid the demands of *three* surveyors in the Port of Newry (a guinea each). Towards evening we had got to the northward of Copeland Island, when the wind failed and soon after dark the tide was drifting us direct on the islands, which did not a little alarm me, but through mercy a light air helped us to clear it, but did not gain Belfast Lough till daylight the next morning, when we obtained a pilot who conducted us to Gramail, being the nearest anchorage to Belfast. Near about the middle of June I returned to Liverpool 1792, and never sailed in the *John* afterwards.

*   *   *   *   *   *

17

He Revisits his Birthplace and is later Employed on a Press Tender

About the month of August the brig *Mayflower*, that I was first master of, returned from Lisbon to Liverpool with a cargo of cotton. The Master that left England with her was put into prison at Lisbon with some other British shipmasters who in a drunken frolic shot a Portuguese boatman. As I was not to leave Liverpool for Quebec till the spring of the year 1793, I was requested to superintend the *Mayflower* and the delivery of her cargo, great part of which was wetted with salt water, the vessel being thirty-seven years old and very leaky. When the vessel had discharged her cargo I was asked whether I had any objection to make a voyage to Bristol. I replied in the negative, as I much disliked an idle life. I was therefore again appointed Master of this brig, and having obtained a cargo of rock salt, etc., sailed for Bristol, but having to carry a press of sail in rough weather to keep off the shore in Beaumaris Bay the vessel became very leaky, so that after my arrival in Bristol I was requested to apply to two of her owners in that city to consult what was best to be done with her. At last it was determined to sheath her bottom. About this time the Bank of England stopped discounting bills, being aware of the great extent of false credit in the kingdom, the consequences of which are well-known by the multitude of bankruptcies that took place in the year 1793. Liverpool was especially affected by the storm, so that business for a while lay dormant and a vast many houses were shut up.

Having got the brig sheathed I sailed for Liverpool, but

NORTH-WEST PROSPECT OF BRISTOL.

had a very disagreeable passage, the vessel still being leaky.

Whilst lying at Bristol I witnessed a curious scene, viz., a merchant had stopped payment, and when this was known to his creditors, without resorting to law, the tradesmen boarded one of his vessels ready to sail for the West Indies and seized on the property that originally belonged to them, and what was more surprising the captain assisted in the delivery, for I saw him attending the hatchway to bear off the goods hoisted up by the tradesmen, and I had the curiosity to stay a while at the vessel and saw a half of a new cable that had been spliced to an old one by a rope maker being cut off on board.

When the French war broke out, Mr. 10. 10 was all agog for privateering, which by no means met my approbation, as I considered it in no other light but a kind of licensed robbery, or as a plunderage of peaceable and innocent individuals. *The Brothers* having been built as an armed ship had all her ports ready, and twenty-six guns were now put on board her, as a privateer. The *John* had bulwarks raised on her and was fitted out as a Letter of marque.

My new mate, whom I shipped before I sailed again for Bristol, was one of the surviving crew of His Majesty's Ship *Guardian*, whose bottom was beat to pieces against the ice in the southern ocean, but still floated to save the people who remained by the vessel.

The *Brothers* privateer soon sent in two prizes, but they proved what seamen term *Flemish*. One was a Swede, which I believe was soon liberated. The other, a Dane with a French cargo for the West Indies, remained for the decision of the Court of Admiralty, but was finally liberated, leaving a loss to the owners of the privateer of some thousands. The officers of the *Brothers* had wantonly tortured the Dane's captain by means of a thumbscrew in hopes he would confess what nation owned his cargo, but they failed of obtaining the desired information, leaving the owners of their ship open to the penalties of the law incurred by their bad conduct.

I was not at all pleased that no other vessel was provided, for me, but my hopes being kept alive by fair promises I procured a cargo and sailed for Bristol about May, 1793, and arrived there safe after a middling passage. After the brig was discharged I was determined to pay a visit to my friends in the west. It was the latter end of May, when I left Bristol in a stage-coach for Exeter; the weather being excessively hot, greatly reduced the pleasure of travelling, and I am not a little surprised that the English should make use of the same carriages for public conveyance both in extreme cold and intense heat, and 'tis truly lamentable to be boxed up during a long summer day in a close coach, and especially in the one that conveys the mail. Other nations with less genius provide different carriages to suit the different seasons.

The following day being the Sabbath no coach went out to the westward, but on Monday morning at six o'clock I left Exeter, well pleased with my entertainment and set off for the west. Among the rest of my fellow-passengers were a London tailor and his son, the father was going into Cornwall for orders. We had not proceeded many miles when the son became sick and emptied his stomach partly on my clothes, but as there was no help for the accident I endeavoured

to make the best of it, but not without lecturing the landsman for his neglect of running his head through the port-
hole of the coach. We breakfasted at Oakhampton and I
was not a little pleased in partaking of some clotted cream
once more. We dined at Launceston and in the evening
arrived at Bodmin. The next morning early I proceeded
on my route, and on our arrival at Indian Queen (a single
house on a common) I quitted the coach as I expected to
find my brother-in-law's horse awaiting my arrival to convey me across the country. By the time I had taken my
breakfast in a damp musty room the horse appeared. We
crossed a very rough country and arrived at G —[1] about
noon, where I was cordially received by my friends and
relations. After staying here a few days I departed for the
extremity of Cornwall with an intention of spending a few
weeks at my native place, with an uncle and his married
nieces, with one of whom he resided (the wife of a surgeon).
My brother-in-law lent me a horse and accompanied me a
few miles towards Truro. On entering this town I found it
much improved since I visited it when a boy, it being now
well lighted and paved at the sides for foot passengers with
flagstones.

I passed on to Redruth, where I dined, seeing some pickled
samphire on the table brought old times to my recollection,
as I had been accustomed to range over the cliffs when a
youth where this plant grew. Having left Redruth I had a
pleasant ride, often in sight of the sea, and arrived safe in
my native town, receiving a hearty welcome from my friends
and townsmen. My friend the surgeon, who was now my

[1] Probably Grampound. – ED.

host, had been my playmate in childhood; he was possessed of an excellent garden and summerhouse delightfully situated for overlooking the pier, bay, and pilchard fishery. In this garden I took great delight and was not a little chagrined and mortified at receiving a letter a few days after my arrival here, to hasten my return to Bristol, as my friend had agreed for my vessel to load a cargo of horse-beans immediately for Liverpool. As I was engaged to dine with H. M. Praed, Esq., the Patron of the Borough, at his country residence,[1] I went there at the time fixed but found myself so unwell that I could eat little dinner, though the table was plentifully loaded with roast and boiled butcher's meat, poultry, venison, potted liver, pastry, etc., and he being a man of great opulence, possessing extensive gardens with hot-houses, etc., I need not say the dessert abounded with varieties.

After a few glasses of wine were drank, the company retired to the bowling green, where I remained a looker-on. This commanded a view of the beautiful park well-stocked with deer, some of which were browsing while others were reclining in peace under the branches of wide-spreading trees, with which the park was well stored; it also contained ponds of water in which doubtless there were many fishes, as they appeared well laid out at a great expense for that purpose. We had our tea in the bowling green house.

About the latter end of June I commenced my journey for Bristol; my host accompanied me as far as Camborne where we took our tea and parted. Soon after I left Redruth night came on, when a gentleman joined me and proposed con-

[1] Trevethoe, in Lelant parish. – ED.

tinuing in company 'till our arrival at Truro, which I was glad of, being a stranger on this road. Soon afterwards a third horseman joined us, and being acquainted with my companion they entered into conversation, and as my horse was small and unable to keep pace with the others I was soon left in the rear to find my way alone in a very dark night. The highway being skirted with tin mines and gravel pits rendered my travelling unpleasant, and I was not a little pleased when I arrived at the turnpike-gate at the entrance of the town. After supping at the inn, for want of room I was conducted to a bedroom in a private house, which appeared to have been occupied lately by an Army officer, whose breast-plate and other apparatus lay in disorder on the toilet. The next day after breakfast I was standing at the inn door awaiting the arrival of the Falmouth stage, when I saw the landlord reconnoitring the movements of a person whom I found was his female servant and who had saved a little money, but that now she was repairing to the church to be united to a *married* soldier – knowing him to be such! – then under marching orders. At length the coach arrived without a single vacancy, but as several men were waiting for places I agreed with two gentlemen to proceed in a post-chaise to Exeter, and therefore immediately preceded the stage. After journeying a few miles I found that one of my companions was a London wine-merchant and the other a clergyman, who informed me that he was also a chaplain to an illustrious personage, but had he been dressed in another garb his manners and conversation would have led me to suppose that he was a man of a very different character. We travelled the following night in hopes to save the Bristol coach from Exeter, but during the last stage we began to despond as the chaise moved slowly, and we could not prevail on the post-boy to drive quick. However, we were not a little pleased at seeing the stage-coach at the door as we approached the inn door at Exeter. We dismissed our driver without his usual fee, as he had used impertinent language.

At six o'clock my companions mounted the top of the coach to enjoy a view of the country, but being far from well, I preferred an inside berth to avoid the direct rays of the sun. The only passenger I found in the carriage was a girl about fourteen, returning to a boarding school at Taunton, and from her hair and complexion was doubtless a native of India. She conducted the conversation with a reserve not usual with young ladies of her age, but was not at all deficient in politeness. At breakfast, without solicitation, she took the management of the repast and appeared no more embarrassed than if she had been used to the superintendence of the table for many years. I once travelled with a lady that had just quitted school, of a very different behaviour, which was doubtless the effect of an improper education. We found the weather very hot, and I heard that a number of horses had been killed in the stages during the past month from the great heat.

On our arrival at Bristol, at seven in the evening, I repaired to the quay and found my vessel in great forwardness for sailing. The steerage had been broken open at night by a rogue, who carried off some clothes. This man was known to make use of a boat on the tide in which he carried off his prey unmolested.

One day an American ship hauled alongside my vessel, and as the tide ebbed she leaned heavy against our top-side, doing much injury. I therefore called a survey to enable me to recover damages, when to my great surprise I discovered that the top timbers or ribs of our vessel had disappeared, being long since returned to dust. There being now nothing to fasten the planks to a few chocks were fixed, and I was determined, if I got safe to Liverpool, to abandon this bundle of boards for ever, she not being seaworthy and her condition highly dangerous. As soon as we cleared Customs I proceeded with the brig to Pill, to be ready for the first fair wind. Two or three of my crew were Swedes, which were in general secure from the Impress, and always considered so by the Admiralty, but while I was at Bristol the gang boarded the brig and carried off the foreign seamen, knowing them to be such. As soon as I heard of my loss I applied to the two lieutenants for their release, in vain. I then made a humble application to the regulating captain, who heard me with indifference and finally dismissed the petition. I was therefore under the necessity of hunting for other men. After much trouble I met with a landsman who agreed to go with me if I would permit him to take his Welsh wife to Liverpool, having been married about three weeks. To this I consented, not knowing where to get another man. I advanced him a little money to buy tea, sugar, etc., and got them on board, but in a night or two after the man absconded leaving his spouse as a legacy to me. On inquiry I found she was so extremely ill-tempered and quarrelled so often with her husband that he thought best to leave her without a change of clothes. I therefore ordered her to leave the vessel contrary to her inclination.

I now removed my brig to Morgans Pill and was visited by Captain Ducket, commander of a privateer in Kings Road, who insisted on my company to dine at Lamplighters-hall with the noted privateer, Captain John Shaw, who formerly commanded the *Lion* from Bristol, but cannot say I was highly entertained with the conversation, it being in a style I much disliked.

At last the wind moderated, and having got under sail we reached the Flat Holmes by low water and anchored under the lee of that island before night and proceeded as far up the north channel as the Skerry light, when an easterly wind forced us to run for Holyhead, where we anchored. We lay here a few days, during which a Parkgate packet and a Liverpool pilot boat were forced into the harbour. I went on shore to this poor place, and in hopes to find some enter-tainment I visited the hotel and do not think I saw a single person belonging to the house nor a newspaper, and as no one would answer to my requirements I left it as I found it, not very clean.

The people here make use of oatmeal cakes, but the principal inhabitants draw their provisions from Dublin, and I have seen loaves of bread landing from the packets.

After our arrival at Liverpool I declined sailing again in the vessel, which was finally sold to a Portuguese. After I had remained a few weeks unemployed I felt like a fish out of water – restless. I was in the habit of spending my evenings at my lodgings (a boarding house for shipmasters). One night a boy came running into the house saying that our host was at the west-country coffee house where two men were beating him. His son-in-law (a shipmaster) and myself ran immediately to the public-house. On the road, knowing my companion to be a violent young man, I cautioned him against involving himself in trouble till he knew the cause of the affray, but he bounced into the room with the greatest impetuosity, and seeing two men in their shirts he seized hold of one of them and began to buffet him; the other being his companion ran to his assistance against the intruder which brought me into contact also, our host having left the room previous to our arrival. One of the stripped boxers now struck me, and having seized him by the collar we both fell on the sanded floor, which prevented firm footing. My antagonist now got his fingers inside my mouth and endeavoured to disfigure my face, making three furrows in my cheek. As several people and a watchman had now entered the room we were separated. On inquiry I found the man who had wounded me was a block maker, a noted boxer, and the other was his journeyman, but what was the reason of the original quarrel with my host was not worth my notice, as I knew him to be a tippler. A few minutes before I had been peaceably in my dwelling, prudent in advice and an enemy to tippling, but notwithstanding this from the folly of a rash young man I was now wounded, bleeding and disgraced in an ale house. My face the next day was decorated with three black plasters as an emblem of a rioter. I was ashamed for some days to appear in public, and the scars on my face remain to this day.

After being about three months idle I was unexpectedly put into full employ. A letter arrived from the mate of the

Thetis tender, dated Sheerness, saying that her master had gone into the hospital at Plymouth, sick, and the mate requested that Mr. 10.10 would send him money to purchase clothes that he might appear respectable in his new situation as master. As my relation was now in Liverpool, Mr. 10.10 wished him to go to the vessel, but I imagine he did not like being in a fighting ship. Having collected a few clothes in my trunk I set off per coach, and was two nights and a day in getting to London, where I arrived with a sore throat. Having dispatched my business I took coach at noon the next day for Chatham; my fellow-travellers were of various characters and descriptions. One was a lieutenant of Marines, returning unsuccessful from the recruiting service. Another was a Highland sergeant who had been on the Dunkirk expedition. There was also a farmer and two talkative women of the lower class. The lieutenant had little to recommend him but vulgarity, which he seemed to delight in as his natural element, and in the course of conversation I found he was a ci-devant Guinea-Pig[1] from an East India ship. The sergeant was a well-informed, sensible man, and gave me a farther account of the expedition to Flanders than I had seen in the news-papers.

I was landed at Sheerness dockyard, and went on board my vessel, and though the decks had been recently washed the footmarks thereon certified what I was to expect below. I found the lieutenant, a man apparently verging on dotage, with a heavy head, who gave himself no trouble about the state of the vessel, being arrived at that age in which the

[1] Guinea-pig; midshipman of an Indiaman. – ED.

grasshopper is a burden. I perceived he was much afflicted with asthma and seldom left the ship, being fond of peace and quietness. After we had conversed a while he informed me that he feared I was come too late to mend a bad business, as he had every reason to expect that the ship would be dismissed the service. I found the mate (who had written for money to buy fine clothes) a slothful drunkard with his hands well-covered with the itch, and fearing to catch this musical disease, I sent him to the *Union* hospital ship for cure. Both the ship's crew and lieutenant's boats crew (properly denominated the Press Gang) were short of their number, and many of those on board I perceived towards evening were drunk on their allowance of beer, especially the boatswain on his watch, who was not capable to give me an answer, though he appeared to walk steadily. I soon reduced those gentlemen to sobriety by reducing their allowance, and got the vessel brushed up to appear a little after the rate of what she was expected to be. One of the midshipmen was a rough, tippling, vulgar seaman, the other a pert, conceited, ci-devant attorney's clerk. The latter gentleman soon gave me an opportunity of curbing his impudence ! He had stayed beyond his time on shore, which I reproved him for. He replied that I had no authority to call him to an account as my appointment originated with the merchants, but that he was a regular naval officer. I reported the conversation to the lieutenant. He replied I had equal authority in rank with sailing-masters of men-of-war in the sixth rate, and if I required it he would order one of the midshipman's legs to be put in irons that he would then be tried by a court-martial and broke. The midship-

man was now ordered to attend the tribunal of the commanding officer and was informed of his liability to punishment, and as I wanted nothing more than his humility, I
forgave him. One of the apprentices ran from the boat
and another had deserted before my arrival. I was well
assured that they were on board one of the armed ships and
one of them was discovered on board a brig. On going on
board her I found both the lads were there and I demanded
them of the lieutenant, who was not willing to give them
up; but on application to the Admiral I soon obtained
their release, and to prevent their desertion in future I
kept them on board and locked them in the Press room
at night. The old lieutenant read much in his Bible and I
believe often went through the service in the Liturgy of the
establishment, but at other times I could perceive he was
far from being a pious man.

As I was now the purser he expected me to find him in
several articles of food, etc. As he was not an epicure requiring dainties I indulged him in his little wants, and having offered to bring forward his accounts for him he was
highly pleased and we agreed like Darby and Joan. On my
arrival I had inquired about the sails and was informed
they were in the hands of a sailmaker at Queensborough.
When the sails came on board I took the trouble to inspect
and measure the new canvas over, and found an overcharge
of about fifty-seven yards of cloth, and therefore took liberty
to cut off about £14 from his bill, which he would not allow.
I therefore withheld the payment. One day in the dockyard
a drunken gunner abused me sadly as a rogue and a cheat,
for not paying his friend the sailmaker.

After being here several weeks orders arrived to prepare for paying off the crew, as the ship was to quit the service. When the stores were delivered the Admiral's yacht came alongside early in the morning and all but the mate (who was left as ship-keeper) quitted our ship and the pendant was hauled down. The lieutenant left his old Bible as a legacy to me. The midshipmen and cutter's crew being King's men were turned over to the men-of-war. I now collected my little crew, about five or six in number, and proceeded to the packet house to wait for the evening's tide to return to the ship. My men having now money I need not say that I was fully employed all the afternoon in keeping them together. Towards evening I got the drunkards into the passage boat. My mate had contrived to get some Geneva on board and I found him to be a mere beast in drunkenness, but as quiet as a mouse, laying about the deck like one dead, except in the appearance of his eyes, which were lively. We were now ready for sailing, but could not attempt it for want of men. I was therefore determined to apply to the Admiral to lend me some to conduct the ship to London, and accordingly I obtained an order for a midshipman and two seamen out of an armed ship. The midshipman went on shore to Sheerness and absconded, so I had only two in addition.

A master of an armed ship invited me on board here and I was not a little surprised at the appearance of the cabin, which was decorated with the implements of war. Even the ceiling was crowded with rockets, false fires, etc., and as much spirit was used in this floating dwelling it was rather astonishing that it did not operate at some nocturnal hour in exploding this collection of fireworks.

R

The garrison and dockyard at Sheerness appear to stand on made ground in an eligible situation for commanding the entrance of the river Medway. The side of the yard next the water is planked and caulked to keep out the tide. As there were few houses for sheltering the great number of men employed in the yard, two or three old ships of the line were hauled upon the beach and there propped upright to receive them and their families; many little tenements were also erected on their upper decks.

Returning from the shore one day on going down into the cabin, I observed the deck on fire near the stove chimney. Had it not been discovered in daylight the ship might have been burnt during the night, as I had little watch kept by the drunkards.[1] Having obtained a pilot for London we got under sail. As we drew near Lee Road the *Comet* brig fired a shot across us and brought us to. Her launch with sails soon boarded us under the command of our late midshipman, the ci-devant attorney's clerk, who had a grudge against my best apprentice, they having quarrelled in Chatham yard, and notwithstanding I had an Admiralty protection and two men lent me by the Admiral to help me to London, this vile chap took away the lad in the boat and I never saw him

[1] During the American war, three fire ships were laying in Falmouth Road, and about two o'clock on a fine day I saw smoke arising from one of the ship's main hatchways, which continued increasing till I saw fire running up the shrouds, and she was soon in a blaze. When the guns got hot their shots were discharged at the town and country. The other ships slipped and went to sea. About four o'clock she exploded with a tremendous noise and great concussion. When her cables burnt she drove on shore opposite the town, and as my chamber window commanded her about ten at night, I saw her whole length glowing to the water's edge. The crew was saved.

after. As my mate was laying about near the forecastle speechless with drink, which now reduced my crew to the same number they were before I borrowed the men. During our run up the Thames my men were obliged to lift the mate from place to place out of harm's way, as he was like a dead man. This was the gentleman that wanted money to buy fine clothes to appear in his new situation as master. We got to Rotherhithe before dark and moored there.

Near Griffins wharf was a public-house frequented chiefly by west-country men; there I went occasionally to meet townsmen and old acquaintances. Here I met my father's tailor who made my clothes when a boy, and as he was carrying on his business in the Borough I gave him an order. I also met a Turkish captain, who had accumulated large property since I sailed with him, when he was second mate of the Lisbon packet, his father being at the same time the boatswain. Here I saw an idle, dissipated clergyman, with a coloured pair of breeches on, which he had received in charity from the captain! 'Tell it not in Gath, publish it not in the streets of Askelon!' Amongst the rest of my old acquaintances I recognized the phiz of T. E., the packet's mate, who often treated me with great brutality. I made myself known to him, and being now able to 'speak with the enemies in the gate,' I soon discovered that his crest had fallen, and that he now bore the badge of a sychophant. A number of masters of vessels of my acquaintance, at the adjoining wharves, belonged to a society known by the appelation of 'Odd Fellows.' As the fee of admission was only thirteen pence I was induced from curiosity to become a member, and was accordingly proposed and admitted, when I found it to be merely a Bacchanalian club, under professed rules of morality, the members being masked during the ceremony of admitting a new brother.

The last time I saw the lieutenant was at a porter house near his lodgings. I found him solitary in a public company, and when I accosted him, his sight being dim, he knew me not; but after I had seated myself near him he discovered his late shipmate. He still being desirous of employ was afterwards stationed at a telegraph, where he died, and I was informed had amassed a fortune of about ten thousand pounds. Whilst with me he appeared an object of charity, being very bare of necessary clothing. His uniform, hat, and coat appeared old friends, and as he was fond of ceremony the former had performed as much service as a Frenchman's *chapeau de bras*. His poor cockade had been long like himself, drooping its wings. When he put on a neck handkerchief to attend orders from the Admiral, I observed that it was unhemmed, and I imagine it had formerly been a piece of a shirt. The only pair of hose that I had ever seen, he wore daily. They were a coarse pair of speckled stockings, which I was informed he had drawn from the slops, value 2*s*. 3*d*., professedly for his servant, but actually for himself. I never saw his valet, and should have been ignorant of his having one, had I not heard that he always happened to be on shore on a muster day!

On passing a booksellers in the Strand, I saw a volume in the window, relative to the loss of the *Antelope*, East India packet, on the Pelew Islands. This brought to my recollection that I had been solicited at Falmouth to take a situation in this ship, the voyage on which she was lost, and being curious to know how I should have been treated, I purchased the book, and still keep it as a momento of the kindness of Providence to one of the unworthiest of its servants. On the last day of our loading we were taking on board bobbins of flour and, after having given the necessary instructions, I left the ship to prepare my business for leaving London. I did not return till 8 o'clock at night, and on entering the ship I perceived the main hatchway open with the flour piled irregularly therein, higher than the deck. I could find no person to answer me, and on entering the cabin found the doors open, but no light there. As I was groping in the dark, I kicked something with my foot, and examining farther found it was my log of a mate, again in a state of 'How came ye so!' Had the river depredators been aware of our situation they would doubtless have visited the ship and carried off a great part of the cargo. If a person wishes to know what trouble and anxiety means he may find an index to it during war in the countenance of a careful conscientious shipmaster.

18

He becomes Master of the 'Thetis' and Visits the Scilly Isles

A BOUT the beginning of May 1794 we sailed for the Downs.

After we anchored off Deal the *Hawk* (twenty gun ship) made a signal as a convoy for the westward. I therefore repaired on board and was introduced to the captain (an uncommon circumstance). After he had asked me a few questions, he left me on the deck to order my instructions. The sailing-master having a little recollection of old times when he was in the Merchant Service was attracted towards me and invited me to the gun-room for refreshment. One of these sea animals from the Merchant Service is required for every serviceable ship in the Navy, and his responsibility is very great, as there are few transactions in the ship but what he has something to do in. The ship's carcass, clothing, accoutrements, provisions and seamen are under his immediate care. He berths the ship in the harbour, navigates her at sea and directs all her movements in battle. After all, he is only considered as a Warrant Officer, and is often looked on with disdain and contempt by his superiors who are honoured by commissions. This sea monster makes much use of peculiar phrases, many of which are as unintelligible to a landsman as Greek would be to an American Indian, and I have been informed that should he (when on shore) find occasion to have a tooth extracted he must employ an interpreter, as perhaps he would describe it to be 'The aftermost grinder aloft, on the starboard quarter!'

A day or two afterwards the *Hawk's* topsails were loosed

and she soon after stood to the northward. As she fired no signal guns, we kept fast, observing her motions with astonishment, but suppose she had received counter orders and therefore slipped away silently. An armed ship without a figure-head now displayed the western signal, and the following morning the fleet sailed; we followed with all our might and strength, but could not overtake the convoy, neither did she appear to consider it her duty to attend to any merchantmen, but made the best of the wind for Portsmouth. On passing a sloop off the Owers, I inquired of his master if he knew the destination of the armed ship, and as soon as he replied I discovered it to be the well-known voice of my old persecutor T. E.!

As soon as Spithead appeared in sight I discovered Lord Howe's grand fleet[1] coming out. I therefore ran in amongst them and looked no more after the late convoy. The wind continued fair till night, when it came to the westward and blew fresh, and as we knew nothing of the signals of this fleet, and as it was very numerous (the East and West Indiamen being under the protection of Lord Howe), I thought it prudent to keep within them during the night. Towards morning the wind was northerly, and when the day broke I found our ship abreast of the *Royal Sovereign*. Soon after, near the Eddystone, the Plymouth division joined, when Admiral Macbride in the *Minatour* (newly painted) ran between us and the Commander-in-Chief and they exchanged salutes to my great gratification, being admirably well situated for a view, or rather too near for our safety from the wads of Admiral Macbride's guns.

[1] Grand Fleet: old name for Channel Fleet. — ED.

As we approached Falmouth the ships laying there for convoy were getting under sail, frigates having been dispatched the day before to draw out the merchantmen in readiness. The Grand fleet now shaped a course for Ushant, previous to the action of the 1st of June, whilst we steered for the Land's End. As we passed before the Looe-pool and near Porthleven, I had an opportunity of discovering many spots, houses and churches well-known to me when a schoolboy. Whilst my eyes were roving over the different parishes in view, my memory revived many a happy scene and caused me to recollect many an unpleasant circumstance. On yonder eminence I often ranged with jovial youths, many of which have long since left the habitation of mortals, and slipped into vast eternity. From the dreadful cliff, whose jutting rocks lurk in ambush to wreck the weather-beaten bark, often have I stood secure to view the shattered fragments of stately vessels dashed upon the beach below, and at its base lays many a grave of gallant seamen. There in that town I have been the dread of one who now sits on the Bench of Justice, and on that green I have engaged in trifles with another who was afterwards a Counsellor. In yon church on one of the lower hills, for more than six long years I heard, once a week, a dry, sluggish lesson on morality. In those fields to the right I have often strayed with many a dear relation now gone to rest, and in those various hamlets still lives many a known face in rural peace and cheerful solitude.

Having rounded the sunken rock Rundlestone,[1] as we opened the Bristol Channel, the north-east wind began to

---

[1] Runnelstone. – ED.

freshen, which soon brought us under low sails. The night was dark and unpleasantly spent by me, between the dangerous reef of rocks known by the name of Seven Stones and the Longships. The morning following I observed several vessels bear up for Scilly, and seeing no prospect of doing better I ordered the helm aweather and steered for St. Helens gap. Near Round Island I was happy in getting a pilot on board and cast my cares to the wind, under an idea that every danger was past. We were now gliding along before the wind and waves with the greatest rapidity, and were got within a few hundred yards of the desired port with the water there as smooth as a millpond. We had yet to pass a narrow gut, between two large rocks. 'Port,' says the pilot, but the helmsman's art was now vain, the wheel-rope was jammed by one turn round the barrel riding on the other. The ship was now rushing apparently on inevitable destruction towards the left-hand crag; the pilot had given himself to despair, exclaiming 'the ship is lost,' 'the ship is lost!' Not so myself. I had long known that a grain of exertion in the time of danger was of more value than a load of unavailing lamentations. I therefore called loudly for a knife, which was instantly handed me by a seaman, the mischievous rope was cut in twain, when seizing on the tiller I pushed it hard to port and, a kind Providence being the director, the ship immediately answered the helm and swung clear of Scylla, without running into the gulf of Charybdis. Had the tiller been in a gun-room the ship would have been dashed in pieces, as we could not have taken hold of it so quickly. And I never knew that ever the wheel rope got jammed by the parts riding on the barrel, either before or after riding on the barrel, either before or after this period, though I had from time to time been four years in this ship.

When the tide flowed we moored farther up the pool and obtained from the pilot some eggs, a small rabbit and a rock-fish, but found provisions in general scarce and the inhabitants very poor. I found a Chepstow shipmaster here of my acquaintance, who undertook to be my guide on shore, he being well acquainted with the people of these islands. In the afternoon we landed on Tresco and called on an Irish widow who kept a public-house, but her accommodations were wretched. We ascended the hill above her house from whence we had a fine view of the Siluves, the dry rocks and islands being above a hundred. This eminence commanded a view of new and old Grimsby harbours, St. Mary's road and town, the different sands and bays. The view was both pleasing and terrific, while the inhabitants' details of shipwrecks were melancholy and dreadful. Great complaints were in circulation against a revenue cutter that had captured many smugglers belonging to the islands, but though so many losses had taken place, yet brandy and India handker-chiefs appeared in plenty. Recollecting that I had now an opportunity of procuring a voucher for fresh beef supplied the tender at St. Mary's I was determined to go in quest of the man who had furnished the beef. My friend Captain N – agreed to accompany me and, as the navigation was critical, even in a boat, from the numerous sunken rocks and shelves, we hired a boat at Tresco with two men. We landed on St. Mary's pier and found the town in a bustle on account of its being muster day, with about thirty invalided

CORNISH SMUGGLERS (BY ROWLANDSON).

(*From a print in the possession of* Mr. J. A. D. BRIDGER.)

soldiers composing the garrison of the chief island. We therefore had an opportunity of observing the army go through their evolutions.

On enquiry I found that the person I wanted respecting the vouchers lived on the far side of the island and as a young man offered to walk with me to the farm I left my friend in the town to order dinner against my return and departed for the country. As we walked along we had a fine view of the Island of St. Agnes, on which a lighthouse is erected with a reverberating light to distinguish it from the constant light on the Longships. Having executed our business we walked down to the spot where Admiral Sir Cloudesly Shovel was buried after losing his ship and his life in the Gillstones, being the western labyrinth of rocks. He was afterwards removed from this island and afterwards interred in Westminster Abbey, as I recollect having seen a monument erected in that repository of kings, statesmen, heroes and play actors, to his memory. I think the Admiral is laying in a recumbent posture in white marble and may be known by his dirty face, arising from the juice of tobacco thrown at his face by British tars out of revenge. He having been the first promoter of Burgoo[1] in the Navy, which seamen much dislike.

Hearing the commander of the garrison had good potatoes on sale I ordered two or three sacks from him.

The town of St. Mary's is little better than a large village and few good houses therein. They draw many of their necessary articles of food and clothing from the town and

[1] Burgoo: a dish of boiled oatmeal seasoned with salt, butter and sugar. – SMYTH.

market of Penzance in Cornwall, to which place there is a weekly packet. As the Duke of Leeds has a steward settled here I imagine much landed property in these islands belongs to him. We got safely to our ships and the day following we were visited by gentlemen from St. Mary's, with whom we took a walk before dinner on the Island of Tresco. I observed one of the company was much disliked at this place and that he was known here by the name of Satan, of whom the inhabitants were extremely shy, but I did not learn the reason why he was so called, unless he held an office in the customs. We called in at a small public-house in the afternoon and being seated in the parlour I observed a fine decorated dresser there, on which their fractured china, silver spoons and cream jug were exhibited to the best advantage. To teach the landlady wisdom we crammed the silver ware into some of the basins, teapots, etc., and there left them, expecting her fright on missing them would cause her to take better care of them when again discovered.

We lay at St. Helens four or five days and, as our ship was armed with six guns and six or eight swivels, the small craft bound for St. George's channel were watching our sailing to accompany us in hopes of some protection. At last a southerly wind began blowing, which cleared the different harbours. We sailed towards evening and the next forenoon saw the Irish land within Tusker and we soon reached Liverpool. I now paid off my drunken mate and crew, and delivered the cargo in good order from an old leaky ship.

One of my friends endeavoured to persuade me to take a mate's place in a Guineaman, the law not allowing the appointment of masters, unless they had previously been either surgeon or mate two voyages. This proposal I declined, being well aware of the iniquity practised in that trade.

The *Brothers* Privateer belonging to Mr. 10. 10. had returned from her cruise. She was now sailed as a Letter of marque to cruise in the Bay of Biscay for a given time, and then to proceed to New York to load for Jamaica.

Having hauled our ship into the graving dock I found she was past her prime and, during her repairs, I had much trouble in keeping the shipwrights at work, for when I was on one side they were idle on the other. I have often observed suspicious people visiting the bottom of the docks to carry off ironwork, etc., left on purpose by the carpenters, who shared in the spoil.

I was once informed by an acquaintance of a Custom House Officer that he had in his dwelling a room well stowed with saucepans, kettles and various other articles taken from vessels on which he was boarded. One of these officers boarded on a West Indiaman seized a small keg of rum from a boy, which he did not take from the ship till dark. The poor lad, not willing to give up his loss quietly, followed the officer at a distance and saw him stop at his own door with the rum, but not being able to obtain entrance, his wife being from home he covered the keg with his great coat and repaired to a neighbour's house, probably for the key. As soon as he was out of sight the boy shouldered the keg and the great coat and bore them off in triumph, and I was further informed that the next day the mate or another person nailed the coat or hung it to the mainmast; but as no one thought proper to lay in a claim it became the boy's property from finding it in the street!

I now recollect another set of depredators in Liverpool, viz., the women employed in cleaning ships' cabins previous to their being painted. These ladies I never suffered to come on board but once, having discovered that they made frequent journeys on shore in the day, their petticoats covering many articles that I did not miss till they were paid off.

My owners were quite at a loss how to employ the *Thetis*, and having lost much money by shipping lately had made them timid and wavering. At length I was questioned whether I had any objection of going to St. Domingo, as vessels were wanted there to load coffee, etc., for Britain. I did not much like going to a sickly country, but never liking to shrink from duty, I informed them that if it was their desire to send the ship there I would certainly go in her. This voyage was soon after determined on and a cargo was to be put on board consigned to my disposal. I was first to proceed to Cape Nichola mole in Hispaniola and endeavour to sell the cargo in the various ports in that island possessed by the British troops, to invest the proceeds in coffee and take whatever freight might offer for Great Britain. In case of failure I was ultimately to proceed to Kingston, Jamaica, and do the best in my power.

My lodgings were near one of the naval rendezvous, which gave me an opportunity of witnessing an unpleasant transaction. A carpenter had been impressed and was lodged in the press-hole at the bottom of Water Street. This circumstance being communicated to the shipwrights, a large body of the trade assembled at night with a long spar which they used as a battering ram against the prison door, which soon burst asunder and all the men within were liberated. They then proceeded to the rendezvous in Strand Street which they broke open and literally gutted the house, the feathers of the beds were emptied into the streets and the furniture broken to pieces or carried off as booty, in which business a number of women assisted, as well as in drinking the beer and liquors, and even the windows were demolished. At last a magistrate made his appearance and dispersed the mob. The gang had made good their retreat at the back part of the dwelling. As I lived near the old dock I was often disturbed at night with riots in Strand Street, a noted place for Irishmen's lodgings in cellars. On Saturday nights especially the watchman's rattle was well exercised. We had frequently disturbances in our dwelling, occasioned by taking in irregular lodgers who frequently came home drunk at all hours of the night. The next bedchamber to mine was occupied by a well-educated man who was a brandy merchant. This person's time for coming in to his lodgings was between twelve and four o'clock in the morning. He took his milk breakfast in bed and rose near midday. One early hour he knocked at my door and requested that I would turn out to see something curious. I instantly obeyed and repaired into his room, where I found a terrier bitch (belonging to a Guinea captain in the house) had turned off all the upper bed-clothes and had deposited her newly born litter on the under sheet to our great diversion.

As I had boarded at this house (when in port) for seven years past, I exerted my influence occasionally to adopt regulations for the control of ill-bred, illiberal lodgers, but, as the inmates were frquently changing, the good I had introduced one voyage was all undone by the time I returned. I had observed that one of the yearly boarders, a great epicure, always placed himself close to the carver's right hand at dinner, and from custom was always helped first to the best. I also observed that this same man forestalled the supper under a pretence that he would not wait till the proper hour. I therefore made a motion to counteract his schemes by requesting a fair chance for each boarder being helped first in turn at dinner, and that if any person wanted supper before the usual time he was to take what was handed him by the servants without being permitted to select or help himself, and as these regulations were deemed fair he could do no other but submit. Another time a rare dish was placed before a surgeon of a Guineaman who, being greedy, helped himself to at least three people's share. The next day a similar dish was placed near him again, which I took the liberty of removing to the other side, repeating some little pleasantry by way of rebuke without giving offence, and in this manner I checked many a greedy ill-behaved lodger.

One day a captain of a Guinea-ship arrived at our house, and while he was at dinner a bailiff enquired for him. The mistress of the house, knowing the officer, said the captain was not at home, but an officious servant, to rectify the lie, said 'Is not he sitting there?' He was therefore taken into custody. On enquiry I found that this captain and another, on the coast of Africa, having had some altercation with the natives, the crews of both ships were sent on shore, armed, at night with their faces blacked and attacked the village, doing much injury. The natives, being aware of their enemies, repulsed them and found means to cut off one of the ships. The other captain, who lost his ship, afterwards returned to Liverpool, and being the principal transgressor, the present arrest was at the suit of the underwriters for the recovery of their loss. This captain was liberated after examination and was afterwards blown up in his ship whilst engaging a French privateer, and I believe most, if not all, of the crew and the cargo of slaves perished. How awful !

I now shipped a young mate, no eligible one offering. This young man had a fair character from his late captains, with whom he had served his apprenticeship in the Kingston trade. I soon found in loading the vessel that he was extremely vain, ignorant and assuming, but I did not know how to better myself, as both mates and seamen were very scarce. As it was war-time I endeavoured to procure a few stout apprentices, but could meet with none but boys under fifteen years, three of which I engaged, making altogether four boys.

After laying several weeks at the dock gates I was permitted to prepare for sea, and as we were armed for a running ship,[1] was allowed to have a puncheon of rum without duty. I now sent the ship into the river with the few men I could muster, and when I could ship another he was sent on board ; but when I had got all but two, I was completely at a loss. During a whole day's hunt I could not procure a man, I was therefore (for the first time) obliged to resort to a Jew crimp to try what he could do for me. He therefore set to work and I was not a little surprised at seeing a man of

[1] Runners: ships which risk every impediment as to privateers or blockade, to get a profitable market. – SMYTH.

his procuring who had refused to go with me when I had before, in the course of the day, applied to him direct. I now took a carpenter for the first time since I had been a ship-master.

*   *   *   *   *   *

19

He Sails to St. Domingo

ON September 4th, the wind being at south-east, we sailed for St. Domingo. My order was to endeavour to go through the north channel to avoid French cruisers. During the night of the 5th we had sometimes light airs and calm, and at other times strong gales, which brought us under double reeft topsails, the weather being foggy, but when it cleared a little we found ourselves to the southwards of the Isle of Man. On the 6th, the wind being to the northward of east, I gave up my attempt for the north channel and ran to the southward. The 7th, at 3 a.m., we passed the Smalls light with a strong breeze at E.N.E. The 14th we had a fresh gale from the westward with heavy squalls and rain, and the following day being rough we struck top-gallant masts and ran in the jib-boom. The 16th we split our fore top-mast stay-sail and bent another. The 18th the wind continued rough from the westward. From the 18th to the 28th we had much contrary winds and unpleasant weather, on the latter day we spoke the brig *Mayflower* of and for Newcastle-on-Tyne, from Jamaica, out nine weeks, having carried away the head of her mainmast. At 8 a.m. the wind shifted suddenly to the westward, when a wave burst in our cabin window, though they were highly situated, and the water did much damage in the cabin. For a few days after this we had moderate weather with a fair wind. On the 4th October we saw a brig in the southern quarter which gave us chase, but in about an hour after she stood to the eastward. The 5th being in the latitude of 37° 59′ N. and longitude 43° 46′ W., we saw two tropical birds, which generally frequent the torrid zone. They are white, about the size of a gull, and have a long tail terminating in a point, with some red between their eyes and bill. One of this species examined me very closely when I was a boy at the mast-head of one of the West India packets, but they are generally shy. On the 6th October we began to see flying fish, having crossed the Azores to the westward to avoid the French cruisers. On the 7th we got amongst the Saragossa weeds streaming S.E. and N.W. On the evening of the 8th a flying fish fell on board. They are much like a mullet about the head, with long fins or wings from their shoulders, which they spread on rising from the sea. They eat much like a whiting. They are caught in nets by the fishermen at Barbados and are brought in the morning alongside shipping ready fried by the huckster women. This day we spoke a brig from Charlestown for Gibraltar, out twenty-two days. The 11th October the wind being westerly and fresh we began to experience heavy dews at night, and though the sun shined warm and bright through the day, the ship was very damp and we found it difficult to keep our iron and steel things from rust. This day a large shark, several dolphins and old wives[1] were playing about our vessel. The 13th, finding we were got into fine, warm weather, we bent the oldest of our sails. The 14th we began to experience a regular trade wind from south-east, being in the latitude 30° 41′ N. The sea was now covered with Saragossa weeds in an irregular manner. Finding our shrouds getting slack we set them up this day. The 15th we saw few weeds and 'tis difficult to determine where the Saragossa weeds originally grew.

[1] Old wife: a fish about 2 feet long, with a broad dorsal fin and blue body. – ED.

but I think they either come from the African coast or Cape
de Verde Islands, as they are to be seen less or more through
the limits of the easterly trade winds. This day we caught a
dolphin measuring four feet two inches long, and after being
gutted weighed twenty-five pounds and a half. The following day we caught another weighing ten pounds. When
these fish are seen swimming in the water their colour is
green and brown. When they are caught and hauled in they
are yellow like turmeric. When laying on the deck they
tremble much and their colour changes frequently from a
silver to a pink, yellow and crimson, and I have seen their
flesh trembling long after being gutted.

The 17th we had much lightning round the compass with
heavy rain. The 19th we had a great swell from the northward, which made the vessel roll so deep into the water as to
oblige us to take in our lower studding sail. The 20th we
had variable winds with heavy squalls, rain and thunder and
lightning, a large whale keeping us company. The 22nd,
the wind was variable and at 2 p.m., after a storm had been
brooding for some hours in the Northern quarter under a
dismal black sky, it came on with fury, bringing with it
thunder, lightning and rain. To prepare for the worst I got
the sails clewed up and as it cleared away we saw a schooner
standing to the southward and afterwards saw two other
vessels standing the same way. This day the weeds streamed
east and west. I had made up my mind not to make Turks
Island as is customary with British vessels intending to run
to the northward of Porto Rico; but to run down to the
southward of the Plate reef, or Silver Keys, so called from a
Spanish ship with silver on board being wrecked on it. It is

the easterly bank or rocky shoal of the Bahama Isles, and through this passage the French ships bound to Cape François often run. Had I run for the Turks Island passage I must have laid to during the night, but by making my latitude sure I could run through the Plate wreck passage all night. I think it would be a great acquisition if the British Government would cause a lighthouse to be erected on the north-west point of Turks Island, which would in a great measure insure the safety of vessels running at night for that passage, but I think it would be also requisite that the light should be reverberating to distinguish it from other lights made by the Bahama vessels that lurk about these islands to decoy and mislead the unwary. Few vessels I believe would object to pay for the support of it, and it would be highly advantageous to the Americans bound for Cuba, Hispaniola and Jamaica. For want of such a light many vessels get to leeward and sometimes run on the Island of Grand Caicos.

The 23rd we had our cables on deck to clean and scrub. The 24th the wind was light and we saw much lightning in the eastern quarter. The 25th we saw large beds of weeds. The weather was now very warm and sultry and the ship had much long marine grass growing about the water mark. The 30th hoisted out our boat to scrub the bends and scrape off the grass. Several dolphins were sporting about, one of which I struck with a barbed instrument of five prongs, known by the name of the grains, but it afterwards in struggling got away and during the afternoon kept close to the edge of the water, as if unable to sink deeper The 31st October we caught a small shark and as sailors are fond of variety they made a mess of it. This day the wind was light

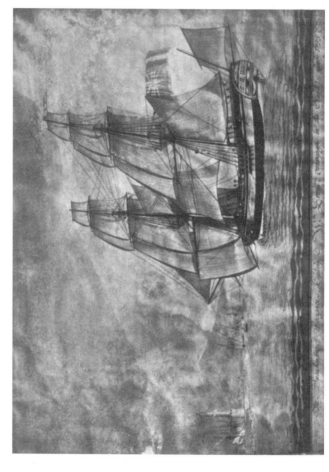

A CONTEMPORARY TRADER: THE 'SPACKMAN' OF PENZANCE.

(*From a painting in the possession of* Mr. C. R. Broad.)

and the weather warm and cloudy. On the 1st November, under a supposition that I was drawing near Hispaniola, I ordered the cables to be bent. The 3rd we had strong breezes and towards sunset I thought it prudent to take in all our studding sails to prepare for falling in with the land, but as Mr. Self-sufficiency's (my mate's) reckoning was not near out, his countenance exhibited a wise or rather contemptuous grin, which I had often noticed during this passage when his opinion differed from mine. About an hour before daylight, according to my instructions given on my retiring to rest, the mate came below and informed me that the land was bold on the larboard bow. I immediately ran on deck and found it was three or four leagues from us, and after the day broke I found it was near Old Cape François, in Hispaniola, this being the island where the famous Christopher Columbus established his first colony, and where the Spaniards afterwards hunted the inoffensive natives, driving them into the thickest forests, where they were shot at like animals or devoured by dogs and it is supposed that in a few years between two and three million of the inhabitants were destroyed.

The 4th November with a fresh breeze at north-east we were running down the island nearly abreast of Monto Christo, when suddenly we discovered a sloop lying a hull,[1] Under a supposition that she might be an enemy (as there was no chance of our dull sailing vessel escaping) I ordered the helmsman to steer directly for her and asked the crew if they would stand by me to engage her, if necessary. They

---

[1] A hull: a ship stripped to her hull, under bare poles. A favourite trick with privateers to render themselves less visible. – ED.

replied in the affirmative and one or two said they would much rather die than be confined in a French prison in this unhealthy climate. The sloop now set her foresail to endeavour to get a sight of our broadside, which I endeavoured to prevent. It was now near sunset and we perceived the sloop had twelve guns, whilst our number was only six guns and six swivels. An English ensign was now hoisted at her masthead and she fired a gun to leeward. We soon ran alongside her and found her name to be the *Bermuda* from Bermuda on a cruise. The captain requested I would visit him, accordingly we tossed out our boat and I went on board and was not a little surprised on going alongside to see such heavy guns as she had on board. Her deck was also well crowded with stout able men, many of which were people of colour. The master was an elderly man apparently well calculated for his employment and seemed possessed of great vivacity. He informed me that at first sight he took our ship for a French sloop of war that had been some time cruising in the Mona passage, but that our ship had taken a sheer by which means he had discovered our force, which must have happened while I went below to get some musquetoons out of the arm chest, having been very careful whilst on deck to keep the ship right end on to the privateer. He advised me by all means to keep a sharp look-out as we approached Port au Paix, as there were many small brigand privateers within the Island of Fortudas. He also gave me to understand that St. Marks was again fallen into the hands of the brigands. The captain was desirous of having some potatoes, I therefore sent him a bucketful, and having hoisted in our boat we made sail about an hour after dark to the westward. Having a piece of fir balk on board I ordered the carpenter the next morning to turn to and expedite his work in making eight wooden guns, the seamen I employed in making and painting cloths to spread fore and aft as bulwarks so that by sunset we had made great progress in showing fourteen guns with the crew covered from sight in a great measure, as it was not prudent to expose the miniature band of warriors, consisting in all of thirteen persons, four of which were boys and two of the men were lame!

The 5th November the wind was light from the northwards at 3 p.m.; we caught a shovel-nosed shark which was dressed and partly ate by the crew. At 6 p.m. we saw a vessel in shore, near Cape François, which I imagine was a British frigate. At 6 a.m. we were abreast of the west end of the Island of Fortudas, but saw none of the privateers from Port au Paix. At meridan we were in sight of the table land of Cape Nichola. On the 6th at 5 p.m. we saw two schooners beating towards the Bahama keys. At 6 we shortened sail in sight of the British men-of-war laying in the Mole as there was no probability of working up to the anchorage during the night. After dark we caught a Baracoota with our fishing line and dressed it for supper, with silver boiled with it to ascertain whether it was poisonous, which is often the case with many fishes in this part of the world. The silver proving bright on trial we ventured to eat the fish, the flesh of which was white and firm. Round the Island of Hispaniola are a great number of web-footed birds, known by the name of Noddies. They approach to the size of a thrush and are of a dark grey or sable colour, but the top of their heads are white. These birds generally fly on board at night and as

soon as they find firm footing compose themselves to sleep
and are caught by the boys, but do not live long, as I never
found one that would eat after being caught. About 8
o'clock in the morning of the 6th we entered the Mole with a
light breeze which soon after increased to a fresh gale blowing right out, and though it was desirable to reduce our sails
we had no opportunity, but were under the necessity of
carrying a press of sail to work up to the town. About 10
o'clock a boat from the *Belliqueux* came alongside, and soon
after a boat from the *Intrepid* boarded us. A licensed pilot
then came with his boat, so that we had three boats to drag
along. Both lieutenants expressed their astonishment that
our topmasts did not go over the side, but they held good.
We had now got abreast of the town point and expected in a
board or two more to fetch the anchorage. In standing towards the town we attempted to tack, when the ship missed
stays and was so near the beach in veering that she turned up
the sand after her. Our pilot immediately requested me to
anchor before the vessel drifted off the bank. We let go
the anchor as fast as possible and veered away a great part of
the cable without bringing the ship up. We were therefore
obliged to let go the best bower which secured her. Being
well aware I was now in the lion's mouth, I paid the lieutenants great attention, and the *Intrepid's* boat soon after left
us. The other lieutenant informed me that he was under the
necessity of taking one seaman from me and left it to me to
say which he should take. Finding I could not divert him
from his object I gave him one who had given me much
trouble.

After dinner some British gentlemen from the town visited

us, from whom I got a poor account of my future prospects. I found the garrison was feeble and the inhabitants of Cape Nichola sickly, the hospital being well filled with soldiers and seamen.

After breakfast I landed to pay my respects where required. I found it requisite to call on the public officers of the old French Government assembled in a kind of court-house in a large open square in the centre of the town. From thence I was directed to the dwelling of the British Governor or Commandant of the garrison, whom I found reclining on a mattress near an open window out of which he answered applicants, but I was admitted to a seat within, near his bed-side.

My own private adventure mostly consisted of cheese, potatoes, onions and bottled porter, a great part of which I disposed of.

The day after my arrival, one of the army surgeons, in hopes of private practice, introduced himself to me on board and I had soon occasion for his services, as two or three of my men were attacked by sickness. Having occasion to visit this surgeon one morning at the hospital I perceived a hoop with a net under it, suspended by a rope from the rafters, which he informed me was for securing his provisions from the ants. To prevent their descent on the rope it was either tarred or anointed with some defensive composition.

One morning, early, having sent my men to fill water, before the stream was disturbed by the inhabitants, one of the *Belliqueux'* officers thought proper to plunder me of another seaman, though I had two more ill on board at the time, which reduced my seamen to *three*, besides boys. About this time a ship arrived here from Liverpool, the

master of which I had known in the Mediterranean. The
captain being drunk a night or two after his arrival, quarrelled with his cook and seeing a naval lieutenant on the
beach requested him to take away the man. As our ships
lay near each other, and witnessing the folly of the master, I
exerted my influence to divert the officer from his game, stat-
ing the distressed state of the ship and hoped he would not
take the advantage of a drunken man who had not his wits to
be aware of what trouble he was bringing on himself. On the
other hand, the lieutenant wanted men to recruit the losses
by death, and was not easily persuaded to give up the cook.
However, I at last got the lieutenant on board my ship to
take some refreshments and the poor cook escaped. The
captain fell at Port au Prince by the fever.

From the time of my arrival two gentlemen here had paid
me great attention, at whose tables I frequently dined. One
was a merchant of the name of Brandy, belonging to the
house of Brandy & Dubourg. This Mr. B. recommended
me to take bitters to fortify my stomach against the prevailing sickness, and also requested that I would call daily about
eleven o'clock at his dwelling for that purpose. The other
gentleman was the naval contractor, who purchased some of
my goods. His house lay at the east end of the town to which
I was going one day under the burning rays of a meridian
sun. To cut short the distance I quitted the path, and was
proceeding over a patch of grass which concealed a great
number of hornets or black bees, that had burrowed in the
earth. These insects, not being accustomed to be disturbed
by the foot of man, instantly quitted their strongholds and
attacked me with the greatest fury, one of which stung me

violently under the eye, the pain of which was so acute that I hardly knew what to do. However, I left the grass as fast as possible and on my arrival at the house washed the swelled part with rum, but the pain continued long.

At this place I had the opportunity of being in company with the man who once held the office of Governor of Port au Prince, but alas! no vestige of his former grandeur remained save his gold headed cane. He now held an army commission, under the British Government for a maintenance.

One day, at the request of the commandant, I paid him a visit, he being in want of some articles. I found several army officers in the breakfast room discoursing on the hazardous excursion of the Governor, who had just returned from a long ride without the lines, to endeavour to discover the brigands, and I imagine from the subject on the carpet, no officer of the garrison but himself would have ventured five hundred yards without the advanced post on any consideration whatever. I think the only two roads from the town proceeded from its two ends, each of these passes were flanked by the guns of a line of battle-ship, and these men-of-war were the only protection to be depended on, as I imagine the garrison did not exceed two hundred men, many of which were in sickly circumstances.

After being a week in the Mole, during which time I had made little progress in sales, I made up my mind to hasten to Kingston in hope of obtaining some remnants of the last crop. The town of Cape Nichola is built on the south side of the Mole about three or four miles from its entrance, on a low, flat plain projecting into the Mole, apparently of made ground. On the low sandy west point is a fort adjoining the corner of the public square, where most of the principal inhabitants reside. This square has several walks in it and many trees, though not sufficient to shelter from the sun. A sluggish stream of drinkable water runs through this square. The houses consists of a ground floor only, which is divided into several apartments, but how the French residents found means of subsistence I know not, as there was little appearance of business going forward. On clearing at the custom house I perceived a charge of ten dollars for the fort, a certificate of which was given me; taking this document as a clearance to pass the lower fort I repaired there and lodged with a subaltern. Towards evening I waited on the commandant to inform him of my departure and to make a tender of my service for Jamaica. I found him and a captain of the navy seated at their wine and a chair being provided for me, I was requested to partake. The commandant having promised to forward his despatches I retired, and as I was going to the eastward an army officer accosted me, saying that I had done wrong in depositing the paper at the lower battery, and that it was necessary for me now to visit the eastern fort. I accordingly proceeded thither, where a further demand of ten dollars was made on me as a fee to this fort!!

* * * * * *

20

He Sails to Jamaica

HAVING procured two French mulatto women and a negress as passengers for Jamaica we left this sickly imposing place on the morning of 17th November, 1794. We experienced a strong breeze from the northward with a great swell of the sea.

The 18th at meridian Cape Roseau, bore east seven leagues. We got a sight of the Mountain of Grand Ance in the island of St. Domingo, which I think is higher land than any hill in Jamaica. In crossing the Bite of Leagan a schooner chased us. When she came near enough we fired a shot at her, which caused her to haul to the eastward.

The 19th we passed the island of Navassa in the forenoon, and at meridian got a sight of the Jamaica mountains. On the morning of the 20th near the east end of Jamaica, a Falmouth packet passed us for the windward passage.

The night of the 20th we lay off and on near the White Horse cliffs and early in the morning received on board a negro pilot belonging to Campbell and McEwin of Port Royal. For some time past I had been troubled with a violent retching without discharging anything from my stomach, which our pilot perceiving, he requested me on arrival to get some green ginger and pound it, then boil it, using the decoction as tea, which advice I followed.

The 22nd, at 2 p.m., we entered Port Royal. The *Siren* sloop of war boarded us here and impressed three of my seamen, leaving me only the mate, the second mate, carpenter, and a lame sick man, besides the boys, three of which were thieves. About sunset we arrived at Kingston.

The 23rd November we moored the ship abreast of Princes

Street and unbent our sails. Seeing a Liverpool ship near one of the wharves, I went on board to get some information from the master. I found by him that I was come to a bad place for freights. Had I arrived a month sooner I should have had a better chance.

I found myself now surrounded by slave ships from Africa, the stench from which about daylight was intolerable and the noise through the day very unpleasant. I therefore removed the ship to the windward and eastward of the nuisance. About a week after my arrival my carpenter came to me in the evening and informed me that the lame man and the second mate (who had also a sore leg) were intending to leave the ship. I knew well it was useless to notice it, as I could not prevent them if they were so inclined, but on going on deck the next morning I was not a little surprised at finding the boat had been carried off, not only by the two men but the carpenter was absconded also. I was now left with only my young mate and four small boys. As most of the ships in the harbour had the yellow fever on board I contracted with an apothecary to attend my mate and boys during our continuance in Kingston harbour for ten pounds, should they at any time be sick.

Whichever way I looked now my prospects were dreary and discouraging. The colours of different ships were almost daily hoisted in mourning, but it would have been much more prudent to have kept their losses secret and buried their dead in silence. I do not recollect going on board my ship without seeing the sick laying on the quarter-deck under the awning, and the Guinea ships particularly suffered by the fever, as many who had escaped the fevers on the

African coast got ill on their arrival here and several of their surgeons fell victims to this climate. I particularly noticed a fine healthy stout African captain one day playing billiards, but before the week ended he was buried.

About the middle of December my four boys were attacked by the yellow fever and I was obliged to hire a negro named King to assist the mate and myself to attend on them. At last I got lodgings for two of them on shore and in a day or two after landing them my stoutest boy (Ned) died. Having hired a ship's carpenter to make his coffin on board our vessel I sent the mate and King to see him buried. When they returned from the funeral, the other boy being convalescent and wishing to leave the lodgings, was brought on board, where he found his companions also recovering from their illness, and so little were they affected at losing Ned that they plundered his chest. I was sorry to find many articles in the deceased's chest that he had plundered from the cabin. Amongst the rest was a bottle of bark from the medicine chest and the glass mustard pot, neither of which being of any service to him, shews that he was notorious for pilfering. I had taken off my chain and seals from my watch on leaving Liverpool to prevent their being injured by the bilge water, but could never find them afterwards. Probably they had been sold on shore to a negro. Two of the other boys I had chastised on the passage out for thieving from the cabin.

I was informed that the parson who read the burial service at the boy's funeral was afraid to enter the burying ground and therefore performed his duty (as it is called) without the gate. At the latter end of the week, when I paid King his

T

wages he refused taking any pay for the day he put Ned in his coffin and assisted in the burial. I enquired his reason for his generosity; he replied 'It was God Almighty's work and I will have nothing for it.' Will anyone say after reading this that negroes are void of bowels of mercy and compassion? 'Tis probable this man was in the habit of attending on the Methodist preaching, or on the black Baptist minister, Mr. Lyle, who had a meeting to the eastward of the town, at which place I have sometimes attended on the Sabbath, and had the pleasure, in company with two other shipmasters, of protecting his congregation from insult. We were standing at the door in the afternoon on a Sunday when several young men (apparently clerks) approached the door, one of which was on horseback, and they had evidently been drinking to excess. The horseman requested that we would make room for him to ride into the chapel, but finding us disposed to protect the assembly they retired crestfallen. I saw some decent free blacks in the congregation, especially a family with second mourning gowns on the females. I observed that the men bowed to the minister on entering the chapel and the women took off their shoes and curtsied. The singing was very bad, as few understood the words, but the service was conducted with the greatest order. I was informed that there was a trap-door near the pulpit to retire by in case of an assault from the drunken white inhabitants, who are more frequently intoxicated on the Sabbath than on any other day in the week. Mr. Lyle appeared aged and was much beloved by the negroes. I think he was by trade a mason in good credit, and had several students who preached occasionally, one of which I heard discoursing in a reasonable manner respecting death and its consequences. For the benefit of sociability, as there were several ships in the same predicament as ours, six masters, including myself, entered into an agreement to dine alternately with each other, which enabled us to live better than we could afford singly. This daily intercourse tended to keep up our spirits, but at times it had a different effect, there being so many people laying about the quarter decks of one or other of the vessels.

A new Lancaster ship was moored alongside of us, the master of which was a Quaker, and he lodged on shore. He sometimes came to his vessel whilst the crew was sick on board, and at last caught the disease and in a few days after died on shore. His mate being a diffident man, declined taking command, the second mate was therefore appointed who, forgetting all decency, gave a drunken frolic to his acquaintances a few days after the Quaker master died.

I was here informed that the ship *Brothers* Letter of marque, belonging to my owners, was condemned at Montego Bay. The newly appointed master on his passage from New York had run the vessel on shore on a reef near the great Caicos and had afterwards got her afloat and proceeded to Montego Bay, where she sunk.

In the month of January, 1795, several vessels sailed without convoy for different parts; amongst the rest was the *Jamaica* for Liverpool, a constant trader. These ships were mostly captured by a privateer off the west end of Cuba and a ship in ballast was given to their crews, who returned to Kingston in her.

We could now see in calm mornings that numbers of marine plants were growing on the ship's bottom very long, so that it would be impossible for her to beat to windward. As the Ports in Jamaica were now open to the Americans, the ships of that nation glutted the island with their produce. A brig belonging to Philadelphia, laying on our starboard bow, had just delivered her cargo and had received on board a few hogshead of sugar, which her captain imagined was sufficient to stiffen her without striking his top-gallant masts. The next morning, whilst my mate and myself were painting our ship, we observed the sea breeze advancing with rapidity and as soon as it reached the American brig she began to heel to the wind and continued to lay down till her masts reached the water. She then stopped a little and afterwards turned bottom up, her royal masts being in the mud at the bottom of the harbour. She then blew at the cabin's windows and when the air within was discharged her masts returned to the surface and she lay quietly afloat on her side. Our boat was despatched to the assistance of her crew, and to pick up the floating articles ejected by the air from her cabin. Sometime after I saw her captain approaching his vessel scratching his head, apparently in great distress. In the afternoon the harbour master applied to me to permit the wreck to come alongside our ship to endeavour to free her from water, but as our ship was nearly finished painting I at first was unwilling, but my humanity overcame my carnal policy and I agreed to admit her alongside and assist in raising her. Her anchor was therefore lifted and she was hauled alongside and I received her captain and crew on board my ship to accommodate them with lodgings, etc. The next morning, early, we got our derrick purchase on her mast and hove her upright, and a sloop hired for the purpose hauled alongside to assist in lifting her. Between the two vessels we raised her main hatchway out of the water, and then set the pumps to work, and some negroes hired bailed at the hatchway. When things were in a fair train I left the ship on some business and on my return found my mate and the captain as merry as grigs, quite at their ease, not troubling themselves to examine who was at work or who was at play. I soon roused them from their slumbers and pointed out to the captain where his attention was required, who was no more fit for a shipmaster than I was for an admiral. Towards night she was well freed from the water and I believe the next day after striking her masts, she hauled from us, which I was not sorry for, as I much disliked my company.

Some mornings at daylight we had a chance of obtaining mullets, which were caught in the following manner. When a fishing canoe discovered a shoal of these fish sporting on the surface the negroes surrounded them with a net, the boat having also a perpendicular net spread lengthwise, as a wall above the men's heads. The fishermen being now prepared made a noise with sticks on the boat's side which made the fish leap out of the net in every direction. The fish that took the direction towards the fishing-boat struck against the net hung up and fell into the canoe, but all that took a different direction were lost to the fishermen; but many of them fell into the ship's boats that generally collected round the net. This bustle was a great treat to the boys from the ships. These mullets were about the size of small mackerel, but I could not eat fish from the harbour with any satisfaction, as the slave ships were numerous around us.

One day a message was sent me that an old friend of mine

in the Government would be glad to see me on board the *Perseverance* Guineaman, of Bristol, just arrived from Africa and the Windward Islands. I accordingly paid him a visit. The female slaves appeared very cheerful and contented on board this vessel, far more so than what might have been expected from their situation.

The merchants on shore were now much distressed for clerks, the mortality amongst them being very great, and the few remaining were obliged to work on the Sabbath. All white men and boys were required within six weeks after their landing in this island to enrol themselves in the militia. I often attended the parade ground where the town militia were embodied. The drum-major was a black man past the middle age, and wore a dark curled wig; he often made me smile by his strut and manœuvres. All the whites, except two companies of Jews, were obliged to find their regimental clothing, which cost a private about ten pounds. The Jews were in rags and too poor to purchase clothes. They occupied a part of the parade ground distinct from those regularly accoutred. I sometimes visited the barrack yard of an evening to hear the remains of the band belonging to the regulars, who consisted of four musicians, the others having reached their long home. I found the inhabitants in general proud and licentious and given to tippling and gaming, and many of the men in trade were void of honour and honesty, and most of the European clerks soon after arrival adopted these evil practices, which soon destroyed their health and brought many to an early grave.

About the end of March, 1795, as I could see no prospect of obtaining an early freight for to sail with the May fleet for Liverpool, I engaged to load at Old Harbour for London, and as our top seams were very open I hired some caulkers. I also got the ship heeled to scrape off the marine plants and shell fish from the bottom; the former were a foot long. A small boy having offered himself, I took him, but where to get a ship's crew I knew not, nor indeed could I find a single man but a few vile outcasts from the Spanish main.

About two days after my new mate came on board on the 7th April, being in a Jew's shop I was taken very ill and on leaving the house I repaired to Mr. Tinker's (the apothecary's) who lived near, and he lent me his gig to carry me to the house of my friend Mrs. M – who gave me a kind reception, and as I was not able to return to the ship my messmate and friend, Captain Bird of the ship *Mary*, of Liverpool, undertook to dispatch my ship for Old Harbour with the mate. Six Spaniards were engaged to proceed in her and to continue by the ship one month, their wages being immediately advanced, their landlord giving security. My mate also shipped an Irish carpenter with a bad sore leg.

On the 19th my new mate's ill-usage drove all the Spaniards and my four boys from the vessel. He was therefore obliged to hire negroes to load the ship. On the 23rd I was informed of my loss and as soon as possible I got my friend to persuade the Spaniards to return to the ship, and their landlord sent them by a boat; the boys were not to be found. When I got a little recovered I went in search of the boys, and was informed by a friend that he had seen two of them on board the *Rachel* brig, of Lancaster. During my illness I was attended by Mr. Broughton, the partner of Mr. Tinker, whom I found to be a man of feeling and possessed of great abilities for his profession. At night his negro was sent to apply a blister to my back, who ordered me a tumbler of cold water, which he requested I would drink at the time he stuck on the plaster; as I could not conceive the service of this water, I requested the doctor when I next saw him to explain its use, when he expressed his astonishment at the negro's conduct, and was as much at a loss to account for its expected effects as myself, it being a mere whim of the servant. My wound was dressed with leaves from the Palma christi tree which grew in Mrs. M – 's court. The house of my friend, M – g – n belonged to a merchant, who was at this time with his lady in England. There was a large yard on three sides of the house in which were numerous offices. In the centre of the largest piece of ground was a pond in which, on pillars, a pigeon house was erected. Several trees and cotton bushes grew in the enclosure, in which a cow was also kept.

A gig and two horses were also kept in the yard. Two gentlemen boarded in the house, one of whom, when I began to recover, drove me in the gig at daylight before the sun was very warm, about two or three miles into the country, during which I visited the encampment at which I formerly (when a boy) sold my walking canes! The roads were so thronged at this early hour with invalids and convalescents with pale faces and emaciated bodies that a stranger on entering the suburbs would be apt to conclude that Kingston was a vast hospital. One morning the gig was lent me, in which I was proceeding with the usual ride when a light-horseman stopped my career and gave me to understand that no person was permitted to leave the town that morning. I found that a strict search was being made by the militia to dispossess

the French emigrants of their arms, as a rumour was in circulation that these refugees had it in contemplation to
encourage a revolt of the slaves. Between two and three
hundred warlike articles were secured and many suspicious
Frenchmen were sent to the British possessions in St.
Domingo.

One morning I borrowed the harbour-master's boat, and in
her proceeded alongside the Brig *Rachel*, to demand my
apprentices. The boys, having discovered my approach,
jumped into the boat the opposite side of the vessel. As I
perceived their intention I called to them to come back or I
would severely punish them. They begged for mercy and
returned. On questioning them about their desertion they
gave me a bad account of the mate's behaviour, whose cruelty
had forced them from the ship. Not being inclined to trust
much to their promises, I tied them together with a cord and
got them lodged in the workhouse till I could convey them
to the ship. A day or two afterwards I paid them a visit to
see that they were not ill-treated and found they were in good
spirits and employed in picking oakum.

One of my messmates who had been taken by the French in
January was now ready to depart for Old Harbour in a prize
ship. Accordingly I embraced the opportunity and having
taken my boys from the workhouse we sailed the 6th May,
and arrived on board the *Thetis* the same day at noon. I
found the sails still bent to the yards, my wine, etc., nearly
exhausted and things in general denoting the want of a
careful manager. I found one of the casks of sugar stowed
had a hole in its side to which the negroes and Spaniards
resorted, and I imagine from one to two, or even three

hundredweight was missing, the slaves being very fond of drinking sugar and water, which I immediately put a stop to.

We were now going on smartly in our lading, when my hopes of saving the convoy were quashed by the rain continuing to pour down with the greatest impetuosity during two days in succession. Our boats were filled alongside and all hands were obliged to continue below deck. A current ran through the bay carrying away with it trees and other floating substances. The roads were destroyed to a great distance which were obliged to be *repaired* before any more sugar could come to the wharf.

Just as the weather cleared a young gentleman from Kingston made his appearance on board in borrowed clothes from the tavern; he having been overtaken with the rain after he left the town and arrived at the bay like a drowned rat. His business was to solicit a gratis passage to England, as he said he could not pay for his passage and he was afraid to stay any longer in such a hazardous climate. I found he had visited Jamaica by the solicitations of a schoolmate, who had got an estate left him in this island, and after taking possession had written to request his friend to quit England, and on his arrival in Jamaica he would do great things for him; accordingly the young man paid his passage out, but instead of being handsomely provided for, the estate owner had returned to Britain without making any kind of provision for his reception. He therefore accepted the situation of book-keeper in the contractor's employ, for which he was previously qualified in a Jamaica merchant's counter in London. As I could not help feeling for his situation, I informed him that if he would lay out what money he could spare in pro-

visions, and would engage to pay five pounds to the ship
owners on his arrival in London, I would require no money
for myself, but would take him with me, he therefore returned to Kingston rejoicing.

The 16th May Providence sent me three seamen, who had
deserted from ships at Port Royal to obtain the run to England. On the 20th three Swedish seamen came to the vessel
and agreed to take the run. The convoy being appointed to
sail the 28th of May, I was under the necessity of going to
Kingston by land to clear the Customs. I slept at the Bay
Tavern and early in the morning started in a gig with a negro
footman for Kingston. After proceeding about half a mile
the horse would proceed no further and for nearly a quarter
of an hour we were baffled in all our attempts to urge him on.
At last he started again. I found the bad effects of the late
rain on the roads as we proceeded, but the country appeared
in the highest state of beauty, the dust having been washed
off the trees and grass, caused a great liveliness in the vegeta-
tion and the many rivulets we met with had a cooling appearance. The grass was near a yard in length in some of the
meadows and I saw large herds of black cattle, but notwithstanding the luxuriance of the grass they appeared lean and
large-boned with wide-spreading horns. I saw one ill-fated
youth known by the name of a book-keeper superintending
a field gang of negroes. I did not envy his employment
under the rays of a burning sun. We arrived at St. Jago de
la Vega, or Spanish Town, about nine o'clock and remained
there during the extreme heat of the day, but I was too feeble
to walk about the place. I just walked to a house to receive
the amount of a draft for hogsheads of coals sold at Old Har-

bour, and about three in the afternoon proceeded to Kingston. The next morning I went to the Customs and got my business in a train for clearing, and having settled all my affairs I took up my passenger about three in the afternoon and finally quitted one of the most unwholesome, stinking places I had ever visited. We passed through Spanish Town about sunset, but found it impossible to reach Old Harbour, as the poor horse was completely exhausted. We therefore stopped at a miserable tavern by the roadside for the night. Being much fatigued I soon retired to my bed in a room honeycombed by the rats, and stinking abominably. During the night they made a great noise and I slept uneasy. At daylight we proceeded on our journey to the Bay Tavern. After leaving our gig, I was walking across the court when I heard some dollars chink behind me and looking round saw them laying on the ground; as I had thirty or forty with me I examined my pockets and found the rats had eaten through the outside of my coat to get at some crumbs of biscuit in the pocket.

The morning of the 27th I joined my vessel and to my great joy found all the coffee on board and ship in great forwardness for sailing the following morning. Having returned on shore, I waited at the Tavern in expectation of seeing Doctor Miekle from Old Harbour township to pay me for some thousands of building bricks that I had sold to him, and on expressing my fears that he would not appear to a shipmaster who knew him well, he replied that he had no doubt but he would visit the bay in the course of the day, but he never came, and as he died soon after, the bricks were never paid for. This is a common trick in Jamaica.

KINGSTON HARBOUR.

After our ship was unmoored and the long-boat hoisted in, my crew came on shore to get a few necessary articles, and I promised them the same sum for their run home as was generally given by the fleet. Being short of provisions I obtained here two barrels of beef without pickle, the fat was turned rusty, and tasted like an old tallow candle, but I could obtain no other. My passenger laid in but a paltry sea store, but supposing he was governed by his circumstances I was silent, though I had every reason afterwards to be well convinced that he had a considerable sum of money in his possession ungenerously secreted.

Before I quit Jamaica, I wish to remark that if the magistrates of Kingston paid a little more attention to the welfare of the inhabitants by employing the negroes of the workhouse to remove or consume the accumulating masses of filth from the wharves and entrances of the streets and lanes next the sea, it would doubtless increase the health of the people. It is well-known that all the floating filth from Guineamen and other ships anchored before the town is driven on the beach and under the wharves the whole extent of Kingston, besides the filth of the land floods. The blood from the market slaughter wharf, quantities of putrid animal and vegetable substances, mixed with cart-loads of straw, are constantly laying to windward of the town, therefore instead of getting a pure breeze from the sea, it is first tainted by the exhalations of this extensive putrid hot-bed which breeds and harbours myriads of common flies and other insects, and when I was a boy allured flocks of vultures to prey on dead dogs, cats, etc., and used to perch in rows on the fences adjoining the sea. To correct this evil in a great measure I would recommend the workhouse negroes to be employed in collecting *all filth day by day*, laying to windward of the town, and as soon as the land wind commences, consume it by fire, that the sparks and scent may be carried across the sea. This would be of great advantage to the inhabitants in general, especially to the merchants and their clerks, the whole length of Port Royal Street. The filth on the land side might also be consumed by fire, during the continuance of the sea breezes. No salt fish or other articles liable to putrefaction should be stored to the eastward of the wherry wharf, and then all the mangy hogs would cease from rooting amongst the rubbish to the great annoyance of people on the wharves. The cattle should be slaughtered at the west end and their blood and garbage buried under a penalty for neglect. Should these hints be acted upon with vigour and extended, I verily believe that sickly Kingston would be a **very** different place.

21

He Sails to England

ON the 28th May, 1795, at 4 o'clock in the morning, having previously obtained a negro pilot from Port Royal, we got under sail from Old Harbour after laying in Jamaica nearly seven months, and had not a wise and watchful Providence undertaken my preservation, I had doubtless descended to the regions of the King of Terrors in a polluted sinful land. On the 29th, at daylight, we joined many ships, and at noon anchored at Bluefields. This bay is surrounded by sloping high land, well cultivated, and exhibiting delightful scenery. There is a small town on the beach with a fine stream of excellent water from the mountains. Soon after we anchored, canoes with live-stock came alongside, from which we purchased a few hogs and fowls, and I obtained a quarter of beef from an overseer of a plantation, who informed me the mortality amongst the whites had been so great in this neighbourhood that the estates were distressed for want of overseers and book-keepers.

The 31st at noon we saw the convoy with the Kingston ships in the offing, but for want of wind could not reach our anchorage. At 8 p.m. a boat arrived from Admiral Ford in the *Europa* requesting the ships in Bluefields Bay would follow him to Negril Bay, where he intended collecting the whole of the merchantmen from both sides of the island. My mate was very urgent for me to allow him to bring on board a puncheon or two of rum for smuggling into Britain, but I would not admit of it. At 5 p.m. I ordered the anchor to be lifted, but the mate and crew refused to do anything till I gave notes for the 'run' money. The mate, I found, was at the head of the mutiny, and was a most barefaced rogue ingrain. He went to his cabin and continued obstinate till he obliged me to give him a note for fifty guineas, and each of the crew required a note for forty-five guineas, which I was obliged to comply with before I could get up anchor and join the fleet. What a lamentable thing it is, that the legislator has not found means to put a period to this evil, which has existed year after year for quite half a century, to the great distress of shipping and to the incalculable loss of shipowners. Ever since I can remember it has been the practice of English seamen to sign articles to remain by the ship to the West Indies and back to Britain, without the least intention to perform their contract. They obtain two months' advance before they sail from England, and consequently on their arrival in the Islands they have no wages due and take the first opportunity to desert to obtain the customary 'runs' from all distressed ships. The money my crew was now to have for conducting the ship to London was the enormous sum of £383 5*s*. sterling, whereas their monthly wages would only have amounted to the sum of £86 18*s*. 9*d*. Each of my seamen was now to have 45 guineas, the greatest part of which would probably be spent in drunkenness and debauchery to the great injury of soul and body, and though I was the subject of all the anxiety and trouble in navigating and directing the ship I was obliged to be content with a quarter part of a seaman's wage, viz., only five pounds per month for the passage to England with my constitution irreparably ruined by the hardships of the voyage!

On the 1st June at 1 p.m. having got under sail we had to beat to windward to clear Blue Fields' Bay, and next morning joined the Admiral to leeward of Negril Point.

On the 2nd at 2 p.m. I went on board the *Europa*, for instructions for which I paid the clerk I think three dollars. At 9 a.m. the fleet made sail for Europe, being 120 merchant-men under convoy of the *Europa* and *Belle-queux* two deckers, *Magicianne* frigate, and *Swan* sloop of war.

The 3rd we experienced squally weather with rain. We got our derrick spar lashed across our stern to prevent being boarded by the enemies' privateers frequenting the coast of Cuba.

The 4th we saw the island of Grand Cayman.

The 5th at 5 p.m. we were about five miles from the S.W. end of the Cayman, and the leeward ships procured many green turtle from the boats belonging to the island. Before sunset a heavy squall came on which split our foretop sail in pieces. The night was very dark with rain, thunder and lightning, and the fleet lay to. At midnight made sail, the wind having settled to the eastward. As we passed the Grand Cayman we saw a ship on shore on the west side of the island. We were obliged to bend another topsail.

The 6th June we had pleasant weather. Under a supposition that all was not right on deck I left my bed about midnight and found the mate and every person in his watch asleep, the wind being light. I took the liberty of rolling the officer from the hencoop down on deck, to his great astonishment.

The 7th and 8th we saw some high land on Cuba within the Isle of Pines.

The 9th the wind was light. This day we caught a shark,

U

six feet in length, with a dolphin fishhook and part of the line in his stomach.

The 11th at meridian we had got about five leagues to the westward of Cape Antonio, being the west point of Cuba. We had light winds till the 15th. At midnight heard several guns fired for assistance to leeward. At daylight saw the *Bellequeux* towing a transport without a bowsprit, she having carried it away by running on board another vessel in the night. Found a current setting to the north-west.

The 16th at meridian the notch of the Coxcomb mountain in Cuba bore south-east about nine or ten leagues from us.

The 17th, seeing many ships with their colours in mourning, I imagined the yellow fever was still prevailing. One of our men seeing a mattress bed floating near us, hooked it as a prize, but I made him throw it overboard again, being well convinced it had been the bed of a person who had died in the fever. At meridian the Dolphin Head on Cuba was in sight to the eastward. The winds continuing light, the fleet made little progress.

On the 19th we had rain, thunder and lightning.

The 20th we had fresh breezes with frequent squalls. At 4 p.m. the lowland to the westward of the Havannah bore south-east distant four leagues. At 2 a.m., having left my bed, I found the mate and all but two in his watch asleep, though the weather was boisterous. This day we broke our main top-gallant yard.

The 21st we got up a new top-gallant yard. At 7 p.m. the fleet hove to till 1 a.m., when the wind shifted from the southward to north-west, when a signal was made for the fleet to veer and lay to with their heads to the northward till daylight, when we made sail. At 6 a.m. the wind shifted to the eastward, and at meridian the Admiral made the signal for seeing land on the Martyrs which I imagine was about Key Looe. We now entered what is properly called the Main Florida stream between the Bahama Islands and Florida Reefs, the most dangerous part of this navigation. Sometimes the stream in this part runs like a torrent to the northward; and its influence is felt far to the eastward of the Banks of Newfoundland, and at times near the coast of Ireland. Want of due attention to this current occasions great errors in ships' reckonings: some vessels falling in with Ireland or England before expectation, and others bound to America looking out for a sight of that continent when they are ten degrees to the eastward of it.

During my continuance in the American trade I paid a great deal of attention to this current. Near the coast of East Florida I have experienced a drift of about seventy miles to the northward in twenty-four hours, but it runs weaker as it proceeds along the American coast, and runs much to the eastward off the Capes of Virginia, but is governed in its velocity by the different winds. To ascertain the direction of the current in general I observed the direction of the streams of floating substances such as weeds, straw, feathers, etc. After taking the sun's altitude and having ascertained the difference of northing or southing from our regular course steered, this difference in latitude and the course of the current enabled me to ascertain how many miles I had also been carried to the eastward, and this method corrected my reckoning amazingly. Sometimes when the trade winds are strong for a considerable time.

together, the water accumulates in the Mexican Gulf, and rises very high, even to drown some of the Florida Islands. It would be easy to erect poles or beacons on the principal parts of both sides of this labyrinth of rocks and islands at a trifling expense which would greatly conduce to the safety of shipping passing through the Florida passage into the Atlantic Ocean.

The 22nd at 7 a.m. we saw two hummocks or small round hills on the main-land of East Florida, about Dry Inlet. The sight of this land brought to my mind the days of slavery I had passed in this province whilst I assisted in the evacuation and belonged to the *Jason* Transport.

On midsummer day, as we had a long passage through the gulf, I put our crew on an allowance of provisions. This day (the 24th) spoke a brig belonging to Liverpool (one of the fleet). From the captain I learned that one of the vessels under convoy had been captured by the French during our passage along the coast of Cuba. This day we caught a dolphin.

On the 27th at midnight I again detected the mate asleep in his watch, he being much given to tippling. As the morning advanced we experienced squally weather from the north, with rain, thunder and lightning. As our ship sailed very bad we had work enough to keep up with the fleet, being obliged to carry a press of sails which often caused their splitting.

The 1st July the leech rope of the foretop sail gave way in three places which we repaired aloft. Three of the men-of-war had each a merchantman in tow this day.

The 3rd my mate pretended that one of the puncheons of

rum stowed in the steerage had leaked out many gallons, which caused me to examine the cask. I found the bung had been started since it was shipped, and I have little doubt but my mate knew the road to the spirit. At 9 p.m. I found him drunk on his watch and discovered that he had spilt some grog on the head of a cask of coffee stowed in the cabin. On examining our stock of water we found a considerable deficiency by leakage; I therefore put all hands to an allowance of two quarts per diem. At meridian there being no wind the brig *Elizabeth and Ann* fell on board us and carried away our jib-boom; and she gave us much trouble before we got her clear from our rigging.

The 4th we repaired our damage and got out a temporary jib-boom whilst the carpenter was making a new one. The 5th we had squally weather from the eastward, saw a great many grampuses sporting around us. The 6th we got out our new jib-boom.

On the 8th we had fresh gales with frequent squalls and rain. At midnight the wind shifted suddenly from southwest to the northward, and as soon as we got our sails regulated we heard two vessels firing distress guns. At daylight the *Bellequeux* passed us with the ship *Ocean* of Bristol in tow, having lost her head and bowsprit by running on board the Admiral's ship. On the 13th the wind again shifted from the north-west to north-east, which brought our vessel from the rear to the van of the fleet and ahead of the Admiral, but instead of shortening sail as required, I was determined to push on, being a heavy sailing vessel. But this breach of etiquette was soon corrected by shot from the *Swan* sloop.

The 14th we had moderate breezes and were far enough astern of the *Commodore*.

The 15th we had strong variable breezes with heavy rain, the Admiral being out of sight ahead. At daylight saw the *Bellequeux* astern, and only twenty vessels in sight. At 8 a.m. the *Bellequeux* made sail ahead to endeavour to discover the Admiral, and we carried a press of sail after her which strained the ship so much as to require hourly pumping.

The 16th at 1 p.m. we experienced rough weather, the wind blowing strong from the northward, there being only twenty-five sails in sight. At 7 p.m. the weather clearing we discovered the main body of the fleet to windward. Being now in the habit of pumping every hour at 10 p.m. discovered that the ship had spring a fresh leak and that there were two feet of water in the hold. After clearing the water we found it requisite to pump every quarter of an hour, and I had some apprehensions that we should be forced to abandon the ship. During the night a large flying-fish fell on board. As the daylight appeared the wind moderated and we found ourselves as customary in the rear of the fleet.

The 17th at meridian we could only see four vessels to windward, the wind blowing strong from the eastward and very hazy weather, pumping half-hourly under double reeft topsails.

The 18th at 1 p.m. we experienced fresh gales with frequent squalls and rain. As the sun set we could only see five vessels from the mast-head. At 4 a.m. we had two of the fleet in company. I sent to the mast-head, from which place four sails close together were discovered in the S.W. quarter. I stood for them, our companions following us. At 8 a.m.

we counted one hundred and six vessels, and at meridian joined the fleet.

The 19th we had the pleasure of being abreast of the 'Admiral,' which was an unusual treat. At 9 p.m. our leak suddenly ceased, doubtless by drawing some substance into the hole. At 9 a.m. hoisted out our boat as the wind was light to procure some provisions from my acquaintance. I accordingly obtained two tierces of beef and two hundred and fifty loaves of bread from the ship *Uxbridge*, and a keg of rum from the ship *Mary*, both of Liverpool. The former ship had brought to Kingstown a cargo of lumber from Philadelphia, and on her passage near St. Domingo she had beat off a French Privateer and arrived much damaged.

Our sails had been so often split and mended that our canvas was nearly expended, and I had been under the necessity of using the men's hammocks to repair the damage. Before we hoisted in our boat we scrubbed our ship's bends, to remove the marine grass and barnacles growing thereon.

The 20th July we were astern of the fleet. At 6 a.m. the *Swan* sloop of war came down to us and veered a hawser astern requesting we would make it fast. We accordingly got hold of it and exerted ourselves to make it firm, but before we could get it secured they filled their sails and hurt my arm and it was a great mercy that it was not jammed in pieces. The captain of the sloop of war informed me that the ship *Britannia* was so leaky after her sailing from Montego Bay that the captain had run her on shore on the Isle of Pines, and that the *Success* of Belfast had gone into Havannah leaky. I informed him of two other vessels belonging to the Kingston Division being missing, which he appeared ignorant of, and about 4 p.m. on the 21st ordered us to cast off the tow-rope that he might speak to the 'Admiral' before night, and promised to see me again when I should want his assistance to tow us into the fleet.

The 22nd July as we were now approaching the banks of Newfoundland we experienced foggy weather. This day we had a strong gale with frequent heavy squalls, and as we were uncertain how far we were astern of the main body of the fleet, we carried a press of sail and were well exercised in reducing and extending our canvas to endeavour to keep up with the convoy. At 8 a.m. a heavy squall laid us nearly on our beam ends, its approach not being observed owing to the fog. As I was at my post watching the sails I called loudly to let fly the main sheet, but no one being quick enough and seeing the carpenter panic-struck, I was tempted to seize hold of his jacket and fling him to leeward to execute my orders. The sheet was accordingly cast off and the sail immediately rent to pieces.

By urging my carpenter to his duty I had now laid myself open to the discipline of the gentlemen residing in Doctors Commons, who give no allowances for any situation a master of a ship may be placed in to save the ship and cargo as well as the lives of the crew. But they keep close to the letter of the law, embracing every advantage of the harassed and perplexed situation of the poor shipmaster.

The 23rd saw a ship in the fleet that had lost her main and mizen topmasts, perhaps in the storm of yesterday. This day we had fresh gales with squalls and very foggy weather. At 11 a.m. we passed several vessels at anchor on the Grand Bank of Newfoundland.

The 24th we had a strong gale with frequent squalls from the S.S.W. with heavy rain. At 7 p.m. we lay the ship to, and got down the top-gallant yards, a heavy sea running. At 8 p.m. a wave struck the afterpart of the ship and which threw the steersman over the wheel but providentially his life was preserved though much bruised. At midnight the wind having shifted to the westward we set our topsails and foresail. Whilst laying to we got soundings on the Bank in 34 fathoms. At daylight on examining the rudder we found it sprung in the rudder case; we therefore woulded it with rope and did our best to repair the damage. Having discovered the fleet hull down ahead we made sail to endeavour to overtake our convoy. On the evening of the 25th we overtook the 'Admiral,' our ship being very leaky.

From the 25th to the 30th having moderate weather we kept up with the fleet, and on this day the 'Admiral' made a signal for all masters of merchant vessels about 8 a.m. Whilst our crew were busily employed in clearing our boat to hoist her out the ship *Thetis* of London passed us, and informed me that I had no occasion to answer the signal, it being confined to those bound for Bristol and the St. George's Channel, which was good news for me, as I found myself very feeble.

The 3rd August we were obliged to pump every half-hour, and the 4th and 5th we were left the stern-most of the fleet.

The 6th we experienced very rough weather, but was obliged to carry a press of sail to keep the fleet in sight, though the waves were making a free passage over us and our crew much fatigued at the pump, which now required

almost constant attention to keep the water under. The
convoy seemed to care little for the slow-sailing ships, but
kept pushing on and sometimes ran ahead out of sight.

The 7th and 8th the wind blew strong with rain and thick
weather. Towards meridian we spoke a ship, and was informed that we were in soundings, the depth 74 fathoms,
my longitude by account being 7° 46' W. which will ascertain that my method of allowing for a *constant easterly current* is correct. As the *Swan* sloop was about 4 degrees
astern of me when I last spoke her I imagine she must have
been 8 degrees to the westward on striking soundings, not
having allowed for the easterly stream. Indeed, few naviga-
tors know anything of it, nor will they give themselves the
trouble of enquiry, how their reckonings are so often
erroneous. This day we had been just ten weeks from
Jamaica, and a signal was now made for the ships bound
for the Bristol and St. George's Channels to separate from
the 'Admiral,' and proceed to their respective ports.

On the morning of the 9th we discovered three line-of-
battleships and a frigate coming into the fleet, one of which
spoke our Admiral, and afterwards steered as the other
ships. As we had now a strong convoy the *Europa* took
French leave, and made the best of her way for Portsmouth.

The 10th and 11th being fine days we employed our
crew in repairing our shattered sails and rigging.

The 12th found ourselves deserted by all the men-of-war.
This day a Dover cutter came alongside, but the weather
being foggy we could not see the land. My passenger being
tired of the sea, agreed to give some guineas for the cutter
to land him. It will be recollected that when this young

man applied to me in Old Harbour to give him his passage to England, he represented himself in distress and without the means of paying for his passage. He could now find money to pay the cutter for taking him on shore and to defray his expenses to London. During our voyage he saw me frequently reading in my Bible, and as he had imbibed principles of infidelity, he endeavoured to ridicule the Scriptures, saying they had been proved a fabrication, erroneously translated from the original text to mislead the ignorant, and as a proof of their inconsistency he informed me that the Head of the Almighty was represented in one place as white as wool and in another part as black as a raven. This representation staggered me, and I began to think all was not right, not being aware at that time that these descriptions were only figurative, and not to be taken as the literal sense.

Towards evening a sloop of war laying in wait for homeward-bound ships fired several shots at us, wantonly, to bring us to, when one gun would have answered every good purpose, but young men in arms are fond of hectoring over those from whom there is no danger of retaliation.

Three of my English seamen had previously hid themselves amongst the cargo before the boat boarded us, and as no British could be found a Swede was taken, but after examination on board the man-of-war he was sent back to me, and I was allowed to proceed up the English Channel. At meridian we saw the Needle Point plain.

On the 13th at 2 p.m. the wind became variable, inclining to the eastward, I therefore thought it prudent to proceed to Spithead for a convoy. About dusk we gained South

Yarmouth road, within the Isle of Wight, and anchored near a Liverpool ship bound also for London. After dark my mate was laying about the deck drunk and helpless; being a complete tippler, it was this man's practice during our passage to watch for my coming on deck, which as soon as he perceived he hastened below to the rum bottle, and being on my guard I used to detect him. One night in the dark he caught me in his arms, not knowing what he was doing, being generally what seamen term, 'Half seas over!'

The 14th the tide answering at two past noon, we got under sail in company with the ship *Mary* to work to windward for Spithead, the wind being light. We endeavoured to decoy a shark to our fish-hook, but it would not come near the ship.

I saw the *Europa* laying at Spithead with yards and top-masts struck, and the 'Admiral' was probably safe in London. Three of my crew hired three fishermen from Ryde to proceed in the ship to London to officiate on deck whilst their employers hid themselves in the hold from the Press boats.

The 16th as we passed Hastings we had a good view of the encampment in its vicinity. One of the boats from the town visited us with fish; but more particularly they were in quest of goods for smuggling, and were not a little disappointed at finding they had applied at the wrong shop. In the afternoon a Dover boat boarded us, and having enquired of our men whether our ship had received any damage on the passage, and having learned that the rudder was sprung, etc., they endeavoured to persuade me to go into

Dover to get the damage repaired, and that if I would be governed by them I should receive a handsome sum for myself. However, I resisted their dishonest advice, and dismissed them as rogues in grain!

At daylight on the morning of the 17th we rounded the South Foreland and stood for the Downs, where we discovered a Russian fleet of sixteen men-of-war at anchor there.

The 20th we discharged our pilot at Gravesend, and obtained a pilot for the Pool. At 10 o'clock in the morning we weighed with the flood, and at five in the afternoon we anchored near the convict ship at Woolwich, having two Custom House officers and two excise men on board from Gravesend to keep each other honest. This night my three British seamen landed on the Essex side and proceeded to London.

The 21st at six in the morning we again made sail from above Woolwich. Soon after passing Blackwall the pilot ran the ship on shore on the Isle of Dogs, but as the flood tide was running we got her off by the help of a kedge anchor during a great fall of rain. Before sunset we entered the Pool. We had been twelve weeks from Jamaica, and as I had been sadly harassed during the whole time with a slow-sailing, leaky ship, and an unprincipled crew, I was much rejoiced at finding myself safe in the Thames.

The 22nd we hauled the ship to the Guinea chain. My crew now demanded their run money: I informed them they should be paid as soon as I could ascertain the average sum that was given by the fleet; they therefore quitted the ship, and having made acquaintance on shore with men of bad character, I soon received several summonses from proctors in Doctors Commons.

The 24th we got our sails unbent by lumpers, and on going on board in the evening found the mate had taken 'French leave,' who afterwards met me on the exchange, and civilly handed me a proctor's letter, and sneaked away like a dog with his tail cut. As my owners were desirous to pay the runs without trouble, I paid the amount of £383 5s. to the crew for twelve weeks' wages. Each seaman receiving 45 guineas, whilst my wages in the same space of time did not amount to £15. While Mr. 10.10 was in London he received advice from Montego Bay that the whole of the cargo landed from the unfortunate ship *Brothers* had been consumed by fire and was a total loss. As I gave a very bad account of the condition of our ship, Mr. 10.10 agreed to advertise her for sale as soon as possible. Accordingly on exhibiting a broom at the mast-head many people came to inspect her.

As my health continued to decrease I applied to Mr. Hawes, an apothecary in Tooley Street, who gave me some medicine, and requested me to use less exercise for awhile. A person who came on board to inspect our ship about this time discovered the apron of her stem was decayed, and as this was a defect of great consequence her bad condition was published far and wide. However, at the time appointed she was put up for sale at Lloyd's coffee-house, and as no person would bid near the amount expected she was bought in by the owners.

About this time my host with whom I boarded in Liverpool, came to London on business, and invited me to dine with him at his sister's in the Borough, who was married to a surveyor in the Excise. I accordingly accepted the invitation, and as Mrs. J — saw that I was poorly, she invited me to stay at her house a few days, and she would use her endeavours to restore me to health again. I therefore agreed to sleep on shore a few nights, and she made me some beef-tea to drink. On the Sabbath afternoon her husband proposed a walk, and conducted me to Kensington Gardens; we took tea with one of the Household in St. James's Palace, and after drinking a glass or two of wine with a butler to a great man in office near Hyde Park, I returned to the Borough much fatigued and injured by my excursion, instead of being benefited by my walk, but I could have expected no other had I considered that I had been breaking the Sabbath.

I had now been seventeen years regularly at sea, exclusive of my first voyage to South Carolina with my father previous to the American War; and, on a rough calculation, I imagine I have sailed more than one hundred thousand miles on the Atlantic Ocean. During this time I was never in a vessel that was stranded, wrecked, or that lost a mast by the board, larger than a topmast, and believe that the Underwriters never lost a sixpence by me during the whole of my seafaring life, which calls loudly on me for gratitude to my great Preserver. I left school at the age of fourteen. I was then sent to sea, and for the first four years sailed in the Falmouth packets; then I sailed about three years in the Transport Service, and during these several years I suffered innumerable hardships and ill-treatment.

The remainder of my sea-life I spent in the service of a

merchant from the Port of Liverpool; the first three years
I was chief mate and the latter years I was shipmaster. At
fifteen years of age I earned my livelihood, and from this
period never received five shillings as a gift from any
relative, nor ever sailed from a port to the best of my
knowledge one shilling in debt.